TRAUMA-INFORMED EVALUATION AND RESEARCH

TRAUMA-INFORMED EVALUATION AND RESEARCH

A PRACTICAL GUIDE

Martha A. Brown
Aaron W. Kates

THE GUILFORD PRESS
New York London

A Division of Guilford Publications, Inc.
www.guilford.com

Printed in the United States of America

This book is printed on acid-free paper.

For product and safety concerns within the EU, please contact *GPSR@taylorandfrancis.com,* Taylor & Francis Verlag GmbH, Kaufingerstraße 24, 80331 München, Germany.

Last digit is print number: 9 8 7 6 5 4 3 2 1

Library of Congress Cataloging-in-Publication Data is available from the publisher.

ISBN 978-1-4625-6352-4 (paperback) — ISBN 978-1-4625-6353-1 (hardcover)

Preface

Research conducted by Drs. Robert Anda and Vince Felitti (Felitti et al., 1998) put childhood trauma at the forefront of child development and public health concerns. In their groundbreaking study, they found that more than 60% of people living in the United States had experienced one or more adverse childhood experiences (ACEs), which include but are not limited to abuse, neglect, household dysfunction, separation or divorce, and incarceration (Centers for Disease Control and Prevention, n.d.). In addition to childhood trauma, humans individually and collectively experience other acute and chronic traumas as they progress through adulthood, such as accidents, poverty, domestic abuse, racial trauma, sexual trauma, natural disasters, military service, law enforcement service, secondary trauma, and the traumas caused by war, refugee camps, and displacement.

Because we are human beings, evaluators and researchers—including the authors—are not exempt from experiencing trauma—in childhood, as adults, or in our line of work. However, most do not yet acknowledge how primary and secondary trauma affects us and how we design and conduct research and evaluation. Trauma-Informed Evaluation and Research[1] (TIER) is not a standalone evaluation methodology; rather, it is a principled framework—a lens—that informs how evaluators conduct their work across various approaches. TIER applies the Substance Abuse and Mental Health Services Administration's (SAMHSA; 2014) trauma-informed principles to help evaluators acknowledge and minimize potential trauma while maintaining methodological rigor within their chosen evaluation design. Throughout this book, evaluators and researchers will learn about trauma—their own and that of other individuals and groups—and how to apply SAMHSA's Six Principles of Trauma-Informed Care (2014) to themselves and their work.

[1]We credit Bosk (2023) with the origin of the title of this evaluation lens.

SAMHSA's *Concept of Trauma and Guidance for a Trauma-Informed Approach* (2014) describes the history and evolution of the Six Principles in detail, and we provide an abridged history here. SAMHSA was motivated by a desire to provide the government and service sectors with a way to connect trauma to behavioral health issues and create a trauma-informed system. They conducted an environmental scan of trauma definitions and trauma-informed care that guided the beginning of a framework, which was then discussed at numerous conferences in the early 2000s. The American Psychological Association (APA) was a critical partner in this endeavor. Decades of research, public input, and work led to the clearer definitions of trauma and trauma-informed care as described in SAMHSA's Guide, which provides the foundation for our philosophy and the terminology that we use throughout the book. These are SAMHSA's Six Principles:

- Safety (physical, psychological, social, moral)
- Peer Support (create healing-centered connections among staff)
- Trust and Trustworthiness (keeping one's word, valuing and listening to others)
- Collaboration and Mutuality (shared decision making, shared power, co-creation)
- Gender, Cultural, and Historic Issues (gender and culturally responsive methods)
- Empowerment, Voice, and Choice (a person's own inner wisdom)

Any researcher or evaluator can apply the Six Principles regardless of the methods they use or their environment/context. We believe that wearing a trauma-informed lens throughout the entire research and evaluation process is transformational and healing for participants and researchers alike. TIER will help mitigate power imbalances, increase awareness and connection to self and others, eliminate or minimize triggering words and questions, increase authenticity, promote healing and empowerment, and improve a study's validity.

In this book, we share the same principles-based lens currently worn by many mental, behavioral, and physical health professionals with researchers and evaluators regardless of field, specialty, approach, or method. We assert that TIER has universal applications, and the extent to which TIER is used is limited only by the knowledge and experience of the researcher or evaluator.

Additional Principles

We bring other principles to this work as well. Author Martha Brown integrates restorative justice philosophy and practices into her research and evaluation methods (Brown, 2015). At the heart of restorative justice is the indigenous belief that we are all interconnected; we are all worthy of dignity, respect, and mutual concern; and are therefore accountable to each other (Evans & Vaandering, 2016; Zehr, 2002). This means that we should do all things in good ways that promote community and connection. This is especially important with TIER because trauma causes disconnection, and to heal from trauma, one needs healthy, trusting, and caring connections with others (Eastern Mennonite University, 2023). The following are the restorative principles grounding this work:

- We all function better when our core needs are honored and met.
- Within supportive environments, we become accountable to one another.
- Experiences of justice and injustice affect people's sense of community (Evans & Lester, 2013; Zehr, 2002).

Additionally, both of us co-created and agreed to follow the principles below that guided how we worked together to coauthor this book:

- We offer new thoughts and ideas, as what we think and believe is important.
- We center the individual and make the individual relevant.
- We elevate voices of LGBTQ+/BIPOC scholars and practitioners.
- We blend the personal and the academic, the theory and the practice.
- We make this book accessible, practical, and readable.

It is also important to note that the traumas and subsequent healing journeys that both authors have experienced and continue experiencing inform this work. Stories matter because they shape who we are and how we present ourselves to the world. We did not write this book as outsiders, or "objective" researchers (a myth we confront repeatedly), but as trauma survivors who choose to share their experiences and lessons learned so that others can be helped and healed. *This work is personal.*

It is worthwhile to explain our first principle: what we think and believe is important. We do not confront or dispute scientific findings about trauma. And we acknowledge that we are standing on the shoulders of many researchers and evaluators as well as those individuals and groups who have survived trauma and thus contribute to this evolving work. But for us to also continue our own healing journeys as academics, evaluators, and humans, we must give ourselves permission to believe this work has value; that it is indeed important; and that people, programs, and organizations can and will benefit from what we offer in this book. To that end, where the research may not be completely clear, or where it ceases to speak at all, we do not shy away from making conjectures and stating opinions. We do, however, use caution when doing so and make it clear that any such passages are just that. Because TIER is a relatively new concept, we humbly put forth what we think and believe, and encourage others to build on, challenge, and expand the work.

Pedagogical Features

We have intentionally designed this book to be practical, so we provide many opportunities for readers to connect with and reflect on the content and to bring the theoretical and academic teachings to life:

- Case studies: contributions from researchers and evaluators who have employed TIER practices in their own work
- Bolded words: vocabulary used in trauma-informed work
- Activities: designed to promote practice and deepen learning
- Reflections: opportunities for readers to pause, think, and perhaps write or journal
- Accessible language that brings the authors and readers together

Whom This Book Is For

This book has a broad reach across disciplines where research and evaluation are taught and practiced, including but not limited to the following:

- Nonprofit, human services, health organizations (mental, behavioral, physical, public)
- Arts Education programs and organizations
- Education and Educational Psychology programs
- Social Work programs
- Criminal Justice programs
- Government agencies and programs
- Research methods and evaluation courses
- Current working practitioners
- Any employee with no formal training whose job includes gathering and analyzing data, especially those in nonprofits, human services, and public agencies

Because TIER is a lens rather than a complete method, this book could be a supplemental text in any course where research and evaluation methods are taught, even if trauma is not the focus of the course. The book requires that the reader have some prior knowledge of research and evaluation methods because we refer to methods and approaches but do not teach them.

Work in Progress

Although anti-racism is not specifically named in the Six Principles, it is an important practice to integrate. Kathomi Gatwiri and Virginia Mapedzahama (2022) describe an anti-racist pedagogical practice that entails three core transformative elements: self-reflexivity, storytelling, and collaboration with people of color. Throughout the development of this book, we have made every effort to practice those elements ourselves and to provide readers with the same opportunities. We encourage readers to take the time to think about the reflection questions we provide and to perhaps journal or discuss those questions with others. We emphasize the importance of deeply listening to participants' stories and responding mindfully and empathetically. Last, through our collaboration with all the contributors to the book, we have had the joy and honor of partnering with diverse evaluators and researchers, who are overwhelmingly female, whose perspectives were (and are) central to our thinking and learning about TIER practices.

Ours is a work in progress, as is theirs, as is yours. Even as we wrote this book, more relevant articles were published on this topic, and we scrambled to keep up with and include the newest literature. Although there is no "there" on this journey, we can confidently assure our readers that this book will change how and why you do the work that you do. In the many conversations we've had with each other, with colleagues, and with our contributors, we've deepened our passion for this work and hope that you too will be inspired, emboldened, and challenged to integrate everything you can into your work and life. It will look and feel different for each of us. However, we are part of a growing movement of practitioners and teachers striving to foster healing, resilience, empowerment, and transformation in a world that desperately needs all those things.

Thank you for joining us on one the most important journeys you may ever take.

Acknowledgments

This book truly took a village to write. We thank workshop participants who informed our thinking, as well as our colleagues we quoted or who wrote examples and case studies. These are people doing the work building the TIER plane as it takes flight.

We could not have done this without the support of C. Deborah Laughton, our editor at The Guilford Press, or of our spouses and partners who have supported us over the years it took to write the manuscript.

We are very grateful to those researchers and evaluators who are hungry to learn more and who inspired us to keep going every step of the way and to those professors who are anxious to include this text in their course curricula.

We both have turned our lenses inward and have done a significant amount of healing work from our own respective traumas. This has taken place through introspection, confiding in friends and family whom we trust, engaging in therapy, and even writing this book. While we would never claim to be "totally healed" (if there is such a thing), we have both experienced a sense of transformation and increased resilience. Our hope is that this book can spur on others in the field to walk the same path.

Above all, we write for those who have suffered and continue to suffer trauma. This work is for you, for us.

Contents

I. Understanding Individual and Collective Traumas—Including Our Own 1

1. What Is Trauma? 3

Defining Trauma 3

Individual Traumas: ACEs and PTSD 5

Collective Trauma 11

Epigenetics 14

The Cultural Context of Trauma 15

CASE STUDY 1.1 Resiliency and Breaking the Cycles of Intergenerational Trauma 15
CELENA DONAHUE

A Traumatized Brain and Body 16

The Autonomic Nervous System 19

Symptoms and Stress Responses 19

2. How Our Own Traumas Influence Our Work 24

Introduction 24

Being Trauma-Informed Starts with Ourselves 26

Secondary Trauma: The Unspoken Hazard of E&R 28

Secondary Trauma in the Literature 29

CF, Burnout, and STS Defined 29

Our Vulnerability to CF, Burnout, and STS 30

CASE STUDY 2.1 Challenges of TIER in International Development Programs 31
MARIAN WARE

The Significance of CF, Burnout, and STS in E&R 32

Methodology Does Not Eliminate Risk 34
STS and Our Partners 34
CASE STUDY 2.2 Centering Healing and Activating Resilience: Shifting Our Transformative Evaluation Process during COVID at Centro Hispano of Dane County 37
EVELYN CRUZ AND VIVIEN AHRENS
We Can Be Dangerous 39

3. Foundational Principles of TIER 41
Why TIER? 41
The Four R's of a Trauma-Informed Approach 42
The Six Principles of Trauma-Informed Care 44
Guiding Principles for Evaluators and Researchers 47
Ethical Decision Making 47

II. The Evaluation Landscape 53

4. Representation of Trauma in the Evaluation and Research Literature 55
Introduction 55
Searching and Coding the Literature 56
Surface-Level Engagement: Early Patterns and Their Persistence 57
Emerging Themes in Recent Literature 59
From Literature to Practice: What We Suspect but Cannot Confirm 63
A Call to Transformation: The Time for Trauma-Informed Evaluation Is Now 63

5. TIER's Congruence with Evaluation Approaches 66
What Is Theory? 67
How TIER Fits 68
TIER and the Evaluation Theory Tree 68
Approaches and the Six Principles 72
A Good Approach Does Not Always Mean a Trauma-Informed Approach 77
Restorative and Transformative Justice in Evaluation Practices 77

6. Equity-Focused and Trauma-Informed Evaluation and Research 80
MELANIE WARD, RUCHA LONDHE, and KATRINA BLEDSOE
Introduction 80
Centering Equity through Equitable Evaluation Processes 81

Equity- and Trauma-Informed Approaches 82

Implementing an Equity-Centered, Trauma-Informed Equitable Evaluation 83

CASE STUDY 6.1 Cultural Adaptation of Trauma-Informed Research Practices 89
RACHAEL JACKSON

CASE STUDY 6.2 Mandatory Reporting 91
ERIKA KEAVENEY

III. Doing TIER 93

7. Being a Trauma-Informed Researcher and Evaluator 95

A Trauma-Informed Practice: Box Breathing 95

What Is Resilience? 96

Healing Trauma Wounds 97

Recognizing Our Window of Tolerance 99

What Is a Trauma-Informed Researcher and Evaluator? 101

Holding Safe and Brave Spaces 103

CASE STUDY 7.1 Wisdom of the Heart: Working through Grief toward Health Equity during the COVID and Racism Pandemics 104
EVELYN CRUZ

Incorporating Resilience Practices 109

8. Designing and Framing TIER 112

Power and the Purse: Issues of Power, Oppression, and Funding 112

Trauma-Informed Convening 114

CASE STUDY 8.1 Ethical Riders in Your Contract 120
STEPHANIE EVERGREEN

Framing the Evaluation 121

CASE STUDY 8.2 Values in Action 125
AARON KATES

9. Making Surveys Trauma-Informed 127

Introduction 127

Trauma-Informed Survey Design 128

Ongoing Informed Consent 128

CASE STUDY 9.1 A Trauma-Informed Approach to Informed Consent Procedures 130
CARRIE FISHER AND SOFÍA ALEJANDRA LADNER

Survey Length and Built-In Resilience Breaks 132

Phases of Survey Design 133

CASE STUDY 9.2 Navigating Cultural Differences When Collecting Demographic Data 137
AARON KATES

CASE STUDY 9.3 Beyond Required Answers 138
MARTHA BROWN

Conducting the Survey 140

What about Purely Quantitative Research? 141

10. Trauma-Informed Interviews and Focus Groups 145

Interviewing Staff 145

CASE STUDY 10.1 Designing Trauma-Informed Interview Tools 146
ERIKA KEAVENEY

Example of an Insensitive Interview 148

Being Trauma-Informed, Even When the Protocol Is Not 149

Preventing Shaming 150

Listening versus Listening Deeply 152

Responding with Empathy 153

CASE STUDY 10.2 Creation of the Interviewer Processing and Reflexivity Group within Wilder Research 153
NORA JOHNSON

Focus Groups and Circles 155

CASE STUDY 10.3 Circle Did What a Focus Group Could Not 156
ELYSE FUERST

CASE STUDY 10.4 Reframing Field Interviewer Thinking vis-à-vis Trauma-Risk Populations 157
KAREEM KYSIA

11. Trauma-Informed Analysis and Reporting 161

Introduction 161

Analysis 162

Reporting 166

IV. Growing TIER 177

12. Trauma-Informed Programs, Organizations, and Systems 179

Introduction 179

Expanding the Work in Your Sphere of Influence 180

How Can Organizations within Systems Change? 189

CASE STUDY 12.1 Trauma-Informed Systems Change at the Jewish Federations of North America 189
CARMEL RABIN

CASE STUDY 12.2 Trauma-Informed Approaches at Wilder 190
NORA JOHNSON

Time to Go to Work 192

Appendix A. Recommended Literature Referencing the Six Principles 195

Appendix B. Trauma-Informed Coalitions and Organizations 198

Appendix C. Resources for Deeper Learning 200

Appendix D. What About Fawning? 204

TIER Glossary 207

References 219

Index 233

About the Authors 243

Contributors 244

PART I

Understanding Individual and Collective Traumas—Including Our Own

For some readers, this may be your first introduction to understanding trauma, its effects, and how it affects individuals, groups, and ultimately whole communities. This part is dedicated to helping you understand how individual and collective traumas change the brain and body (Chapter 1) and cause physiological/physical, not solely psychological, responses. In Chapter 2, we look at how our own traumas play out in our work as researchers and evaluators, including our risk of secondary trauma (Chapter 3). We conclude this part with messages of hope and healing by explaining the foundational principles of trauma-informed care (Chapter 4)—principles that, when employed, not only minimize the risk of retraumatization but also create pathways for healing.

CHAPTER 1

What Is Trauma?

If we just change our definition, can we get it to go away?

WHAT YOU'LL LEARN

The word *trauma* means "wound," and getting wounded is an inevitable part of life (DeWolf & Geddes, 2019). We all experience trauma in different forms, and what is traumatic to one person may not be traumatic to another. It's complex. But the Substance Abuse and Mental Health Services Administration (SAMHSA; 2014) and many other organizations and authors have made trauma-related neuroscience and behavioral science accessible to those of us who are not mental health or medical professionals. In this chapter, we define trauma and discuss many causes of trauma to individuals and groups. Once we understand what trauma is and how it affects our genes, we turn to neuroscience to fully understand trauma's effects on our brains and bodies. We summarize and simplify a very complex biophysiological response and encourage you to learn more by exploring our recommended resources.

Defining Trauma

Trauma occurs when an individual or a group experiences a highly stressful event or series of events over which they have no control. They feel powerless and threatened in the face of a situation that feels unmanageable, terrifying, or insurmountable. Such feelings overwhelm one's ability to cope in the moment and after the event (Atkinson, 2002; Craig, 2016, 2017; DeWolf & Geddes, 2019; Yoder, 2005). SAMHSA (2014) defines trauma as "what results from an event, series of events, or set of circumstances that is experienced by an individual as physically or emotionally harmful or life-threatening and that has lasting adverse effects on the individual's functioning and mental, physical, social, emotional, or spiritual well-being" (p. 7).

According to Mears (2012), "the degree of powerlessness felt by individuals in the face of various dangers influences the level of psychological trauma they experience" (p. 16). This means that two people can be present at the same event and yet experience it differently. Scholars are also increasingly warning against universal conceptions of trauma that assume all individuals experience and respond to distressing events in the same way, especially given how responses are highly influenced by factors such as gender, race, ethnicity, and historical context (Briant-Davis, 2019). Yoder (2005, pp. 15–16) lists common traumatic events or stressors that affect both individuals and groups of people, including but not limited to the following:

- Abuse or assault: physical, emotional, sexual, including rape
- Accidents
- Causing harm to others deliberately: criminals; torturers; abusers; terrorists, including state-sponsored or sanctioned terrorism, abuse of power
- Causing harm to others in the line of duty, such as that done by law enforcement officers, executioners, military personnel
- Economic policies, poverty
- Homelessness, being a refugee
- Human-caused disasters: chemical spills, dams or levees that break
- Living under occupation or in conditions of servitude or slavery; human trafficking
- Mass violence: assaults, massacres, genocide, wars
- Natural disasters: hurricanes, earthquakes, tornadoes, tsunamis, wildfires
- Neglect of those who cannot care for themselves
- Serious illnesses; pandemics and epidemics such as AIDS, COVID-19; bioterrorism
- Structural violence: social structures and institutions that deprive people of their rights and ability to meet basic needs
- Sudden loss of loved ones, status, identity, possessions, home, territory
- Sudden changing of the rules, expectations, or norms: social revolutions
- Surgical, dental, and medical procedures, including difficult births
- Torture
- Witnessing death or injury

In perusing this list, we can see how likely it is that we—evaluators and researchers—have experienced traumas, just as the people with and for whom we conduct research and evaluation. To understand how trauma affects our lives, we ground our work in **trauma theory**, which describes a scientifically informed and complex biopsychosocial understanding of what goes wrong for human beings under conditions of overwhelming stress. Trauma theory presupposes a cause for one's difficulties, and that cause is not an individual character flaw, a moral weakness, or an innate malevolence but a result of injury. This is especially important if those injuries have occurred in childhood because normal development of body, brain, and mind is likely to be derailed (Bloom & Farragher, 2013).

Because trauma that remains unhealed can manifest and compound over a lifetime and generations, we will first discuss **adverse childhood experiences (ACEs)** and posttraumatic stress disorder (PTSD), followed by a discussion of how collective traumas compound individual traumas, affecting entire groups and populations.

Individual Traumas: ACEs and PTSD

Adverse Childhood Experiences

From 1995 to 1997, Drs. Robert Anda and Vincent Felitti (and their colleagues) authored the seminal ACEs (1998) study to determine whether 10 adverse experiences before the age of 18 were related to negative physical, mental, and behavioral health outcomes in adulthood (Centers for Disease Control and Prevention [CDC], n.d.). These 10 experiences were put into three categories:

1. *Abuse:* emotional, physical, sexual
2. *Household challenges:* mother treated violently, household substance abuse, mental illness in household, parental separation or divorce, criminal household member
3. *Neglect:* emotional, physical

The original ACEs study has been criticized because, having been done in partnership with Kaiser Permanente, the study participants were mostly white middle-class people with health insurance. A result of this critique was the replication of the ACEs study in more cities, regions, and countries, resulting in a more diverse sample and an expanded list of traumatic events children may experience, including but not limited to the following:

- Experiencing violence, abuse, or neglect
- Witnessing violence in the home or community

- Having a family member attempt or die by suicide
- Instability due to parental separation or household members being incarcerated
- Food insecurity/hunger
- Homelessness or unstable housing
- Experiencing racism and gender discrimination
- Being bullied by a peer or adult
- Living in a war zone or unsafe neighborhood
- Losing a family member to deportation (CDC, n.d.; Eastern Mennonite University, 2023, p. 69)

Prevalence of ACEs across Populations

We have established that ACEs are common in general, but we also know that the rates vary across genders, ages, geographies, races, and ethnicities. This is because all of us are exposed to different life circumstances that are associated with these attributes. Given the results of multiple studies, we know that more than 64% of U.S. adults reported experiencing at least one type of ACE and that over 17% reported experiencing four or more types of ACEs (CDC, n.d.).

A recent meta-analysis of 206 articles, mostly from the United States, gives detailed breakdowns of ACE frequencies by subpopulations, highlighting some of these stark disparities (Madigan et al., 2023). The study revealed that the racial/ethnic populations with the greatest burden of four or more ACEs are Indigenous/Native Americans (40.8%), Latinos (25.6%), and Blacks/African Americans (21.55%; Madigan et al., 2023). Women are also more likely than men to experience four or more ACEs (17.5% vs. 14.3%, respectively). The populations who experience the greatest burden of ACEs by far, however, go beyond race and gender, with alarming rates of four or more ACEs being experienced by the unhoused (59.7%), those with substance abuse or addiction (55.2%), and those with a history of mental illness (47.5%) (Madigan et al., 2023).

ACEs' Link to Chronic Health Problems

ACEs are linked to chronic health problems such as substance use, mental illness, heart disease, cancer, diabetes, high blood pressure, and obesity. They are also dose related, meaning that the more ACEs a person has, the more likely they will develop chronic health problems as adults. ACEs affect children's attention, decision making, brain development, and learning and may interfere with their ability to form healthy and stable relationships and friendships, which in turn hinders their education, job opportunities, and earning potential as adults.

Although all children are at risk of ACEs, the inequities linked to historical, social, and economic environments in which some families live affect some groups even more. The cost of ACEs, many of which are preventable, is staggering: The CDC (n.d.) estimates an economic burden of *$748 billion annually* in Bermuda, Canada, and the United States alone. Imagine if that money were spent on preventing ACEs instead.

The lasting effects of ACEs include **toxic stress**, a prolonged activation of the body's stress response that can disrupt the development of brain architecture and other organs and increase the risk for stress-related disease, cognitive impairment, and other problematic long-term consequences well into the adult years (Bloom & Farragher, 2013; Burke Harris, 2021). Throughout life, we all experience physical or psychological stressors that disrupt **homeostasis**, or our balanced state; these are called **stress-response stimuli** (Chu, Marwaha, Sanvictores, Awosika, & Ayers, 2024). As the stress-response stimuli go from adaptive and lifesaving to maladaptive and health damaging, toxic stress becomes entrenched in the brain and body, keeping **trauma-affected people** stuck in the past and hard-wired into a dysregulating pattern that can alter mood, cognitive ability, and behavior patterns (Burke Harris, 2021; Mears, 2012; Menakem, 2017).

Posttraumatic Stress Disorder

Posttraumatic stress disorder, or **PTSD**, is a formal psychiatric diagnosis for traumatic stress[1] that is ongoing and continues to negatively affect a person in a way that the medical community has determined increases to the level of pathology or illness. PTSD symptoms persist over a month; cause extreme distress; or interfere with the ability to function at work, school, or home (American Psychiatric Association, 2022). Symptoms include intrusive thoughts, flashbacks, dissociation, distress when exposed to triggers, heightened physiological reactions (e.g., breathing difficulties, shaking, nausea, headache), avoidance of difficult subjects or stimuli, negative cognitions, and heightened reactivity (American Psychiatric Association, 2022). Galatzer-Levy and Bryant (2013, as cited in Gerhart, Canetti, & Hobfoll, 2015) state that there are over 600,000 possible presentations of PTSD given the various combinations of presentations in DSM-5-TR.

Not everyone who has difficulty with trauma has PTSD, and not everyone who endures a traumatic experience will develop PTSD. Additionally, once a person develops PTSD, it does not mean that they will always have PTSD. According to Gilman (2023), those who have experienced sexual trauma have the highest chance of developing PTSD, although in the public's mind it is most commonly

[1]This may be splitting hairs, but we like to think about trauma as the event, whereas traumatic stress is the effects that follow. An event is only traumatic, and therefore trauma, if traumatic stress follows. We mostly use the word *trauma* in the book as a catch-all, but this distinction is more technically accurate.

associated with soldiers and veterans. Without treatment, PTSD can persist for years and goes hand in hand with depression and drug and alcohol use (Gilman, 2023). PTSD can occur in both children and adults.

Other Trauma Diagnoses

PTSD looms large in social consciousness as the main manifestation of trauma. However, there are four other specified stress-related disorders in DSM-5-TR, including **reactive attachment disorder, disinhibited social engagement disorder, acute stress disorder,** and **adjustment disorder** (American Psychiatric Association, 2022). The manual also leaves room for other specified or unspecified trauma- and stressor-related disorders, meaning that people may experience trauma in ways that cause problems for them but do not exactly fit criteria for any one of these diagnoses. Table 1.1 gives a brief overview of these other diagnoses.

Critiques of PTSD Diagnosis

Not all traumatic responses result in PTSD, and the term is commonly misused. Some are critical of the way in which the *Diagnostic and Statistical Manual of Mental Disorders* (DSM; American Psychiatric Association, 2022) defines PTSD because it "does not highlight the chronic, ongoing stress of particular situations or where the stressors are cumulative over time" (Atkinson, 2002, p. 51). Some individuals with serious trauma reactions may consult the DSM and find that they

TABLE 1.1. Alternate Trauma- and Stress-Related Diagnoses

Diagnosis	Description
Reactive attachment disorder	A rare but serious condition in which young children fail to form healthy emotional bonds with primary caregivers, typically due to severe early neglect, abuse, or frequent changes in caregivers during critical developmental periods (usually before age 5).
Disinhibited social engagement disorder	A childhood disorder characterized by overly familiar and inappropriate social behavior with unfamiliar adults, typically resulting from inadequate care during early development.
Acute stress disorder	A trauma-related condition that occurs immediately following exposure to a traumatic event, with duration from 3 days to 1 month, serving as a potential precursor to PTSD.
Adjustment disorder	A condition characterized by the development of clinically significant emotional or behavioral symptoms within 6 months of exposure to an identifiable stressor, where the symptoms are either disproportionate to the severity of the stressor or cause significant impairment in functioning.

do not meet criteria because their experience is not reflected in what the manual considers to be a traumatic experience. But human experience is broad and varied and difficult to catalog in an exhaustive manner.

Additionally, Yoder (2005) cautions us about overusing the term *PTSD* because "there is also a danger that trauma responses and populations may be underestimated and therefore minimized if PTSD is the standard by which trauma is measured" (p. 31). It is also our contention that overuse may lead to people confusing normal stress and adverse situations and experiences (which are a normal part of life) with PTSD. Such a view of the ubiquity of trauma may also undermine people's conceptions of their own resilience and ability to thrive despite the difficulties we all experience as we go through life.

Retraumatization, Triggering, and Remembering

Much of the evaluation and research (E&R) literature focuses on **retraumatization** as the main driver of the need for **Trauma-Informed Evaluation and Research (TIER) methods**. This is a word that we find thrown around a lot in the literature without much thought given to what retraumatization actually is, how it occurs, or why it occurs. We define retraumatization in accordance with Duckworth and Follette (2012), the authors of the only scholarly book dedicated to the topic: "Retraumatization [is] traumatic stress reactions, responses, and symptoms that occur consequent to multiple exposures to traumatic events that are physical, psychological, or both in nature" (p. 2).

In the evaluation literature, as in many other fields, writers tend to treat any situation in which a participant becomes uncomfortable, anxious, or distressed while recounting or being reminded of their trauma narrative as retraumatization (Duckworth & Follette, 2012; Weiss, 2025). Most often, what most scholars are describing here is the concept of **triggering** or simply **remembering**. Triggering happens when a sensory experience or a situation reminds someone of their trauma and sets off a trauma response (e.g., shaking, crying, becoming unresponsive). Remembering is simply recalling a traumatic incident in one's mind. This can occur on its own or in the course of a conversation and may or may not be accompanied by a trauma response.

We think that confusing these concepts does a disservice to those in the field, as it adds to a level of fear when it comes to engaging with traumatized populations as well as obscuring the actual risks involved in our work. By precisely defining retraumatization, we are better equipped to know what to do when one of our participants becomes uncomfortable or does become retraumatized. Table 1.2 gives some examples of retraumatization, discomfort, and triggering. In the context of a sensitive and well-planned interview process, we would consider retraumatization to be a rare experience, with triggering being somewhat more common and simple remembering (whether accompanied by upset or not) being by far the most common possible occurrence.

TABLE 1.2. Retraumatization, Triggering, and Remembering

Situation	Category	Rationale
Brounéus (2008) describes the experience of female survivors of the Rwandan genocide who shared their trauma narratives in front of truth and reconciliation commissions. These took place in their communities, oftentimes in front of their family members' murderers who were walking free. Most of the women in the study faced retaliation and death threats. They found the experience to be terrifying, and the majority reported worsening PTSD symptoms afterward.	Retraumatization	Recounting their trauma narrative in an unsafe place led these women to real psychological, physical, and social harm. This was not just a reopening of an old wound. This constituted a new wound, which itself would be difficult to heal.
Taylor and Cahill (2002) describe the case of a woman who was in six car accidents in 10 years, causing severe PTSD symptoms.	Retraumatization	The person in this case study suffered repeated trauma events of the same kind. These were not just triggers (e.g., seeing a car, hearing tires screech) but were entirely new instances of trauma each time.
An evaluator asks an interviewee if he has ever experienced sexual abuse. The interviewee responds that he has and explains his trauma in detail while shaking and crying.	Remembering	In this instance, a person has shared their trauma narrative. This trauma narrative lives inside them and tends to reactivate their body (e.g., shaking and crying). They have not been triggered by a sensory experience or situation; they are simply remembering and retelling.
An evaluator who resembles the man who abused his interviewee in the past enters the office where data collection is taking place. The participant feels her heart beginning to race and starts to cry.	Triggering	This represents an instance of triggering. If the evaluation team handles the situation with tact and care (e.g., providing an alternate interviewer, listening to the interviewee's concerns), this can be prevented from turning into a retraumatizing event.

Distinguishing These Responses in Practice

Understanding these distinctions in real time during data collection is essential for providing appropriate responses. Although the boundaries can sometimes blur, certain indicators can help identify what you may be witnessing.

With retraumatization, a new injury occurs during or as a result of the research process itself. This might manifest as interviewer insensitivity that causes additional harm (questioning the validity of their experience, breaking confidentiality); violations of participant autonomy (pressuring them to continue after they've asked to stop, conducting interviews in unsafe environments); or situations where the participant expresses feeling harmed by the process itself, distinct from discomfort about their memories. With appropriate care and trauma-informed protocols, such occurrences should be exceedingly rare.

Triggering often presents as a sudden, seemingly disconnected response. You might observe a marked change in affect or body language that appears disproportionate to the current topic, physical symptoms like rapid breathing or trembling without direct discussion of trauma, angry outbursts, or confusion about why they're reacting. The participants themselves may not immediately understand their response, as it's often activated by something environmental (e.g., a smell, sound, or someone's appearance) rather than the content being discussed.

In contrast, remembering typically occurs in direct response to questions about traumatic experiences. The distress clearly connects to the content being discussed, and despite emotional responses like tears or shakiness, the participant usually remains oriented to the interview context and can articulate what they're feeling. This emotional response to discussing difficult experiences is normal and doesn't necessarily indicate harm or require stopping, although we should always follow the participant's lead.

This framework helps evaluators respond appropriately: Retraumatization requires immediate intervention and follow-up support; triggering calls for grounding techniques and environmental adjustments; remembering may simply require patience, validation, and periodic check-ins about continuing. By understanding these distinctions, we can move beyond fear-based avoidance of trauma-affected populations toward more skillful, compassionate engagement that minimizes actual risk while honoring participants' experiences.

Collective Trauma

ACEs and PTSD are contributing factors to **collective traumas**, which affect entire groups or populations (Yoder, 2005). When trauma remains unhealed and unmetabolized[2] (Menakem, 2017), trauma behaviors become the norm for individuals, families, and entire communities, as "trauma victims adapt their behaviors and beliefs to compensate for their traumatization, compounding their traumatization" (Atkinson, 2002, p. 88). This results in the replication of the individual's impaired function throughout an entire group (Yoder, 2005). Many causes of chronic trauma are still embedded in and compounded by colonizing and racialized bureaucracies, policies, laws, institutions, and systems that have existed for long periods and are slow to change (Atkinson, 2002).

---

[2]Resmaa Menakem uses the term *metabolize* because trauma lives in the body; it has to be metabolized for one to heal from trauma. Think about what happens when someone takes a pill for a headache. The pill enters the body through the mouth and is digested in the stomach and then processed—or metabolized—in the liver. From there the medication enters the bloodstream, where it goes to work. The opposite of this would be to just stay in the illness, live in the discomfort, and/or adapt to constantly having headaches.

Here we list and explain types of collective trauma, which are sometimes interrelated and interchangeable:

- *Structural trauma:* the ongoing violence of poverty and systems that make it difficult to meet basic needs, such as health care, jobs that pay wages that can support families, etc.
- *Systemic trauma:* features of environments and institutions that give rise to trauma, maintain it, and affect posttraumatic stress responses (Goldsmith, Martin, & Smith, 2014)
- *Historical, intergenerational, transgenerational trauma:* the cumulative emotional and psychological wounding over the lifespan and generations from massive group trauma, including slavery, colonialism, persecution, and genocide, as well as attempts to eradicate all or part of a culture or people (e.g., Indigenous peoples, European Jews, Palestinians, Cambodians, Armenians)
- *Participation-induced trauma:* trauma that results from being an active participant in harming others, including committing domestic abuse, police brutality/oppression, child soldiering, gang violence, white supremacy
- *Complex trauma:* the exposure to multiple, recurring, and interpersonal traumatic events over an extended period (Cénat, 2023)
- *Racial trauma and complex racial trauma (CoRT):* experiences related to threats, prejudices, harm, shame, humiliation, and guilt associated with various types of racial discrimination for either direct victims or witnesses and that occur multiple times over an extended period (Cénat, 2023)

Yoder (2005) further describes *participatory trauma* as "the egoism of victimization, the inability to see beyond one's own pain to empathize with the suffering of others. Consequently, there is little guilt about committing retaliatory violence and a failure to take responsibility for the victims and suffering created by one's own actions" (p. 34).

Menakem (2017) offers another name for participatory trauma—**moral injury**, which is the result of a person inflicting harm on another person and committing a moral transgression. To live with or ignore the shame that these actions produce, harmers often repeat harmful behaviors in an attempt to normalize them, thus creating a vicious cycle of violence.

Both Atkinson (2002) and Menakem (2017) use the term **soul wound** to describe the damage caused by historical, intergenerational, and transgenerational trauma. Below, Atkinson describes the transgenerational trauma of Australia's Indigenous people resulting from brutal and violent colonization; these traumas are generalizable to other Indigenous peoples around the world who were similarly victims of colonization.

- Historical trauma is a sociopolitical, genocidal impact of colonization.
- Kin-group or communal trauma includes the diseases and massacres of first contact, removal to reserves, and removal of children to residential schools experienced by whole communities.
- Extended-family trauma includes the articulations of distress of the other unhealed layers of trauma and homicides, domestic violence, rape, child physical and sexual abuse and neglect, and alcohol and drug use.
- Individual trauma includes suicides and suicide attempts, mental illness, and individual victimizing experiences from the above. (p. 81)

Collective trauma seeds violence. Unmetabolized trauma often leads to a deep-seated rage that leads to violence against self (acting in) and others (acting out; Center for Justice and Peacebuilding, 2023). The amount of violence a society or country experiences is directly related to the amount of trauma it has both inflicted and experienced. Atkinson (2002) explains that because colonized and oppressed people are often unable to express their rage at the perpetrators directly, "both their inner compass and their outer maps for what is considered proper behavior are lost" (pp. 53–54).

Posttraumatic Slave Syndrome

DeGruy and Leary (2005) describe **posttraumatic slave syndrome (PTSS)** as the trauma experienced by enslaved people from Africa and the transgenerational effects of those traumas. They posit that African Americans have experienced a legacy of trauma that has been debilitating to beliefs and assumptions about their worth, leading to hopelessness and fatalistic behaviors. "Today, the African American community is made up of individuals and families who collectively share differential anxiety and adaptive survival behaviors passed down from prior generations of African Americans, many of whom likely suffered from PTSD" (p. 119).

Structural, systemic, and political inequalities add to PTSS, especially for women of color in the United States, who are "situated within at least two subordinated groups that frequently pursue conflicting political agendas" and who are easily "erased by the strategic silences of anti-racism and feminism" (Crenshaw, Gotanda, Peller, & Thomas, 1995, p. 375). For example, a 2024 study revealed that Black women in the United States are six times more likely to be murdered than white women (Waller, Joseph, & Keyes, 2024). This implies that some communities and groups are more susceptible to the effects of collective trauma and its ensuing violence than others. Likewise, Levins Morales (1998) writes,

> [i]nternalizing the perpetrator's rationalizations, they may come to believe they are the source of their own problems and treat themselves and each other with disrespect and violence. Drug abuse, alcoholism, gang violence, domestic

> violence, and a stunted sense of what is possible can all be seen as a result of the inability to identify the causes of pain and take an active stance to end them. Only when we are able to take in the cumulative impact of slavery, lynching, and other forms of organized violence, enforced poverty and segregation and the systematic denial of opportunities to African Americans can we find ways to talk about the violence inflicted by young Black men upon each other as caused, not inherent. . . . We need a body of diagnostic know-how, a tradition of recognizing and understanding in detail the harmful nature of oppression. (p. 18)

TIER could contribute to that very body of literature so desperately needed to move policies and programs away from treating symptoms and toward creating systems and institutions that address trauma as the root cause for most social ills and provide opportunities for healing accordingly.

Epigenetics

Meaning "above the genome," **epigenetics** is a relatively new area of research with much yet to be learned. It is the study of mechanisms that switch various genes on or off without changing the underlying DNA (DeWolf & Geddes, 2019; Menakem, 2017). Although it does not change the genome itself, toxic stress from trauma changes the way DNA is read, expressed, and transcribed (Burke Harris, 2021).

Epigenetics explain why no matter how much "impact" programs claim to make and no matter how many social and safety net programs are in place, societal ills caused by trauma still prevail. Unhealed trauma leads to more trauma because trauma changes a mechanism in our genes that predisposes us to trauma responses and behaviors. A social program can't fix that. "Being told you are inferior for hundreds of years can have lasting psychic impacts, impacts that could pass from parent to child, to grandchild, to great-grandchild" (DeGruy & Leary, 2005, p. 158).

Black and brown bodies in the United States are in constant trauma-response mode, as they are repeatedly assaulted with racism in the media, in political dialogues, at the workplace, and in the streets. Grandparents, who thought they had "fixed this," have to shield children from the same harms that they and their ancestors experienced for generations because the same harms continue to happen. The moral injury in white bodies as a result of centuries of violence, soldiers killing and raping civilians, and colonization works to uphold the very structures, systems, and institutions that continue traumatizing individuals and groups today (Menakem, 2017).

Although traumatic wounds carried by people of color may be more obvious and easier to identify, what are the wounds carried by white people, descendants of enslavers, and inheritors of the privileges and advantages that come with having white/light skin pigmentation? What wounds need addressing that come through guilt and shame, whether inherited or experienced in the present or through isolation and separation resulting from the legacy and aftermath of slavery? The wounds inherited by white people are different, of course, but have nonetheless led to generations of woundedness, often evidenced by extreme reactions and vehement denials to any mention of racism (DeWolf & Geddes, 2019).

Racial healing, then, requires recognizing our own wounds and the wounds of others, as well as the role that trauma plays in our societies (DeWolf & Geddes, 2019). Epigenetic research suggests that racial prejudice, rooted in our brains long ago, is passed down through generations and continues to influence our instincts today. It is also believed that epigenetic effects occur in the womb and throughout our lives. However, and most importantly, "*epigenetic changes may be reversed through the choices we make and environmental exposures*" (DeWolf & Geddes, 2019, p. 18, emphasis added).

The Cultural Context of Trauma

The following case study by Celena Donahue, a Native American woman, illustrates how intergenerational trauma passed on through epigenetics can be healed, although it takes several generations.

CASE STUDY 1.1 Resiliency and Breaking the Cycles of Intergenerational Trauma

CELENA DONAHUE

My name is Celena Donahue. I am Pueblo Indian, and my family is Hupa, Yurok, and Karuk. I grew up on the Hoopa Valley Indian Reservation in Northern California. Growing up on a rural Indian Reservation comes with a lot of traumas, struggles, drugs, violence, physical and sexual assault, mental illness, suicide, and so much more. My childhood home did not have central air and heat. We stayed warm with a wood stove, but most of the time we had no firewood to stay warm. I remember many winters when I had to mentally prepare myself to get out of bed and get ready for school when it was 20 degrees outside. We had no heat and only cold water in the shower. Most days I had to walk several miles to school.

Throughout my school years, I was in "survival mode" and had many physical altercations. It was pure survival. I was 14 years old when I became pregnant. I had my first child at the age of 15 and a second by the time I was 18. My high school refused to let me come back to school because "I had a baby" and they wanted me to get a GED.

The one thing I enjoyed was my education. Despite all the trauma I endured, I was still resilient, and I refused to get a GED. Instead, I completed 2 years of high school in 1 year and graduated with my high school diploma when I was 16 years old. I wanted to break the cycle of historical trauma. I started college when I was 16.

Drugs and alcohol are a crisis on our reservation. By the time I was 20 years old, my parents lost our childhood home and I was taking care of them due to their drug addiction. I knew I wanted an education. I knew I wanted my kids to be embedded in their culture. I knew I wanted a better education for my children than I got. I knew I wanted the historical trauma cycles broken. Trying to break the cycle of intergenerational trauma was most difficult.

At the age of 20, I left to pursue higher education and moved into the city 5 hours away from the reservation. It was a struggle living in two different worlds—the city, which was "white man's world"—and in our traditional and cultural ways on the reservation. We managed and did it! How? Knowing if I fail, there is no one to help me. If I fall, no one is there to catch me. If I can't pay my rent or have food on the table, I can't call anyone to borrow money or help me. Knowing if I did not give my kids a better life, who would? That was my motivation and what drove my resilience.

Today, I have been with my husband for 34 years and married for 27 years. Both of my kids are successful, and we have a beautiful grandson. I finished my education and have been working in public health with a focus on cancer prevention among American Indian populations for over 2 decades. Our culture is embedded in our life. Our children are involved in our ceremonial dances, and my daughter had the honor to "pack medicine" and be Medicine Girl at one of our ceremonial dances. We live, eat, and breathe our culture. This is what resilience looks like! This is history, truth, and healing for resilient Native Americans!

CASE STUDY 1.1.
REFLECTION QUESTIONS

1. What role did resilience play in Celena's desire to break the cycle of transgenerational trauma? Where do you think Celena's desire to break the cycles of abuse and trauma came from?
2. Think of how you have been resilient throughout your lifetime. What helped you survive and go on despite what might have happened to you?

A Traumatized Brain and Body

Before we attempt to explain the brain's response to traumatic events, we need to acknowledge that there are constantly new discoveries in the field of neuroscience, and we all need to keep current with new discoveries and information (e.g., Kim et al., 2024). The brain is a complex organ that we are still learning about. Three major independent parts most frequently referred to in trauma studies are the prefrontal cortex, the hippocampus, and the amygdala, seen in Figure 1.1.

1. **Prefrontal cortex**, or higher brain, is our rational, thinking brain. Our executive functions, like decision making, are housed behind our foreheads in the prefrontal cortex. Trauma, as well as conditions such as attention-deficit/hyperactivity disorder, can interfere with executive functioning.
2. **Hippocampus**, located in the lower brain, controls memory storage and emotions and helps to distinguish between past and present. Trauma sometimes can "lock" the emotional brain in the past.
3. **Amygdala**, or "lizard/reptilian" brain, is also in the lower brain. It is our

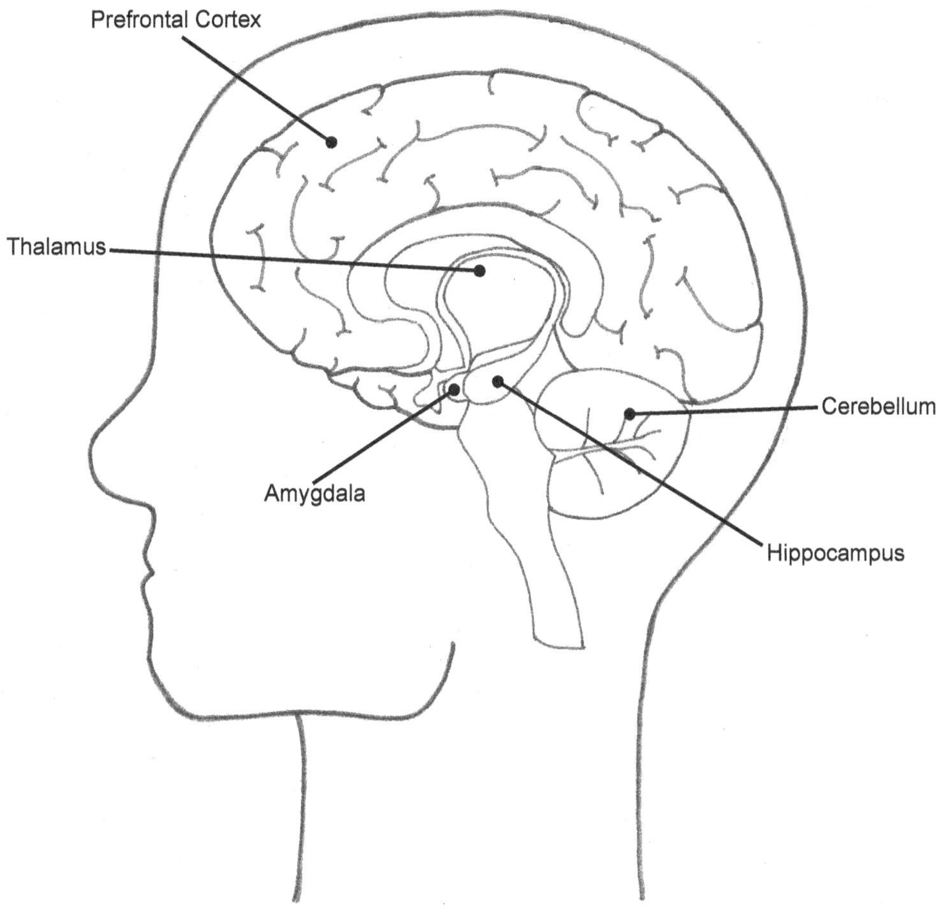

FIGURE 1.1. Sections of the brain. Drawn by Cynthia Nado.

instinctual survival center, controlling automatic reactions we don't have to think about, including breathing; heartbeat; and the **fight, flight, or freeze** stress responses. This part of the brain has no sense of time; everything is now.

Under safe or normal conditions, incoming information is first routed to the cerebral cortex, our rational or higher brain, and then on to the lower brain. In a crisis or stressful situation, the information bypasses the thinking centers in the higher brain and goes directly to the lower brain and amygdala, which registers fear and activates a survival response. DeWolf and Geddes (2019) explain this process:

> Our brains are designed to orchestrate responses to trauma that aim to protect and keep us safe. The amygdala, located in the *emotional brain* (limbic system),

> sends a message to the *instinctual* (or "lizard") brain, which then responds with fight, flight or freeze. This is automatic/instinctual and happens before the rational/thinking portion of our brain can engage. Rational thought is basically bypassed in times of traumatic stress to help us survive, which then affects brain function and group behavior. (p. 10)

Kozlowska, Walker, McLean, and Carrive (2015) refer to the fear reaction as the **defense cascade**, described here:

> All defense responses in the animal model of the defense cascade—arousal, freezing, flight or fight, tonic immobility, collapsed immobility, and quiescent immobility—are responses to threat mediated by neural circuits involving the extended amygdala, hypothalamus, peri aqueductal gray (PAG), ventral pontine tegmentum, ventral and dorsal medulla, and spinal cord. Each defense response has a signature neural pattern that corresponds to a combination of activated connections within a descending neural network. This descending network terminates at the level of the effector organs, where it controls a somatomotor component (which involves skeletal muscle), an autonomic/visceromotor component (which involves the viscera), and a pain-processing component. (p. 264)

Because the brain responds to threats instinctively, trauma memories are not processed or stored in the same way by which memories are stored in a regulated, nonthreatened brain. Trauma memories become fragmented, later producing graphic images on one hand and on the other, an inability to recall (Yoder, 2005). Even though an individual may not be able to consciously recall a specific memory, memories remain *chemically* stored in the brain. Some researchers have likened the effects of traumatic experiences to a sort of brain damage. For many survivors, the chemistry of the brain is permanently altered, giving rise to problematic behaviors and decreasing ability in certain areas (Mears, 2012).

This memory storage issue is why victims of violence are often unable to tell their stories chronologically or why there can be a wide variation in the details when trauma survivors recall their experiences over time—an important fact for law enforcement, prosecutors, judges, researchers, and evaluators to know. The survivor story may change over time as memories are recalled, reprocessed, and reframed. This does not mean a victim is lying but means their brain is attempting to reconstruct a sequence of events that are fragmented in their own memories.

Clinical treatments for past trauma include cognitive-behavioral therapy, eye movement desensitization and reprocessing, and tapping. These therapies help "patients to understand, tolerate, and reinterpret traumatic memories" (Kozlowska et al., 2015, p. 278). The process of shifting the neural pattern is the necessary first step in unlocking the patient's trauma response, in breaking the cycle of suffering, and in helping the patient to adapt to and overcome past trauma.

The Autonomic Nervous System

As described above, the entire **autonomic nervous system** (ANS) is involved in trauma responses, creating a ripple effect that causes various **somatic** responses. When we are safe, we are centered, balanced, coping, and resilient, and our **parasympathetic nervous system** (PNS) is activated. This "space" is called the **window of tolerance** (WoT), defined as the "zone where our nervous system is relaxed, calm, alert, engaged" (Graham, 2010). When we sense a threat, challenge, or new situation (picture the proverbial cave-dwelling human and the hostile predatory animal outside), our **sympathetic nervous system** (SNS) is automatically activated, meaning that we don't have to think about what to do. When our amygdala perceives a threat, be it real or not, it activates the SNS and signals the **hypothalamic–pituitary–adrenal (HPA) system** to release stress hormones such as adrenaline and cortisol.

This is the body/brain response that mobilizes us to act and protect ourselves and that forces our cerebral cortex to go offline (we are now running away from the threatening animal without thinking about it). SNS and HPA activation close our WoT and rocket us into the stress response of fight or flight. If our previously learned patterns of coping are passivity, confusion, withdrawal, and isolation, then we drop into freeze mode, where we shut down and immobilize ourselves (Graham, 2010). Yoder (2005) compares the freeze response to pressing the accelerator and brake at the same time.

However, when a threat occurs when we are within our WoT, we can learn to use strategies that allow us to intervene quickly and return to a more regulated state, especially if we feel connected to others either in the moment or in our minds. However, if we reach the point where we are overwhelmed or feeling vulnerable, then our WoT closes and we move into alarm, panic, anxiety and/or agitation.

Symptoms and Stress Responses

Now that we understand how our brains and bodies react and remember trauma, we can talk more about recognizing symptoms and signs.

A **trigger** is a stress response to something that has reactivated the trauma memory, setting off the cascade of neurological and chemical events we described previously. *Anything* can be a trigger—sight, sound, smell, taste, feel, look, color, place, praise, criticism, touch, proximity—literally anything. Triggers are highly personal and may not even resemble events of the original trauma. Our job as researchers and evaluators is to be trauma-informed so that we take precautions to avoid triggering someone or ourselves, know when and how to respond if someone is triggered, and do our best to care for them or ourselves if it happens (see Table 1.2). Trauma survivors also need to be given the tools to overcome the trauma while not expecting that everyone is going to be able to perfectly meet their needs.

Although we can strive to avoid triggering others, we will almost certainly fail at this goal. The more important thing is to act appropriately when we inevitably do. If we can do this, these difficult experiences can be transformed from instances of retraumatization to situations where resilience was forged in the presence of a calm and accepting other.

Given that in research and evaluation our brains need to be working from the prefrontal cortex most of the time, it is important we know how to calm ourselves so that we can model self-soothing for others. In doing so, we can be the anchor in a situation, allowing all to reestablish a sense of safety. The key is to recognize what is happening and act quickly to return to stability.

Several trauma researchers (Bloom & Farragher, 2013; Brave Heart, 2000; Mears, 2012) have developed lists of symptoms that describe a **trauma-organized individual**, or a trauma-affected person, and common stress responses that we may identify, hear about, or witness in ourselves and others during or throughout a study:

- Inability to grieve
- Problems with authority
- Lack of a basic sense of safety and trust
- Difficulty managing emotions
- Confused sense of fair play
- Depression
- Anxiety and hypervigilance
- Loss of sense of safety
- Anger, irritability, rage
- Oppositional behavior
- Withdrawal from activities and friends
- Moodiness
- Risk taking
- Sensitivity to exploitation
- Sense of a foreshortened future
- Academic difficulties
- Memory loss
- Difficulty expressing self
- Disruption of home life
- Difficulty sleeping
- Impaired concentration
- Impaired ability and problem solving
- Problems with short- and long-term memory
- Withdrawal from prior relationships and routines

Of course, not every trauma-affected person has all these issues. This list creates a framework that should not lead to assumptions and stereotyping but toward designing and implementing studies with awareness of such symptoms and being able to prevent triggers or to intervene with care.

One common symptom, **hyperarousal** or **hypervigilance**, means that a person's alert system is overactivated and the body is prepared to defend itself almost all the time (Mears, 2012). We know that in a state of hyperarousal, the limbic

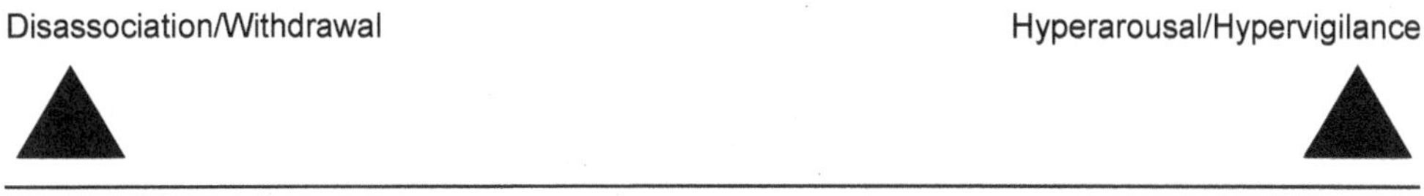

FIGURE 1.2. Stress-response continuum.

system has taken the prefrontal cortex offline. It's like being in a perpetual state of waiting for the next ax to fall. Hyperarousal also leads to serious health problems due to the overabundance of stress hormones.

Think about stress responses as being on a continuum, with hyperarousal/hypervigilance at one end and dissociation/withdrawal at the other (Figure 1.2). Hyperarousal/hypervigilance tends to lead to "acting-out" behaviors such as the following:

- Repetitive violence, military occupation, war
- Domestic abuse and child abuse
- Inability to show empathy to others, be flexible or tolerant of other perspectives, including faith/religion
- Sexual violence
- High-risk behaviors, including extreme sports
- Lawlessness
- Attacks on persons and symbolic property
- Disregard for Earth and environment
- Difficulty and blame in intimate relations
- Hoarding resources

At the other end of the spectrum is **passive response dissociation**, which occurs "when the traumatized individual retreats or surrenders in response to violent or frightening threats and stress. Dissociative states are characterized by avoidance behavior, emotional numbing, and a blank facial expression" (Mears, 2012, p. 20). Dissociative responses often lead to "acting-in" behaviors, where the unhealed pain energy is turned inward on oneself. These behaviors may include the following:

- Substance use, including alcohol
- Overwork
- Eating too little or too much
- Depression, numbness, anxiety

- Self-blame, shame, self-harm, suicide
- Physical symptoms: high blood pressure, pain, headaches, digestive trouble (Eastern Mennonite University, 2023, p. 68)

Trauma responses offer an explanation of the causes of many human behaviors, cycles of violence, and the prevalence of substance use disorders that are difficult to interrupt, no matter the intervention, program, or treatment. Rather than considering these responses as choices or cultural/personality traits, being trauma-informed leads us to understanding that these are learned survival mechanisms—healthy or not. People who adopt dissociative behaviors as a survival mechanism may lack interpersonal skills and judgment, making them vulnerable to exploitation, dysfunctional relationships, and becoming victims of interpersonal violence (Mears, 2012). Thus, programs and interventions that only treat or address symptoms and behaviors without addressing and healing the underlying effects of childhood and/or collective trauma will likely never manifest the long-term outcomes that so many programs and funders say they want to achieve.

WRAP-UP

Trauma is a universal human experience caused by myriad factors that few, if any, escape. This chapter introduced us to various types of traumas and how trauma causes changes in our brains and our genetic responses to stressors. ACEs change brain development, hard-wiring it to expect danger and triggering a complex defense cascade throughout the brain, nervous system, and body. Although people experience and process traumatic events differently, childhood traumas left unaddressed and unhealed lead to significant mental, behavioral, and physical health problems throughout a lifetime. We also learned that marginalized populations experience ACEs at much higher levels than white people and that systemic, racial, and complex trauma interact with and exacerbate ACEs.

Widespread manifestations of trauma symptoms and stress responses in communities and populations are often mistakenly labeled as "cultural traits," demonstrating a lack of understanding, or a racist understanding, about trauma, along with no knowledge of what is needed for individuals and communities to heal. Finally, collective traumas are traumatic events in and of themselves, such as natural disasters, and can compound any unhealed childhood traumas.

Remember, if this topic brings up strong physical or emotional responses, your body may be telling you that there may be issues you want to address by seeking professional help. You can also move your body, take deep calming breaths, and talk to a friend. It is vital that you learn to notice your own body's stress and trauma responses and intervene by breathing, moving, and calming down. *Breathe a little deeper. Let a little tension out. Let your body sink.*

CHAPTER 1 REFLECTION QUESTIONS

1. Think of a time when you perceived a real or imaginary threat. How did you react? Can you identify your dominant trauma response (fight, flight, freeze)? What did you feel at the time? How did you feel after? What did you need to help you metabolize the trauma? Did you get what you needed, or do you have healing work to do?

2. If you are already a researcher or evaluator, think about studies you have conducted. Looking back, were you triggered by anything throughout the course of the study? Do you think your clients and/or participants were triggered? How did you handle that?

3. How does understanding individual and collective trauma change how you look at yourself, others, your community, and the world around you?

CHAPTER 2

How Our Own Traumas Influence Our Work

Evaluators and researchers are immune from trauma . . . said nobody ever!

WHAT YOU'LL LEARN

TIER is not just something you do, but being trauma-informed is something you become, over time, with both practice and self-healing. We bring ourselves into our work; not only our biases but our worldviews have been molded and shaped by trauma. The next two chapters are about you (well, us). We challenge researchers and evaluators to, at the very least, begin your own healing journey if you haven't already, if you genuinely want to strive to do no harm.

In this chapter, we speak candidly of the harm evaluators and researchers can do—and in fact, do all the time—when we are not aware of our own trauma-affected behaviors, reactions, beliefs, and attitudes; when our traumas remain unaddressed and unhealed; when our professional organizations fail to acknowledge the role trauma plays in our work and lives; and when we don't incorporate resilience practices into our daily lives and interactions with others, including our participants. We offer some solutions to these problems and provide several opportunities throughout the chapter to reflect and practice. Throughout this chapter, please take a few moments to practice mindfulness, grounding, and conscious breathing practices whenever you feel tight or triggered. Take breaks when you need to.

Introduction

Although we may like to think of E&R as a force for good and progress, we must admit that it has not always been so. In fact, the E&R fields have harmed and retraumatized participants and communities for centuries by employing colonizing research methods, exploiting people's stories and experiences, extracting data, and leaving communities and programs no better off because of our work (Kostovicova & Knott, 2022). E&R competencies, guiding principles, and institutional review board (IRB) protocols often ignore the fact that we too are human beings with our own life experiences and traumas (Huff, 2025). Our fields—and our academic and professional training—largely fail to acknowledge that our traumas play out in our work, consciously or unconsciously, the same way that culture does (Hood, Hopson, & Frierson, 2015).

We certainly do not see ourselves as caregivers or being in the helping professions, who often experience greater rates of secondary trauma than the general population (Huff, 2025). However, by the very nature of our work, we are often placed—or choose to place ourselves—just outside the reach of our clients, programs, firms, and participants. For this reason, we purposely avoid the tendency to talk about trauma and trauma-affected people as though we, as researchers and evaluators, are somehow exempt from this universal human experience and its effects on ourselves, others, and our work.

Trauma's effect on evaluators has been one of the ways scholars have spoken most meaningfully about trauma. Scriven (2019), on a practical note, acknowledges that trauma can be a factor that impedes evaluators' ability to think clearly and that has potential implications for an evaluator's ability to practice effectively and ethically; thus, he emphasizes the importance of checklists in evaluation practice. But what is it about trauma that might affect an evaluator or researcher and influence the execution of their work?

Some authors note the trauma that can be experienced as an evaluator or researcher who identifies with a marginalized group. Miller and Tohme (2022) address how many LGBTQ+ evaluators "routinely expose them[selves] to the traumatic experiences suffered by their constituents" (p. 147), noting that this can keep evaluators' own traumatic experiences "close to the surface" (p. 148). Phillips, Felt, Perez-Bill, Ruprecht, and Elías Glenn (2022) relate that "pressing for competent LGBTQ+ evaluation can feel isolating, frustrating, and even painful or traumatizing" (p. 17) due to a sense of dismissal or rejection that can resurface old wounds.

Similarly, Boyce and colleagues (2023) and Huff (2025) address the repeated traumas that BIPOC evaluators face in the line of duty, and Walker (2018) notes his early experiences of abandonment and domestic violence as formative for his evaluation style, sense of justice, and way of being in the world.

The idea of examining what and whom we bring to our work is not new and is a foundational tenet of culturally responsive evaluation (Hood et al., 2015). Bledsoe and Donaldson (2014) write the following concerning the importance of such reflection:

> Evaluators often aspire to achieving maximum "objectivity" in an evaluation. But perhaps one of the greatest foundations of evaluation is the evaluator's ability

> to acknowledge his or her personal and professional philosophies and beliefs, and to engage in thoughtful self-reflection about how those philosophies and beliefs can impact an evaluation's design and implementation. Thus, it would seem that the key to conducting a good evaluation starts within the evaluator. (p. 3)

Patton's (2016) review of Ernie House's book *Cherry Street Alley* paints a picture of how trauma shaped House's view of his practice and suggests that his experiences forged his focus on "social justice as a criterion for evaluators" (p. 442). Patton was not the only author to note the role of trauma in House's life. Astbury (2016) writes that "these and other traumatic experiences left a mark, affecting House's character and later his evaluation style" (p. 59).

Although trauma can have a generative and motivational aspect, scholars also warn of the professional and personal toll it can take, especially when left untreated. In a piece on being one's authentic self in evaluation practice, Fierro (2019) warns that childhood traumas can "sabotage" (p. 149) one's personal and professional efforts, underlining the importance of dealing proactively with these issues.

Ideally, before we consider applying the TIER lens to our work, we need to turn that lens inward. Or perhaps we look inward and outward at the same time, as they are intimately intertwined.

Being Trauma-Informed Starts with Ourselves

As discussed in Chapter 1, at least 64% of us have one or more ACEs (CDC, n.d.). As adults, it's highly likely we've experienced additional traumatic events or collective traumas. No one on the planet, save for perhaps a scant few isolated people and groups, escaped the collective trauma caused by the global COVID-19 pandemic of 2020–2021 and the indeterminate periods of sheltering in place. Loss, grief, anxiety, anger, mistrust, and fear were integral components of the pandemic and still fuel global extremism, fed by conspiracy theories and misinformation that lead to toxic stress, hate, and violence. Shelter-in-place orders prevented us from grieving those we lost. Additionally, the threat to our existence as we know it due to climate change is causing increased anxiety and toxic stress, as well as trauma, to those affected by severe weather events.

Although we have managed to live through whatever adversity life has put before us, our philosophies and beliefs are also informed by those traumas, and those beliefs drive our behaviors, some of which may be conscious or unconscious stress responses. Like our culture, our traumas have a direct effect on everything about us, and we need to increase our awareness of how our own traumas and stress responses play out in our work—from design through reporting to deciding what kinds of studies we will conduct and what kinds we avoid. We need to participate in our own healing. Just as trauma affects people differently, people find different ways to heal. Find what works for you. Here are some suggestions.

Therapy and Counseling

Therapy is often a good place to start. Healing trauma and transforming shame is how we can be whole and truly thrive as human beings. Uncovering past and present traumas with the support of a licensed therapist is highly recommended, as healing the kind of pain associated with trauma and shame requires connection and community (Brown, 2012a) and we cannot do it alone. We need to examine our lives and fully understand what makes us tick—and what triggers us. Socrates coined the phrase "the unexamined life," and we believe that our unexamined lives pose a danger to all involved in our work and to ourselves. Even the character Fiero in *Wicked* changed his tune about living an unexamined life when given the opportunity.

Meditation and Mindfulness Practices

One of the most important things to learn is what triggers us, how our triggers manifest as behaviors and words, and how to self-regulate in the moment when we have been triggered. Meditation and mindfulness practices can be used anywhere and anytime we become aware that we've been triggered. It is easy to learn these practices, and anyone can do them. Although it may be challenging to incorporate them into our daily lives, apps like Calm and Headspace are helpful for developing breathing and meditation practices. Evaluators and researchers may feel strange starting interviews or focus groups with grounding and breathing exercises, but it would help alleviate everyone's anxiety and contribute to creating a safe space.

Move the Body—Regularly

Conducting studies often means that we sit a lot. Eating healthy, fresh foods and exercising regularly are important to our overall physical *and* mental health. Exercise and movement of any kind also help move stress hormones and tightness through and out of the body. Remember, trauma responses are chemical, biological, and physical. They are designed to get the body ready to face a threat and survive. So, sometimes we need to stand up and shake it out—literally. Or dance it out. Or run, walk, hike, ride, box, or stretch it out.

Because trauma responses live in our body, we can learn to increase our awareness of where our body is holding the stress by mindfully scanning the body and noticing areas of constriction or tightness. We can learn to notice when our breathing is shallow and our shoulders are up to our ears. Movement helps release what our body is holding. When we are comfortable doing this ourselves, we are better able to sense when our participants may need a movement, breathing, and stretch break as well.

Coming Back to the Breath

Breathing and breathwork are essential to regulating and grounding ourselves when we are stressed or triggered. These practices can be as simple as taking five deep breaths through the nose and exhaling out the mouth, or they can involve working with a breathwork or somatic practitioner for deep self-healing. We may find that after a participant tells their story, we need to take a collective, calming, and cleansing breath before moving on. Again, finding comfort with the practice when we are alone makes inviting others to breathe much easier.

Prevent Burnout and Compassion Fatigue

Balancing life and work are critical to preventing burnout and compassion fatigue (Huff, 2025). Researchers and evaluators often live in their heads and work on deadlines. We often manage multiple projects at once, and some of these projects involve the heavy-lifting work of social justice, which can be emotionally exhausting (Miller, Stiff, & Ellis, 1988). It is easy to develop habits of working late into the night and not getting enough sleep. It is easy to put the work before ourselves, our families, and our physical and mental health, especially if we are independent consultants who depend on billable hours.

In white supremacist culture, productivity is overvalued (Okun, 2021), often at the expense of our own health and well-being. Toxic stress, especially when experienced for long durations, can lead to adverse health effects, including increased risk of cardiovascular disease, anxiety disorders, type 2 diabetes, some cancers, and obesity (Shern, Blanch, & Steverman, 2016). To maximize our energy and effectiveness and minimize toxic stress, we must lead more balanced lives. We need to slow down the pace and question practices and beliefs that lead us to overworking, pushing through burnout, and neglecting our physical and mental health. That may mean learning to say no. It may mean having conversations with our employers or funders about our own needs for health and well-being.

This subject is so important—and so unrecognized—that we want to talk more about it. Dr. Stacy Huff's groundbreaking research on this subject informs much of the next section.

Secondary Trauma: The Unspoken Hazard of E&R

There is a dirty little secret in the E&R communities. And that secret is that sometimes we experience secondary trauma because of the work that we do. It's a secret because our professions and employers have yet to acknowledge this as a risk to ourselves, even if they acknowledge the risk to participants. There are only passive references to this subject in the literature as well as a lack of awareness in academia. And for that reason, it's time to expose the secret.

Secondary Trauma in the Literature

The reality of **secondary trauma**, both as a danger for researchers and evaluators and as a factor when dealing with stakeholders, is addressed by just a few scholars. Hatcher and colleagues (2020) noted the significant violence and real dangers that evaluators in South Africa heard about in their evaluation of a domestic abuse program, stating that "the project itself engaged with death on a regular basis, causing significant emotional trauma" (p. 5). They also called attention to the "heartbreak of trauma work" (p. 169) with victims of sexual violence that impeded a program's effectiveness, as it deflated staffs' ability to effectively implement a prevention program. Likewise, David and Schiff (2015) reported similar patterns of secondary trauma inhibiting effective implementation of a trauma intervention for infants and children in Israel.

Although we *know* that those working in and with the military, Red Cross, nongovernmental organizations, refugee camps, and other monitoring and evaluation contexts experience secondary trauma, our fields lack research on these evaluators and researchers. Although Campbell, Adams, and Patterson (2008) note the role of secondary trauma and professional burnout for those who work with people in hard-to-find populations, these topics are mentioned in passing, if at all.

CF, Burnout, and STS Defined

Exploring compassion fatigue and secondary trauma requires a solid foundational understanding of their key components, which we provide here.

All aspects of someone's occupation can affect their professional quality of life, which ranges from compassion satisfaction to compassion fatigue. **Compassion satisfaction** is the pleasurable feeling that a helping professional experiences when assisting others (Hundall Stamm, 2009). Specifically, it is the good feeling and encouragement about the work done, which involves self-care and stress management strategies. Conversely, **compassion fatigue (CF)** is characterized by emotional and physical exhaustion, reducing one's capacity to empathize and feel compassion for those they serve (Hundall Stamm, 2009). CF often results from feeling unable to provide adequate care to those in need (Ledoux, 2015).

CF is frequently used as an umbrella term for similar job-related stress disorders, such as vicarious trauma, secondary traumatic stress, moral injury, and burnout (Coetzee & Laschinger, 2018; Ledoux, 2015). Differentiating CF from other related constructs can be challenging (Ledoux, 2015). The first subconstruct,

burnout, encompasses feelings of exhaustion, frustration, anger, and depression resulting from work (Hundall Stamm, 2009). Feelings of burnout are related to general work stress, not necessarily the burdens associated with caring for others (Ledoux, 2015). Issues leading to burnout include challenges in the work environment such as time management, caseload burdens, interactions with team members, and inability to achieve goals (Pehlivan & Guner, 2018).

The second subconstruct, **secondary traumatic stress** (STS), refers to stress that occurs when exposure to a traumatic event experienced by one person becomes a traumatizing event for another (Bride, Robinson, Yegidis, & Figley, 2004). **Vicarious trauma**, the stress experienced from listening to the traumatic stories and experiences of others (Pehlivan & Guner, 2018), and similar terms are frequently subsumed within the STS construct. Symptoms of STS include depression, generalized anxiety, avoidance of triggers or reminders, and hyperalertness (Pehlivan & Guner, 2018).

CF manifests in multiple ways, and research shows that these symptoms cannot be alleviated by a break from work, such as a vacation, and can worsen over time. The progression of CF can lead to questioning the meaning and purpose of life, isolating oneself from others, substance abuse, difficulty sleeping, and distress (Ledoux, 2015). There is a lack of consensus in the research on the exact symptoms that fall under compassion fatigue versus those attributed to burnout or STS, but we assert that whatever symptoms you are feeling, you need to recognize and address them.

Our Vulnerability to CF, Burnout, and STS

Researchers and evaluators often confront unique political, systemic, and historical inequities and challenges that heighten our vulnerability to compassion fatigue. As highlighted in a recent blog post by Malhotra, Machado, and Aslam (2023), researchers and evaluators operate in a world where instances of violence stemming from war, conflict, gender bias, racial and ethnic prejudice, and discrimination against various minorities—such as those based on disability, nationality, and language—are on the rise. And evaluators and researchers engage with individuals who have survived various forms of trauma, including refugees, survivors of war and conflict, victims of domestic violence, and even service providers who have been exposed to secondary trauma while working with survivors (Malhotra et al., 2023). Exposure to the trauma experienced by others stands out as the primary risk factor for compassion fatigue (Pehlivan & Guner, 2018). The dissonance between an evaluator's perceived role and practical realities generates distressing emotions, especially if the researcher or evaluator is frustrated that they cannot provide participants with the appropriate assistance (Ledoux, 2015).

Should STS be considered an occupational hazard for at least some researchers and evaluators? We think so. And that means that the entire global E&R

community has a moral and ethical responsibility to provide structures of support that would allow us to metabolize STS and CF and heal (Huff, 2025). The danger of STS is that if left unprocessed and unsupported, it will compound any individual or collective traumas. Case Study 2.1 illustrates this perfectly.

CASE STUDY 2.1 Challenges of TIER in International Development Programs

MARIAN WARE

International development programs, particularly those working in the political realm on issues such as peacebuilding and enhancing democratic norms and practices, create a unique set of circumstances around evaluators' efforts to be trauma-informed. Sensitivity to and understanding trauma becomes even more needed, as the range of restrictive, fragile, and dynamic political environments in which these programs often operate increases the likelihood of encountering experiences of trauma during an evaluation. Such evaluations may engage with political dissidents, marginalized segments of a population, including LGBTQ+ individuals, refugees and internally displaced persons, and survivors of conflict and/or sexual violence. Moreover, cultural norms and power dynamics that vary significantly across contexts make it crucial for evaluators to be thoughtful in how they engage with populations who have likely experienced trauma.

However, evaluators may also face a direct conflict between the program itself and the goals of TIER. Such programs are often funded by the United States government and thus must actively work to avoid perpetuating a legacy of U.S. imperialism and colonialism while operating within the confines of U.S. government interests. Prioritizing trauma-informed practices in these programs requires additional attention to building local communities' ownership and leadership of the program on all fronts—including program monitoring and evaluation. Further, U.S. government-funded programs may default to the government's standard operating procedures, which often lack the human-centered and adaptive practices that trauma-informed evaluations prioritize. This operational context can easily translate to extractive and even colonizing data collection practices rather than using a study as an opportunity to center and amplify the voices of traumatized populations and empower them to be the architects of change in their communities.

One such evaluation that struggled with these pitfalls focused on assessing the effectiveness of a 5-year program that sought to enhance local civic organizations' role in advocating for citizen rights and mitigating conflict amid a civil war. Although the evaluation was clearly operating in a conflict context, the evaluation team was unfamiliar with trauma-informed evaluation approaches. While interviewing civic activists who took part in the program, numerous stories arose of friends and colleagues killed due to their advocacy work over the course of the program. The evaluators were not adequately prepared to respond to these stories. There was no opportunity to pause or adapt the interview and no space to process what had been discussed. Instead, lacking a toolkit to intentionally engage with what was being shared and respond accordingly, they continued with the interviews as planned. Further, when drafting the evaluation report, they struggled to grapple with how—if at all—to capture these stories in the report. In short, the standard practices put in place for this evaluation did not create space to adequately plan for and deal with experiences of trauma.

Examples like this exemplify the necessity of a shift for evaluators and researchers working on international democracy and peacebuilding programs. This shift toward TIER requires rethinking the principles that underlie our monitoring and evaluation efforts (from considerations such as rigor and efficiency to inclusivity and "do no harm"), whose knowledge and opinions we prioritize (from ourselves as evaluation "experts" to the local communities we are seeking to support), and our role as evaluators (from data extractors and analysts to partners and storytellers). With significant forethought, intentional planning, and partnerships with local civic organizations, evaluators can do away with data collection efforts that can be extractive and retraumatizing. Done well, collecting data from trauma-affected populations can even go beyond "doing no harm" to fostering healing and empowerment.

**CASE STUDY 2.1.
REFLECTION QUESTIONS**

1. Put yourself in the shoes of the international evaluation team in the above case study. How would you (like to) respond if you knew a colleague had been murdered or experienced other forms of violence? How can you process the trauma and support others while honoring the confines of the study's design?
2. What came up for you while reading this chapter? Did you identify issues that need attention and healing? Reflect on why you became, or wish to become, an evaluator or researcher. What about the work feels good to you? Does anything about the work feel uncomfortable?
3. Take time and journal privately about how your own traumas may show up in your work. Don't censor—just write. See what bubbles up. At this point, are there any studies or topics you feel you should not engage with because they might trigger past trauma memories? If so, how do you think you might equip yourself to work with those issues?
4. How do you currently practice self-care? How do you feel about breathwork and meditation? What strategies can you use in the moment to help you keep your WoT open? If you don't do these practices now, are you willing to learn and incorporate them into your work?

The Significance of CF, Burnout, and STS in E&R

Understanding the significance of CF, burnout, and STS as "professional hazards" is crucial not only for the well-being of evaluators and researchers themselves but also for the integrity and effectiveness of the study itself. Bledsoe (2021) contends that "an inability to connect with people actually invalidates the data and its credibility. Instead of connecting and understanding the context, society, and issues that comprise a programme, strategy, and the like, we end up relying on our own privileged and often disconnected perspective" (p. 18). The implications of adopting this perspective are significant, as it suggests that if evaluators are suffering from compassion fatigue and are, therefore, unable to connect and empathize with participants, the overall validity of the evaluation may be compromised.

Contemporary evaluation theorists advocate for evaluators to assume the role of change agents, putting evaluators and researchers in much closer proximity to marginalized, oppressed, and traumatized populations. But the call to advocacy does not affect all evaluators and researchers in the same way. Reid, Boyce, Adetogun, Moller, and Avent (2020) shed light on the different experiences of evaluators of color (EOCs), noting that EOCs are often regarded as more trustworthy when engaging with communities of color but may face challenges in being perceived as credible in other contexts, where their voices can be drowned out or marginalized.

In the eyes of EOCs, their roles encompass being change agents in addition to being methodologists, catalysts, and advocates (Reid et al., 2020). However, this perspective can sometimes lead to dissonance between their envisioned role as change agents and the reality of their practice (Reid et al., 2020). When the anticipated change does not materialize, evaluators and researchers, including EOCs, may grapple with feelings of demotivation, potentially diminishing their effectiveness and leading to **moral distress**, characterized by the sense of failing to provide adequate care or achieve valued objectives, which is a risk factor for compassion fatigue (Pehlivan & Guner, 2018; Reid et al., 2020). Empathy—something TIER demands of us—also puts evaluators at risk for CF, and "evaluators who themselves come from the minoritized communities they serve" may naturally harbor heightened empathy (Reid et al., 2020, p. 23).

We summarize some of Huff's (2025) dissertation research findings here:

1. The tension between neutrality and advocacy exacerbates compassion fatigue. Evaluation has a unique stressor in that evaluators feel an expectation to remain neutral and objective, even in highly emotionally charged situations. Evaluators engaging in a human-centered approach, while still experiencing CF for other reasons, seemed to better process these moments. Those who forced themselves into objectivity struggled with anger, guilt, and sorrow.

2. Identity directly interacts with compassion fatigue, and evaluators who share identity with the participants are at greater risk for CF. EOCs often choose projects to work with a specific population, generally a population of which they are a member. The stories they hear are like what they themselves have lived through, increasing their risk for CF.

Knowing this, how do we move forward and change our fields and methods to better support those doing E&R?

Another important consideration is the interaction between CF and the **American Evaluation Association (AEA)** Evaluator Competencies (n.d.-a), which guide evaluators' training, self-reflection, and practice. CF can potentially affect these competencies, and the interaction between CF and the competencies merits further consideration. Symptoms such as decreased compassion, avoidance, and self-isolation may negatively affect an evaluator's competence in the professional practice, context, and planning and management domains. Evaluators experiencing impaired judgment from CF may struggle in the methodology domain, which requires evaluators to use evidence to draw conclusions and make judgments. The interpersonal domain may see the most significant effects, as evaluators struggle to foster positive relationships, listen to diverse stakeholders, build trust, facilitate interactions, and manage conflict constructively. Thus, we recommend that AEA and other professional associations related to E&R strongly consider including being trauma-informed in their competencies *and* financially supporting consultants and organizations that can provide this much-needed professional development (see Huff, 2025, for explicit recommendations).

Methodology Does Not Eliminate Risk

Think about the statistics we see and hear daily: obesity rates, deaths in natural disasters, numbers of unhoused people, poverty rates, school and mass shootings, police murders, missing and murdered indigenous women, sexual assaults and interpersonal violence, diabetes, heart disease, cancer, suicides, hate crimes, undocumented immigrants crossing borders, opioid overdoses, deaths caused by DWI/DUI—the list is truly endless. We are bombarded by numbers—and that means that there are countless people counting things, many of them tragic and traumatic.

So, what about the person at the computer processing and reporting that data? What is the effect of numbers representing horrific things on the person who crunched them? Is that person you? Avoidance and dissociation, also symptoms of CF and STS, can create challenges for data analysisists as well as data collectors, which risks compromising the integrity of the analysis.

Numbers are not benign or neutral. Analyzing data related to traumatic issues, like sexual assault, war, murder, or poverty can affect the analyst, especially if they are close to the issue in some way. Analysts may be horrified or upset about what those numbers represent, especially if they are aware that those numbers are only symbols representing real human beings, animals, or plants. These emotions, like all trauma responses, need to be processed in healthy ways—starting with acknowledging that the emotions exist—and not repressed. Employers need to provide support for their data analysts, regardless of methodology, and give analysts permission to take breaks, get some distance from the data, talk it out with a supportive peer, and metabolize any vicarious trauma.

STS and Our Partners

Although the primary focus of this chapter is on the researcher and evaluator, it is important to understand that the clients with whom we contract and work and their staff may also suffer from CF, burnout, and STS, whether they know it or not. One of the leading causes of turnover in many sectors—including law enforcement, education, and human services—is burnout. That means that as we work with agencies and organizations to determine the effectiveness and outcomes of their initiatives, we are likely sitting with trauma-affected people in our contract negotiations, design meetings, and at all other stages of the project. These people may or may not be the people we survey or interview, but nonetheless they could still experience symptoms of STS, which you need to be aware of and sensitive to.

In fact, CF could lead to turnover in critical stakeholder positions that could slow a study's progress, send it in a new direction, or end it altogether. STS, CF, and burnout will affect the way our clients show up the same as it also affects the way we show up. For example, social workers often serve the same populations as researchers and evaluators, including survivors of childhood abuse, domestic violence, violent crime, natural disasters, and conflict (Hoeper, 2013; Malhotra et al., 2023).

When we become aware of the potential for STS in our clients and partners, we may need to find ways to uncover some backstories. These stories will be shared only if we are trustworthy, which means our focus must be on establishing genuine connections with the clients and partners we will walk alongside for the duration of the project and possibly after. Exploring traumatic backstories could occur informally and off the record over coffee, lunch, or drinks. But understanding our partners' backstories will help us know how to act and support them and possibly minimize triggering them.

We need to go this extra distance for several reasons. First, we could be creating an opportunity to engage in peer support so that partners can talk about what they are carrying into the project with someone who understands. There could be mutuality in peer support as well if there is an understanding that the work affects everyone, including the researcher and evaluator. Redefining what it means to "act professionally" or "keep some distance" may be necessary for developing systems of peer support with our partners. Second, we need to remember the danger that unexamined trauma brings. We could find ourselves suddenly stonewalled and shut out (as a result of shutdown or avoidance behaviors), we may be asked to change the scope of work, we may be asked to delete certain questions from protocols because they are triggering for our client, we may be asked to whitewash findings in the report because they may be triggering for the funder, or our client may ghost us entirely. Is it possible that trauma plays a role in these avoidance behaviors? We think so.

In my (Martha) TIER training workshops with both evaluators and community-based organizations, I invite participants to think about a time they felt they were traumatized doing their work and write what they felt at the time on a sticky note. Participants then put their notes on the wall alongside notes of others. Then, I invite participants to consider what they needed to get through the feelings they had just listed. Next, volunteers are invited to scan the "feelings" and "needs" notes and read themes or commonalities they see among the responses to the group.

It is always a very heavy moment in the room, as we sit in the pain and tension and acknowledge that these feelings and needs are *ours*—not other people's. One (anonymous) participant shared their experience, saying, "I was hired to map suicide data on the census block level in my city and county. The census block three streets over was the highest in the city. These are my neighbors. I felt both deep empathy and sorrow." Sharing our feelings and needs was painful. There were tears. Yet there were also peer support and solidarity because for the first time for many of us in the room, we no longer felt alone.

Over the course of several workshops, I collected the sticky notes and entered the words people wrote into Excel for analyzing and visualizing. I counted the number of responses, not participants, because many people wrote more than one feeling and need (see Figure 2.1). This informal data collection process sheds light on how researchers and evaluators experience STS and what they need to heal—and it is consistent with the trauma literature.

Analyzing the participants' needs was more challenging because the categories often overlapped, like "more time off work" and "time to process with friends," which could fall into more than one category. We ended up settling on nine categories of needs, as seen in Figure 2.2. Data analysis reveals a great need for employers to provide evaluators and researchers with space and time to heal and to connect and process their traumatic experiences—and Dr. Huff (2025) found the same thing in her study. This requires a huge change in how universities and firms do business and treat their researchers.

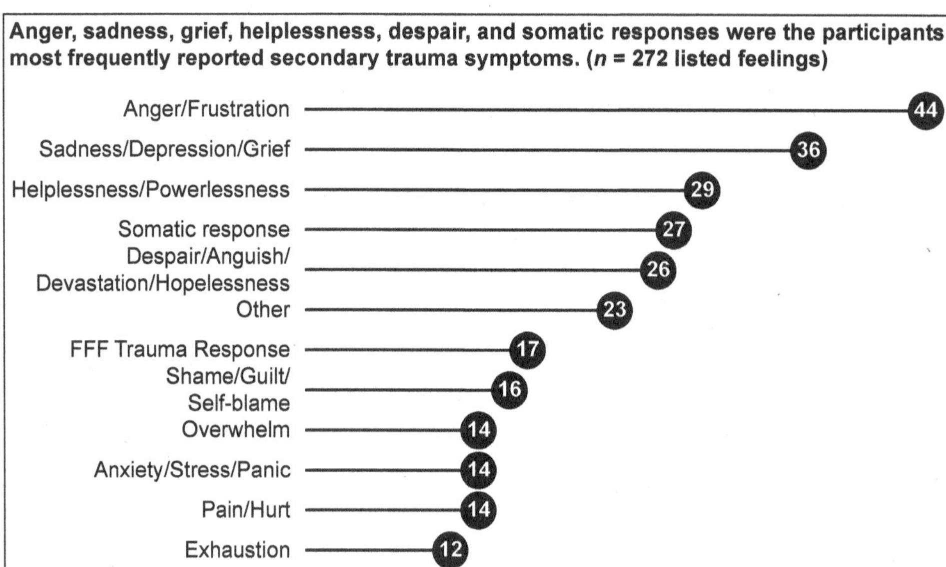

FIGURE 2.1. Type and frequency of emotions felt by traumatized evaluators.

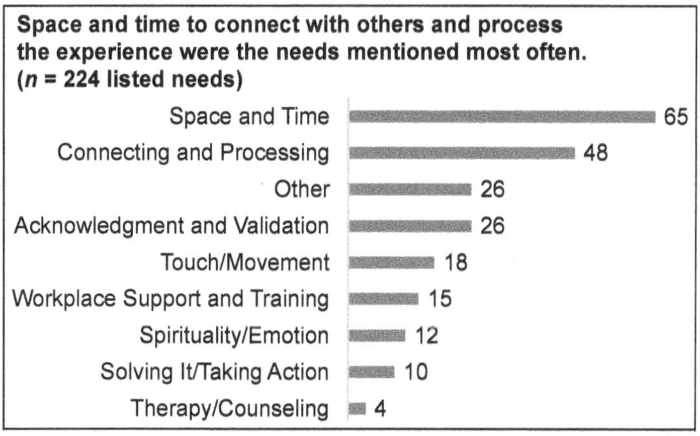

FIGURE 2.2. What participants needed to metabolize secondary trauma.

The next case study provides an example of recognizing trauma and taking the steps to process it.

CASE STUDY 2.2 Centering Healing and Activating Resilience: Shifting Our Transformative Evaluation Process during COVID at Centro Hispano of Dane County

EVELYN CRUZ and VIVIEN AHRENS

Our community has always been in crisis. But during the COVID-19 pandemic, "Se cayó la venda de los ojos." Some of the unseen became seen. The COVID crisis was not, as some mused, an equalizer. It was a visibilizer. The existing suffering became more visible, even more urgent, and existing inequalities more transparent. At Centro Hispano of Dane County ("Centro" for short)[1]—a hub of community services and programs for Latinx residents in Madison, Wisconsin—we had to slow down. The pandemic forced us to pause and center staff well-being in all aspects of our work, including evaluation.

In the spring of 2020, we had just begun a **transformative evaluation** process as part of a 5-year grant funded by the Wisconsin Partnership Program. Centro was able to create the new position of Director of Evaluation and Strategic Planning, for which I (Evelyn Cruz) was hired from within the agency. This was the first time that a staff member had dedicated time to focus on in-house evaluation across agency programs. Before the pandemic, we had started our staff-led transformative evaluation process by brainstorming evaluation questions together. Based on these guiding questions, we then developed an evaluation plan centered around staff well-being and positive narratives about Latinxs in Dane County. We were eager to start telling strengths-based stories: stories of resilience and hope. We also planned to reflect

[1]Centro Hispano of Dane County provides bilingual wraparound services for Latinx families, ranging from case management and youth programs to adult professional development to immigration support. For more information, see *www.micentro.org*.

on how our values supported our well-being through our work. But with COVID, our community, including our staff, was in an even deeper crisis. Under these circumstances, I could not ask staff to make time for data collection. We needed to feel good before we could start thinking about what makes us feel good. We, therefore, paused our transformative evaluation process to center staff well-being.

At Centro, 90% of our staff identify as Latinx. This means that we are affected by the same systems of oppression as the community that we serve. It also means that we can act as multipliers and amplifiers of community well-being.[2] In this situation, we needed to take care of ourselves before we could take care of others. As I (Evelyn) often say, you can't give what you don't have. So, at this time more than ever, our agency focused on staff well-being to ensure community well-being. For our leadership team, this meant many things. Often, we just acted as an emotional sounding board for others. We spent many hours on the phone listening to staff who just needed to talk. Our evaluation team thought about what kinds of information could give us a better sense of what type of staff support was needed during the unique and difficult COVID times.

Centro contracted two experts in mental health and social work who conducted four listening sessions and two qualitative surveys. The assessment uncovered that the COVID pandemic was not only directly affecting the clients that Centro serves but also affecting employees' personal and work lives and how we functioned as an agency. The assessment also revealed that mental health services were needed for both staff and the community. This assessment helped us document and see the effects of COVID on our community within our agency.

As a result, I (Evelyn) completely shifted my priorities. We were fortunate to have the resources, capacity, and flexibility of our grant to pivot and prioritize staff wellness and well-being. For example, we provided more flexibility at work, highlighted our health insurance coverage for mental health, and provided an internal therapeutic support group.

For us at Centro, our transformative evaluation is a way to bring justice to our work by prioritizing wellness. As the COVID crisis subsided, we were happy to take up our transformative evaluation questions again. The COVID crisis gave us a deeper realization of how important it is to tell our stories that help ourselves and others understand the systemic injustices we deal with every day and to show and remember how we ground our work in our values and how that makes us healthier and stronger. COVID is only one of the crises we have overcome. Our story is one of healing and resilience. Let's tell this story loud and clear—at home, in our work, and through evaluation.

CASE STUDY 2.2. REFLECTION QUESTIONS

1. What effects did the COVID-19 pandemic have on you, those around you, and your E&R work?
2. Did you have, and do you currently have, an emotional sounding board, such as others in your field who can help you process feelings?
3. How does storytelling help promote healing and transformation? How can we ensure that people's stories are more than just "data"?

[2]At Centro, we call this idea "wellness from the inside out." For more information, see Glines and Cruz (2019) and Ahrens, Cruz, Pasturczak, Bakken, and Moore (2023).

We Can Be Dangerous

Let's be honest. In some cases, you may not be the right person to be in the room or to do that study—and it takes honesty, humility, and courage to admit that. If you have not begun the journey of healing from your own traumas, or you are unprepared emotionally to handle what emotions might come up, or you have no idea how to hold safe and brave space, you risk doing harm and should probably not be in the room. Throughout this book, we offer many ways you can fold TIER into your work, but that does not mean you can get away with not examining your own traumas and how they have shaped your behavior, worldview, and thinking.

WRAP-UP

Many evaluators and researchers are at risk of compassion fatigue, burnout, and secondary trauma. Period. The dirty little secret is out. The bottom line is that we risk retraumatizing or triggering others and doing harm if we have not healed from our own traumas; if we have not learned to integrate care, resilience practices, and empathy into our work; and if we are unprepared or ill-equipped to hold safe and brave space for our participants. Perhaps reading this book is your first step, or perhaps you've already begun your journey toward being a trauma-informed researcher or evaluator. Maybe you'll find our approach uncomfortable, as it presents a counternarrative to the Eurocentric research methods many of us are taught. Maybe you'll find wearing the trauma-informed lens refreshing and inspiring. Regardless of your comfort level with TIER, we encourage you to examine your own culture, position, privilege, status, and trauma history in safe, supportive ways so that together we can move beyond "resist retraumatizing" and into facilitating empowerment, healing, and transformation.

The widely ignored and unacknowledged problem of evaluator/researcher STS needs to be addressed. Stacy Huff's dissertation research findings correlated with the literature, as did Martha's informal research conducted in her workshops. We have provided data that justify attention and change—changes in graduate programs, professional competencies, professional development, E&R firms, and professional associations. CF, burnout, and STS must be recognized as hazards of the work, and structures and processes need to be created and normalized to provide support for those who need it.

In the analysis of our workshop on participants' feelings and needs, we found that those who were traumatized on the job needed to feel like they had permission to do what they needed to self-regulate, metabolize their emotions and physical reactions, and heal. Although space, time, and peer support were important, 15 respondents specifically called attention to workplace issues that prevented them from getting what they needed. They also expressed a desire for more training and professional development regarding best practices for working with traumatized populations.

Self-care is essential, and the key to self-care is to find what you enjoy and what works for you and do it. On planes, we are instructed to put the oxygen mask on ourselves before helping others. We are so much more than "data geeks," and we are not robots. What we need to metabolize secondary trauma is the same as what our trauma-affected participants and clients need. We are human beings too, after all. We cannot—and should not—engage with trauma-affected people and populations until we have begun working on our own healing. We repeat Socrates' warning that we've modified: *The unexamined life of any researcher or evaluator is a danger to all involved.*

CHAPTER 2. REFLECTION QUESTIONS

1. What is your experience with CF, burnout, and/or secondary traumatic stress? What were your feelings and needs? How can you get your needs met?
2. Have you worked with a client who has symptoms of STS? If so, how did that affect your relationship and your work?
3. Have a conversation with a quantitative data analyst or professor about numbers and secondary trauma. Discuss the publishing and writing standards for academic peer-reviewed journals and graduate theses/dissertations. Do you find any structural or institutional obstacles to reporting quantitative data in a humanizing trauma-informed way? Note any perspectives, questions, or issues the conversation identified.

CHAPTER 3

Foundational Principles of TIER

A good foundation is critical. Just be careful not to overdo it.

WHAT YOU'LL LEARN

Principles. Values. Ethics. Guidelines. Competencies. These are nothing new to researchers and evaluators. Our work is governed and guided heavily by IRBs, governmental licensing agencies, and professional associations, primarily to ensure that our work is done with honesty and integrity and that any risk of participating in a study is transparent. In this chapter, we present SAMHSA's (2014) framework for a trauma-informed approach, including the **Four R's** and **Six Principles of Trauma-Informed Care**, which are the basis for our work, and discuss their alignment with other guiding principles, values, and practices.

Why TIER?

It's true that gender identity, educational levels, socioeconomic status, and race/ethnicity may create power imbalances between researchers and evaluators and our participants, but trauma is, or can be, what connects us. Our shared experiences as human beings are what connect us. However, trauma can also manifest in ways that drive separation. When researchers and evaluators do not realize the effects of trauma and fail to recognize how it affects thought patterns and behavior, we are susceptible to any or all of the following mistakes: (1) doing psychological harm to study participants; (2) misinterpreting body language and other nonverbal signals; (3) underestimating contributions made by participants; (4) minimizing, judging, or dismissing lived experiences; and (5) experiencing secondary trauma without the support and processes needed to metabolize it. Any or all these errors affect not only the experience of those involved in a study but possibly the validity of the findings as well.

Conversely, being trauma-informed in the course of E&R can have the following benefits: (1) promoting psychological safety, (2) increasing the validity of the findings and conclusions of a study in the eyes of various stakeholders, (3) increasing the quality and therefore validity of data collected, (4) decreasing the risk of collateral damage and/or liability for evaluators and researchers, and (5) increasing resilience of traumatized communities and E&R stakeholders. Bosk (2023) emphasizes that trauma-informed evaluation activities could serve as a major bolster to the work happening in trauma-informed programs, as it "could serve to extend experiences of empowerment, collaboration, transparency, and safety for staff and client" (p. 2). We see these as inherently beneficial not only to those with whom we are working but for the integrity of the evaluation itself.

The evaluation field is full of people asserting their special approach as the be-all-and-end-all methodology. We recognize both the overwhelm this can cause for evaluators—*I have to learn a whole other approach?*—and the absurdity of such claims. We all know that in practice, we mix and match what we've learned from many different sources and voices in the evaluation field. We're being realistic about this reality, not shying away from it.

TIER is not another standalone evaluation methodology competing for your attention; rather, it is a trauma-informed lens that can be integrated into whatever evaluation approach you're already using. Grounded in SAMHSA's (2014) Four R's and Six Principles of Trauma-Informed Care, TIER guides how evaluators design, implement, and disseminate their work in ways that acknowledge trauma's prevalence and impact—regardless of whether you're conducting participatory evaluation, developmental evaluation, or any other methodological approach.

The Four R's of a Trauma-Informed Approach

SAMHSA (2014) describes a **trauma-informed approach** as one that is "inclusive of trauma-informed interventions as well as one that incorporates key trauma principles" (p. 9). Research shows that roughly 90% of adults have experienced trauma as defined by DSM-5 (Kilpatrick et al., 2013) and that over half report adverse childhood experiences. Given this widespread prevalence, Racine, Killam, and Madigan (2020, p. 5) argue that trauma-informed care should be "rooted in the assumption that any child or adult could have a trauma history" rather than requiring disclosure or screening first.

Because trauma is so widespread, costly, and harmful, we believe that trauma-informed interventions have a rightful place in E&R as a universal precaution—a practice applied to all participants regardless of known trauma history.

Like universal precautions in health care that assume potential infection risk without testing every patient, *TIER assumes potential trauma presence in every evaluation participant and designs research processes accordingly.* This means creating safe evaluation environments, building trustworthy relationships with participants, offering meaningful choices about participation, and ensuring evaluation activities themselves do not retraumatize. SAMHSA's Four R's lay the groundwork for trauma-informed approaches, as we explain here.

R1: Realize

The first key element is that at all levels of an organization or system, there is a basic *realization* about trauma and how it affects families, communities, individuals, organizations, systems, and groups. It means understanding trauma behaviors and symptoms, coping strategies, and the relationship between unhealed trauma and well-being.

R2: Recognize

The next key component to a trauma-informed approach is to *recognize* the signs of trauma. Although trauma screening and assessment is one way to recognize the specific signs, trauma screenings and assessments are typically done in a clinical setting by licensed practitioners. In the broad context of E&R, recognizing the signs of trauma means understanding that underneath the more obvious signs of dis-ease is the high likelihood of unhealed childhood, individual, and/or collective traumas.

R3: Respond

The third R—*respond*—is the crux of TIER—meaning that we have the tools, knowledge, and strategies to respond to trauma-affected people and groups, and ourselves, in ways that promote resilience and healing.

R4: Resist Retraumatization[1]

The most basic imperative of a trauma-informed approach is to *resist retraumatizing* ourselves, our clients, and our study participants. This aligns with the guiding principle to "do no harm" and is what we consider to be the low-hanging fruit that is not always picked given the propensity of colonizing, extractive methods still employed by many researchers and evaluators today.

[1]Although SAMHA's fourth R is "resist retraumatization," we think it should be broadened to "resist doing psychological harm" because there are harms other than retraumatization. For instance, a researcher or evaluator could act in a way that shames or embarrasses a person but does not rise to the level of a full retraumatization. We would still consider this a harm. We think precision is important when we talk about retraumatization versus other psychological difficulties. Refer back to Chapter 1 for more.

The Fifth R?: Resilience

Because SAMHSA's framework stops at that low-hanging fruit, some trauma-informed advocates and practitioners, like Olivia Teter (personal communication, September 5, 2024), head of Client Innovation at Second Harvest of Silicon Valley, add *resilience* as the fifth R or key component. We agree, as we've already noted the essential role that E&R can have in helping people heal and thrive. To move from resisting retraumatization to actively promoting resilience means fostering authentic connections that promote the formation of new neural pathways and that give purpose, meaning, and hope to study participants. We advocate striving for this fruit that hangs much higher in the tree than "resist retraumatization."

The Six Principles of Trauma-Informed Care

We have previously referred to SAMHSA's Six Principles of Trauma-Informed Care, which we will hereinafter simply call the **Six Principles**. Here, we describe each principle in more detail and explain their interrelationship.

Safety

Safety is foundational to trauma healing and perhaps the single most important of the Six Principles, in that it affects every other principle (Yoder, 2005). *We feel safety in our body.* In the context of TIER, study participants should have the opportunity to determine what is needed for them to feel physically, psychologically, emotionally, and intellectually safe. This means that we ask participants what they need and pay attention to the more obvious attributes of power that make people feel unsafe such as, but not limited to, imposing conference tables, closed rooms with no windows, lack of privacy, and traditionally white spaces that reflect only the dominant culture. Attending to participants' needs for safety must be done at the outset of and throughout any study. For participants to feel safe, we need to create a sense of belonging by expressing empathy and building relationships (Brown, 2012a).

Trust and Transparency

There are no hidden agendas in TIER. Everything we do is done in the light, and we openly communicate the whys, hows, whos, whats, and whens of the study. Participants deserve to fully understand their role in the larger picture and what benefits may or may not come from their participation. Other ways to foster trust include behaving in authentic, unpretentious ways and showing genuine interest and care in others.

Being transparent may also mean that we may sometimes have to tell clients, funders, and participants what they don't want to hear. In other words, some may not want to hear about the effects of whiteness or white supremacy or that their assumptions about the effects of their program fell short. Sometimes honesty is painful and puts the evaluator and researcher in the precarious position of delivering unappealing messages. But TIER holds us to a high standard of honesty. Honesty is required to build trust, and trust builds connection, and connection promotes healing. Our findings are more trustworthy when participants are safe and can trust us to hear and incorporate their truths, perceptions, and stories. It is up to us to cultivate the relationships and feelings that foster a sense of trust between the researchers and the researched.

Empowerment, Voice, and Choice

Empowerment, voice, and choice are interconnected concepts that represent a study participant's opportunity to make choices, express themselves, and be heard throughout the study process. Trauma-affected people often feel powerless and have likely been silenced by people, systems, and institutions that hold power over them. Thus, creating safe spaces for active participation and choice can be *transformative.*

Collaboration and Mutuality

"Healing happens in relationships and in the meaningful sharing of power and decision-making" (SAMHSA, 2014, p. 11). Leveling power differences is important to fostering trusting partnerships among clients, participants, and researchers. In TIER, this means that decisions, procedures, and processes are made together, for the mutual benefit of all. It means participants have a say in things and that they are heard.

Collaborative relationships with trauma-affected individuals create opportunities to promote and model positive coping strategies and increase tolerance of uncomfortable sensations (Craig, 2017), which also means that evaluators and researchers need to be willing to and capable of employing resilience practices in the moment (see Chapter 7). Collaboration can help prevent triggering old traumas and provides a framework for modeling problem-solving strategies, including the need for persistence and optimism when faced with obstacles in meeting a desired goal. "This type of collaborative relationship helps [trauma-affected people] learn to generate alternative solutions to challenging situations. With enough practice, they are able to achieve the cognitive flexibility needed to negotiate the demands of everyday life" (Craig, 2016, p. 67).

Cultural, Historical, and Gender Issues

TIER requires us to learn about and acknowledge historical and current harms and move forward in ways that honor the religion, gender identity, age, sexual orientation, race/ethnicity, socioeconomic status, and so on, of all involved. It also means understanding the effects and signs of historical, inter- and transgenerational trauma and asks us to consciously work in ways that confront stereotypes and biases. For members of the dominant culture, this takes intention, time, work, and self-compassion. For example, how can one study what affects the lifespan of African Americans without discussing the toxic stress caused by racism?

Peer Support

Study participants, clients, staff, and evaluators benefit from available support from others who "get it"—people who know trauma and resilience intimately. In addition to offering empathy to study participants, it may be appropriate, depending on the study, to have a peer or a counselor readily available in a chat room, on the phone, or in the next room. Trauma survivors can offer other survivors' stories of lived experiences that foster hope and safety, connection and belonging, and trust. Given that trauma causes feelings of isolation (Cruwys et al., 2025), peer support is essential for healing.

The Interrelatedness of the Six Principles

Although each Principle is described here individually, we emphasize their nonlinear and interconnected nature (Figure 3.1). Sometimes when you address one, you also address the others. For instance, you cannot build trust without safety. Creating safety is a collaborative and mutual process that empowers participants

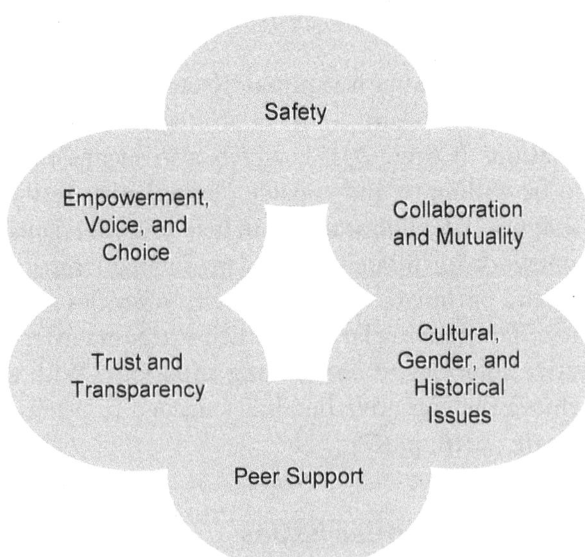

FIGURE 3.1. SAMHSA's Six Principles of Trauma-Informed Care.

through choices and includes attention to cultural, gender, and historical issues. When we wear the TIER lens, we intentionally prioritize the Six Principles, ensuring their incorporation in each stage of the study process.

Guiding Principles for Evaluators and Researchers

Given there is no lack of ethical and professional guidelines for evaluators and researchers, we created a matrix illustrating how the Six Principles *might* align with various existing guidelines—but only if the researcher or evaluator approaches the work with a trauma-informed lens. We chose to represent the AEA's Guiding Principles for Evaluators (n.d.-b) and the National Institutes of Health's Guiding Principles for Ethical Research (2025), as these are large organizations to which many evaluators and researchers look for guidance.

Although these and other frameworks cover areas that are applicable to the Six Principles, there is not a direct one-to-one mapping. At best, the Principles can be inferred from the other guidelines. As we can see, without a mindful *intent* to be trauma-informed, adherence to the SAMHSA Principles could go by the wayside despite other ethical guidelines established to "protect human subjects." Although approaches that point toward equity and justice could be perceived as gesturing toward being somewhat trauma-informed, we believe more explicit fleshing out and application of the Six Principles to E&R practices is needed.

Ethical Decision Making

As Table 3.1 shows, E&R are guided by ethics including informed consent, voluntary participation, avoidance of harm, maintaining confidentiality and anonymity, and the social benefit of the evaluation. However, we present three other factors to consider when deciding how one might engage with study participants: insensitivity, sensitivity, and hypersensitivity. Much of the current discourse in the human services and social sciences fields, and especially in popular culture, centers around these three concepts.

Most of us know insensitivity when we see it. **Insensitivity** is the total disregard for how our actions may or may not affect others. The insensitive individual can be in one of three conditions: (1) believing they have little effect on those around them, (2) realizing they have an effect on those around them but not caring enough to tailor their actions accordingly, or (3) possessing little or no awareness of how their actions affect others. We never want to be insensitive to study participants, no matter our formal and informal training. An example of insensitivity would be to ignore the visible emotional distress of a participant and to push them to answer questions they feel uncomfortable with. Even if distress is not apparent, neglecting to conduct periodic emotional check-ins with our participants could be a sign of insensitivity. Our participants are in our care, and we should demonstrate our openness to their emotional and physical experiences.

We also want to illuminate the contrast between sensitivity and hypersensitivity/avoidance. We define **sensitivity** as the practice of approaching a situation and the individuals involved with an openness to a diversity of reactions while critically examining and anticipating how our actions and words may be perceived and being flexible and willing to make adjustments as needed. Approaching situations and people with sensitivity, even when the conversations or tasks are difficult, is a step toward developing resilience. If done right, it can go a long way toward desensitizing groups and individuals to what may have been very distressing in the past. This includes acknowledging that even with the best intentions, our words or actions may still cause discomfort, as we are not able to predict exactly how they will land.

TABLE 3.1. Comparison of Principles

Framework	Framework item	Applicable trauma-informed principle
AEA Guiding Principles (n.d.)	Systematic Inquiry: Evaluators conduct data-based inquiries that are thorough, methodical, and contextually relevant.	Cultural, Historic, and Gender Issues
	Competence: Evaluators provide skilled professional services to stakeholders.	Safety
	Integrity: Evaluators behave with honesty and transparency to ensure the integrity of the evaluation.	Trust and Transparency
	Respect for People: Evaluators honor the dignity, well-being, and self-worth of individuals and acknowledge the influence of culture within and across groups.	Cultural, Historic, Gender Issues; Collaboration and Mutuality
	Common Good and Equity: Evaluators strive to contribute to the common good and advancement of an equitable and just society.	Cultural, Historic, Gender Issues
NIH Guiding Principles for Ethical Research (2025)	Social and clinical value	Cultural, Historic, and Gender Issues
	Scientific validity	Safety
	Fair subject selection	Cultural, Historic, and Gender Issues
	Favorable risk–benefit ratio	Safety
	Independent review	Collaboration and Mutuality
	Informed consent	Safety; Trust and Transparency
	Respect for potential and enrolled subject	Collaboration and Mutuality; Safety; Cultural, Historic, and Gender Issues

Humility, openness, and willingness to adjust our approach are values that undergird TIER. Healthy encounters contradict the helplessness and paralysis of traumatizing events and help the brain form new neural pathways. We want to provide opportunities to "contradict the habitual way of responding to stressful triggers that further weaken feelings of control and connection" (Yoder, 2005, p. 60). An example of sensitivity in the midst of an interaction would be providing emotional checking, stating, "I know these questions are tough. I want you to know that I am ready to hear whatever you have to tell me, but please let me know if you want to slow down or need a break at any time." If an individual is showing physical signs of distress, one should provide similar check-ins, stating something like, "I can see the tears and hear the pain in your voice. I want to make sure that you're totally comfortable with continuing. It can be good to talk about difficult topics, but I want to make sure that we only continue if you're absolutely sure you're ready for that." This approach acknowledges the agency of the participants and the validity of their experience and places the decision-making power in their hands. It does not assume that because something is difficult or painful that it should be avoided.

An additional stance toward trauma is that of hypersensitivity. We define hypersensitivity as an overprotective stance based on the assumption that traumatized individuals are too fragile to handle difficult conversations or emotions, leading evaluators to make unilateral decisions to shield participants from potential discomfort. **Avoidance** takes this further by deliberately sidestepping difficult topics, sensitive questions, or challenging populations altogether out of fear that engagement might cause distress or invite criticism. Both stances are based in fear, as both hypersensitivity and avoidance mirror symptoms of a trauma response. Although these approaches may possibly help the individual avoid crisis behavior in the moment, in the long run, hypersensitivity can be regressive because it does not promote resilience.

Avoiding studies or participants or hesitating to ask the hard questions is not always beneficial to participants. In fact, avoidance itself is a core trauma symptom we may be inadvertently playing out ourselves when we engage in it. It remains uncertain what effects such avoidance behavior may have on a study if an evaluator or researcher seeks to avoid participants who wish to discuss sensitive or triggering topics or avoid engaging with specific subject areas altogether. As Bledsoe (2021) and others advocate for evaluators to operate from a position of caring and leading with the heart, it becomes vital to understand how symptoms of CF, such as apathy, indifference, and disengagement, affect one's commitment to amplifying the voices of the most marginalized (Ledoux, 2015; Pehlivan & Guner, 2018). Furthermore, it is important to understand the influence of CF on the fields of E&R, considering that CF is known to drive individuals to leave their jobs and the profession altogether (Nimmo & Huggard, 2013).

An E&R culture that relies on the avoidance of difficult topics for fear of creating unpleasant experiences for people, and thus risking criticism, is perhaps, in effect, worsening a core trauma symptom. An example of hypersensitivity would be observing a sign of discomfort, such as tears or a shaky voice, and unilaterally ending the data collection event. Such a move could send the signal that their emotions are unacceptable, shameful or inappropriate. An evaluator should prepare for such moments, self-examining their own capacity to handle others' emotions. If hypersensitivity is the default reaction, this is something you will need to work on before handling sensitive topics with participants.

Table 3.2 compares the messages and effects of sensitivity, hypersensitivity, and insensitivity.

Practically, what does this mean for an evaluator or researcher? It means that no topic is off-limits for an evaluator/evaluation provided that the following criteria are met:

- The topic is *relevant* to the study at hand.
- The topic is *necessary* for answering the research or evaluation questions (which also must be well reasoned).
- The *least intrusive* means of data collection are being used.
- The evaluator/researcher possesses sufficient *background knowledge* to handle the topic/conversation in a tactful and sensitive manner.
- The evaluator/researcher is trauma-informed and able to *recognize* signs of distress and *employ appropriate resilience practices* in the moment.
- All participants understand they have *full autonomy* to participate or not in every or any aspect of the evaluation as they see fit, and this consent is ongoing.
- It is made clear that the *benefits* of gathering the information *outweigh the risks*—and of course, we mean benefits to the individual, not just to the researcher, funder, or client.

TABLE 3.2. Comparing Insensitivity, Hypersensitivity, and Sensitivity

	Underlying message	Short-term effects	Long-term effects
Insensitivity	"Your thoughts, feelings, and opinions do not matter. You are not important."	Discomfort, offense, retraumatization, conflict	Increased trauma in individuals and in the system as a whole
Sensitivity	"I know this topic or task may be difficult. However, I believe in your capability to decide what to share."	Some possible discomfort, but autonomy and agency are maintained for the participant	Increased resilience, decreased trauma in the system as a whole
Hypersensitivity	"You are damaged. You are not strong enough to handle certain topics, conversations, or situations."	Avoidance of discomfort in the moment	Increased sense of vulnerability and fragility, static or even growing level of trauma in the individual and system

Evaluators and researchers must self-screen to determine whether they are able to meet these criteria. These are complex issues, and what exactly one is to do may not always be obvious. We get more into practical considerations for data collection in Part III.

WRAP-UP

TIER, combined with highly democratic and participatory study designs, has immense transformative potential for individuals, communities, and organizations. TIER changes the intention and purpose of a study: Instead of solely focusing on findings and recommendations, facilitating healing is a stated purpose of the study and design elevates attention to the Six Principles. Findings and recommendations would ideally be presented in a trauma-informed manner and agreed on by participants and community members who helped make meaning of the findings. Trauma survivors would be empowered to say what they need to heal and move forward—if it is safe for them to do so. And although most researchers do not have the luxury of working with clients and communities after findings are presented, researchers can still be instrumental in helping to establish processes so that participants themselves are empowered to continue the work of change long after the researcher is no longer involved. TIER provides a framework for climbing up the branches, surpassing the low-hanging fruit of "do no harm," and reaching the golden apple at the top of "doing good."

CHAPTER 3 REFLECTION QUESTIONS

1. Consider SAMSHA's Four R's of a trauma-informed approach. What questions come to mind? Are you wrestling with our claim that trauma-informed interventions have a rightful place in E&R?
2. Do you think resilience should be added as a fifth R? Why or why not?
3. How do you navigate the line between being appropriately sensitive and becoming hypersensitive or avoidant when working with someone's trauma? Can you share an example of where you may have missed that balance, either by being overly cautious or inadvertently insensitive, and what you learned from it?
4. Do you believe that E&R should more intentionally focus on "doing good" than just "doing no harm"? Explain.

PART II

The Evaluation Landscape

This part lays the groundwork for why TIER is essential. But before we head down that road, we need to know where we've been, where we are now, and where the gaps are. Here we make our case for TIER by summarizing the representation of trauma in the literature, showing how little is published on this topic as it pertains to evaluators and researchers (Chapter 4). In Chapter 5, we tie TIER to various evaluation approaches. This part closes with a special chapter on equity-focused TIER contributed by guest authors (Chapter 6).

CHAPTER 4

Representation of Trauma in the Evaluation and Research Literature

We read the articles so you don't have to . . . but maybe you still should.

WHAT YOU'LL LEARN

What does the evaluation literature have to tell us about trauma? To find out, we conducted an in-depth systematic review of the evaluation literature. We find that although discussion of trauma in evaluation literature is increasingly common, much of it lacks depth. This chapter tells you what we already "know" and also identifies the gaps we need to fill with the rest of the book. The topics range widely and there's a lot to say. So, strap in and come along for our deep dive.

Introduction

Does it seem like you've been hearing more about trauma lately? From pop culture to literature to social media, this perception reflects measurable reality. The signs of trauma's cultural salience are everywhere. An indexed search on *podchaser.com* reveals 501,185 podcast episodes with *trauma* in the title released between 2020 and 2025, a 573% increase from the roughly 74,539 episodes from 2015 to 2020. This cultural phenomenon also reflects deeper institutional transformations. While the first U.S. law mentioning trauma-informed practice emerged only in 2010, the following 5 years saw 49 additional bills incorporating similar principles (Purtle & Lewis, 2017). Academic disciplines have experienced parallel growth: Psychology literature evolved from zero trauma-informed care articles between

1995 and 1998 to 116 articles between 2015 and 2018 (McCormack, Ballinger, Valentine, & Swaab, 2022). Yet despite this surge across popular culture, policy, and scholarship, a critical question emerges: Has the field of evaluation kept pace with this trauma-informed revolution? Our systematic review of evaluation literature reveals a complex picture of growing awareness coupled with persistent gaps in practice.

Searching and Coding the Literature

To understand whether evaluation literature has kept pace with the broader trauma-informed revolution, we conducted a systematic review spanning 4 decades of evaluation scholarship. Using Coryn and colleagues' (2017) comprehensive list of 14 scholarly evaluation journals, plus one additionally identified journal, we searched each journal archive for the word *trauma,* downloading every article published before February 2, 2023.

Our initial search yielded four hundred articles published between 1979 and 2023. After excluding articles that mentioned *trauma* only in reference lists, we analyzed 343 substantive articles using thematic analysis to identify how evaluation literature engages with trauma concepts. The growth pattern we discovered was striking: from just two articles in 1979 to 41 in 2022, mirroring the broader cultural and academic trends identified in our introduction.

However, raw numbers told only part of the story. Our analysis revealed a fundamental evolution in how trauma is conceptualized within evaluation literature. Early mentions typically focused on medical trauma, organizational disruption, or war-related PTSD—treating trauma as a discrete, clinical phenomenon. Later articles demonstrate a more expansive, systemic understanding consistent with contemporary trauma-informed approaches that recognize trauma's pervasive effects on individuals, communities, and institutions.

To assess the depth of trauma-informed engagement, we also coded each article for alignment with SAMHSA's Six Principles of Trauma-Informed Care (Safety; Trustworthiness and Transparency; Peer Support; Collaboration and Mutuality; Empowerment, Voice, and Choice; and Cultural, Historical, and Gender Issues). This coding allowed us to distinguish between articles that merely mentioned trauma and those that demonstrated meaningful integration of established trauma-informed frameworks. We've covered the basics of this analysis here, but you can find more details and citations in Appendix A.

Before examining how evaluation literature has engaged with trauma, it's useful to understand the broader evolution of trauma as a research construct. Figure 4.1 illustrates this progression from limited recognition through clinical acknowledgment to today's systematic frameworks. This historical context helps explain both the persistence of surface-level approaches and the recent emergence of more sophisticated trauma-informed evaluation practices.

PRE-1980s
- Limited trauma recognition
- Trauma largely known as physical injury or war-related psychological damage
- Little recognition of widespread civilian trauma or developmental impacts
- No systematic frameworks for understanding trauma's broader effects

1980s–1990s
- PTSD enters DSM-III (American Psychiatric Association, 1980)
- Clinical recognition begins
- Focus on war veterans and discrete traumatic events
- Beginning of psychological trauma recognition

2000s
- ACEs study gains prominence (Felitti et al., 1998)
- Complex trauma concepts emerge (Cook et al., 2003; van der Kolk, 2005)
- Developmental trauma understanding grows (Herman, 1992)
- Foundation for understanding trauma's broader effects

2010–2014
- First trauma-informed legislation passed in 2010 (Purtle & Lewis, 2017)
- Growing policy interest and institutional awareness
- Academic scholarship increases across disciplines
- Building momentum toward systematic approaches

2014
- SAMHSA publishes Six Principles framework (2014)
- Provides concrete operational guidelines for trauma-informed practice
- Marks shift from awareness to systematic implementation
- Watershed moment for fieldwide standards

2015–PRESENT
- Psychology literature explosion (McCormack et al., 2022)
- Cultural mainstream adoption
- Evaluation field evolution: two articles (1979) → 41 articles (2022)
- Only 11.5% of evaluation articles align with SAMHSA Principles
- Bosk (2023) publishes first comprehensive TIER framework

FIGURE 4.1. The evolution of trauma in evaluation, research, and practice.

Surface-Level Engagement: Early Patterns and Their Persistence

The early decades of trauma mentions in evaluation literature reveal a consistent pattern: Trauma was acknowledged but rarely explored in depth. These surface-level engagements reflect the broader cultural understanding of trauma during this period as discrete, clinical events rather than complex experiences with systemic implications for research and evaluation practice. Although this shallow approach dominated early literature, it has proven remarkably persistent, with examples continuing to appear even in contemporary scholarship.

The most prevalent approach treated trauma through a purely medical lens. Sixty-six articles referenced medical trauma (life-threatening emergencies requiring significant medical intervention). But these studies focused exclusively on physical aspects while ignoring concurrent psychological dimensions (e.g., Bergner, Eisenberg, & Hallstrom, 1979; Lewis, Hardy, & Snaith, 2013; O'Leary & Donovan, 1979; Walsh & Walsh, 1982). This narrow conceptualization exemplifies the era's compartmentalized view: Trauma was something that happened to bodies, usually in war, natural disasters, or other horrific circumstances. It was not something experienced, so it was thought, by most people or something that fundamentally altered how individuals might experience and respond to research or evaluation participation.

Equally telling was the instrumental use of trauma as a simple outcome measure. Thirty-five articles employed trauma status as one indicator among many to determine program success, without considering broader implications for evaluation design or ethics. For instance, Spiro, Shalev, Solomon, and Kotler (1989) monitored PTSD symptoms in war veterans to assess intervention effectiveness but left unaddressed how trauma sensitivity might require fundamental changes in evaluator approach and methodology. This instrumental perspective treats trauma as data to be collected rather than as a lens through which the entire evaluation process should be reconsidered.

Even when evaluating trauma-focused programs, the context where deeper engagement might be most expected, the pattern of shallow treatment has persisted across decades. Seventy-two studies examined programs directly targeting traumatized populations, yet most mentioned trauma merely as background context rather than engaging with its implications for evaluation methodology. This pattern appears in studies spanning from the 1980s through recent work, including contemporary examples such as veterans' PTSD program evaluations (Turner, Hardiman, Matteson, & Fletcher, 2022) and family violence prevention initiatives in Bolivia (Stern, Alemann, Delgado, & Vásquez, 2023). These recent studies, while more sophisticated in many respects, continue the tradition of acknowledging trauma's presence without fundamentally reconsidering evaluation approaches. Remarkably, of the studies that referenced trauma-focused programs, only 10 (14%) reported incorporation of any trauma-informed practices aligned with SAMHSA Principles.

Perhaps most revealing is how collective trauma was conceptualized during this period. Twenty-one articles referenced collective or organizational trauma, but most treated it as hyperbole for administrative difficulties rather than recognizing genuine systemic trauma (Kennedy, 1983). Some, however, did refer to more serious traumas such as the tensions in schools resulting from desegregation (Firestone, 1991). More recently, attention has been given to the collective trauma of the COVID-19 pandemic (e.g., Mawhinney et al., 2023). Most of the time, such mentions of organizational or collective trauma did not give full consideration of the implications of such trauma for the programs, nor do they acknowledge SAMHSA's (2014) trauma-informed organizational framework.

This enduring pattern of surface-level engagement reflects how deeply entrenched the traditional understanding of trauma has been within evaluation practice. Despite decades of advancing trauma scholarship in other fields, evaluation literature has been slow to move beyond viewing trauma as an unfortunate but discrete event that might complicate data collection rather than as a fundamental human experience requiring systematic reconsideration of research and evaluation ethics, methodology, and practice.

Emerging Themes in Recent Literature

Although surface-level engagement remains common across evaluation literature, a growing minority of scholars has begun wrestling with more fundamental questions about trauma's implications for practice. This emerging consciousness represents a significant departure from earlier approaches, moving beyond viewing trauma as merely a complicating factor toward understanding it as a lens that should fundamentally reshape evaluation methodology, ethics, and purpose.

The most notable shift involves a deepening conceptual understanding of trauma itself. Rather than the passing mentions or narrow clinical definitions that characterized earlier work, 35 articles now engage substantively with trauma's complex nature, with all but eight appearing in 2010 or later and only four before 2000. This temporal clustering becomes particularly notable after 2014, when SAMHSA's comprehensive framework provided the field with concrete principles for trauma-informed practice, suggesting that evaluation scholars are finally catching up with broader developments in trauma scholarship.

Contemporary evaluation work is now swimming in cultural waters fundamentally shaped by foundational trauma scholars like van der Kolk (2014) and Cook and colleagues (2003), whose work established our understanding of trauma's neurobiological and developmental effects. For instance, Wolfe, Long, and Brown (2020) engage with trauma's systemic nature while introducing readers to SAMHSA's comprehensive definitions. Kubiak, Fedock, Tillander, Kim, and Bybee (2014) ground their intervention work with formerly incarcerated women in sophisticated trauma theory, and Plant and colleagues (2023) explore how trauma disrupts self-regulation development, building on work by Ford (2005) and Ford, Grasso, Hawke, and Chapman (2013).

These discussions signal that evaluators are developing more nuanced perspectives and beginning to tailor their approaches to trauma's complex realities. This conceptual sophistication has generated increased recognition of trauma's methodological implications—acknowledgment that trauma doesn't just complicate data collection but fundamentally alters what ethical and effective evaluation looks like. Twenty-four articles explicitly address these challenges, with 16 appearing after 2010 and only four before 2000. These scholars grapple with profound questions about how trauma reshapes the entire evaluation enterprise.

The challenges they identify are both practical and philosophical. Most commonly cited are concerns about data accuracy, with scholars recognizing that trauma can fundamentally alter participants' ability to provide the kinds of information evaluations typically seek (Bosk, 2023; Simon et al., 1996). Abma and Widdershoven (2005) articulate this challenge with particular clarity, noting that

> traumatic experiences can (temporarily) be banned from the consciousness because they violate the narrator's identity. Survivors of political struggle, war, concentration camps, and sexual cruelties may silence themselves or tell "pre-narratives," stories that do not develop in time and/or do not express what they felt. (p.107)

This insight moves far beyond viewing trauma as a simple barrier to data collection, recognizing instead how it can reshape the very nature of narrative and memory.

Beyond data accuracy, scholars increasingly acknowledge the ethical complexities trauma introduces. Multiple studies identify safety and privacy concerns that extend well beyond traditional informed consent procedures (Campbell, Greeson, & Fehler-Cabral, 2014; Chauvin, Mugajuu, & Comlavi, 1998; Mawhinney et al., 2023; Roholt & Baizerman, 2012). When evaluation activities relate directly to participants' trauma, scholars express heightened concerns about the sensitivity required, recognizing that the need for such sensitivity creates significant tensions between appropriate care and effective data collection (Baizerman, 2012; Bardin, Verma, Wagner, Ruffier, & Morse, 2022; Berends & Wansbrough, 2023; Campbell et al., 2014; LaChenaye & McCarthy, 2022). Additional concerns include risks of undue pressure and distress that can impair participants' ability to engage meaningfully with evaluation processes (Cunningham et al., 2005; Guo, Wallace, Luther, & Wong, 2022; Spiro et al., 1989). Baizerman (2012) extends these concerns to contexts like war-torn regions, questioning whether traditional standards of reliability, validity, and representativeness are even achievable or appropriate under such circumstances.

The practical implications extend to fundamental methodological decisions. Scholars note how trauma-sensitive protections can create recruitment challenges, as Campbell and colleagues (2014) discovered when designing protocols for young sexual assault survivors, finding that protective measures like delayed interviews, while ethically necessary, significantly reduced participation rates. Campbell and colleagues (2008) expand this discussion to various hard-to-reach traumatized populations, including LGBTQ+ youth, unsheltered people, drug users, sex workers, and domestic violence survivors. These access challenges can compromise core methodological elements, creating difficulties in constructing appropriate comparison groups (Toedter, Lasker, & Campbell, 1990) and accessing or developing validated instruments (Tibbitts et al., 2021).

Yet this emerging consciousness also reveals tensions within the field. Berends and Wansbrough (2023) challenge what they see as potentially paternalistic approaches, suggesting that some protective efforts may actually limit participants' access to potentially beneficial experiences. Others note practical constraints, as organizations may perceive they cannot afford the additional precautions, personnel, effort, and time that trauma-sensitive approaches require (Bosk, 2023).

Perhaps most promising is the emergence of thinking about evaluation as potentially empowering rather than merely extractive. Several scholars suggest that research participation could be designed to actively help participants rather than simply avoiding harm. Campbell and colleagues (2014) articulate this vision most clearly, seeking approaches that

> go beyond "standard" requirements so that the resulting methods not only reduce risk but also have the potential to promote emotional well-being, reflection, and insight. In our work with adolescent sexual assault survivors, we needed to pay particular attention to how any and all contact between potential participants and the evaluation team could cause distress—and how we could create a participation experience that could help survivors, even in a small way, in their recovery process. (p. 76)

Berends and Wansbrough (2023) build on this foundation, although they note that the topic of evaluation as an empowering experience for traumatized people remains largely underdeveloped in the literature.

This emerging consciousness, while promising, remains decidedly limited in scope. When we analyzed our literature sample specifically for alignment with SAMHSA's Six Principles of Trauma-Informed Care, only 46 articles (11.5% of our sample) demonstrated any meaningful engagement with these established frameworks. This low percentage underscores how nascent this sophisticated trauma engagement truly is; the vast majority of evaluation literature continues to operate without reference to the trauma-informed principles that have become standard in other fields.

Among those articles that did engage with SAMHSA Principles, the focus was notably narrow (as seen in Figure 4.2). Safety concerns appeared in 57% of these trauma-informed articles, and cultural, historical, and gender issues were addressed in 52%. This concentration makes intuitive sense. Safety represents the most immediately recognizable concern when working with traumatized population: the imperative to avoid retraumatization. Similarly, attention to cultural and gender dimensions reflects broader contemporary academic and social discourse priorities. However, this narrow focus reveals how even trauma-informed evaluation literature tends to emphasize protective measures rather than the more

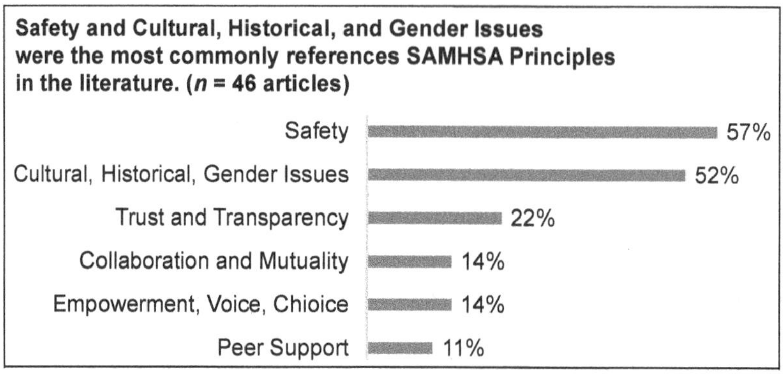

FIGURE 4.2. Frequency of SAMSHA Principles in the literature.

transformative principles like peer support, collaboration, or empowerment that characterize fully developed trauma-informed approaches. This emerging consciousness represents genuine progress in evaluation scholarship: a move toward recognizing trauma not as an inconvenient complication but as a fundamental aspect of human experience that demands systematic reconsideration of research practice. Yet its minority status within the broader literature suggests the field remains in transition, with these sophisticated approaches existing alongside the persistent surface-level engagement documented in earlier sections.

The most comprehensive articulation of this emerging consciousness appears in Emily Bosk's (2023) groundbreaking work, "Creating a Parallel Process: A New Methodological Framework for Conducting Trauma-Informed Evaluation and Research (TIER) in Mental Health Settings." Bosk, a professor of social work at Rutgers University, provides the most extensive discussion of trauma-informed practice in evaluation literature to date, noting the "scant discussion related to the process for conducting evaluations so that they embody [Trauma-Informed Care] principles" and introducing a "new framework for Trauma-Informed Evaluation and Research (TIER) in mental health settings" (p. 1).

Central to Bosk's contribution is her distinction between front-end and back-end trauma-informed work. Front-end work (the service-delivery side including sensitive intervention and screening) has dominated trauma-informed scholarship and practice. Back-end work, however, involves the policy and procedural infrastructure that enables front-end effectiveness, and this is where evaluation resides. Bosk's (2023) review revealed that evaluators were not consciously incorporating trauma-informed practices into evaluation processes themselves, representing an enormous opportunity for programs to become more trauma-informed. As she argues,

> feelings generated in one place or relationship are often reflected, refracted, or enacted in another with reciprocal effects. As [Trauma-informed Care] recognizes, transactional processes ripple throughout a system: policies and procedures

> create the context for interaction, which in turn, shape outcomes. Evaluation procedures, as the SAMHSA guidelines recognize, are a part of these transactional processes. (p. 9)

From Literature to Practice: What We Suspect but Cannot Confirm

While our systematic review illuminates patterns within evaluation literature, it also raises profound questions about the relationship between scholarly discourse and actual practice. The literature provides a window into what we suspect may be occurring in evaluation work across the field, but empirical confirmation remains elusive.

The persistence of surface-level trauma engagement in published work suggests that many evaluators may be giving trauma lip service without implementing systematic trauma-informed measures in their practice. The literature's emphasis on safety concerns over transformative approaches implies that even trauma-conscious evaluators may be defaulting to "do-no-harm" frameworks rather than pursuing the empowering, collaborative practices that characterize fully developed trauma-informed work. We suspect that trauma awareness may be causing some evaluators to avoid difficult topics or shy away from working with vulnerable populations entirely while others continue engaging these populations without adequate consideration of their impact.

Equally plausible is the possibility that many evaluators are employing trauma-sensitive practices intuitively (guided by good intentions rather than evidence-based frameworks) without a systematic understanding of trauma-informed principles or conscious awareness of how their approaches align with established best practices. The disconnect between the 11.5% of published articles that engage with SAMHSA Principles and the likely reality that far more evaluators encounter trauma in their work suggests a significant knowing–doing gap.

Yet we cannot move beyond suspicion to certainty. We lack empirical data about how evaluators actually make decisions when trauma concerns arise, what drives their methodological choices, or the extent to which their intentions translate into genuinely trauma-informed competencies. This evidence gap itself represents a critical barrier to field transformation.

A Call to Transformation: The Time for Trauma-Informed Evaluation Is Now

Our systematic review reveals a field at a crossroads. Although we found encouraging signs of emerging consciousness among evaluation scholars, the overwhelming pattern remains one of surface-level engagement with trauma, a pattern that is no longer acceptable. With trauma's prevalence in virtually every population we serve and with four decades of research demonstrating trauma's profound effects on human experience, the evaluation field can no longer afford to treat trauma-informed practice as optional or experimental.

The stakes are profoundly human. Behind every data point in our review lies the reality of evaluation participants whose traumatic experiences shape how they perceive, respond to, and potentially benefit from engagement. When evaluators fail to incorporate trauma-informed principles, we risk not only retraumatizing vulnerable individuals but also generating invalid data, perpetuating harmful power dynamics, and missing opportunities to create genuinely empowering experiences.

The time for incremental change has passed. The evaluation field must commit to systematic transformation guided by several urgent imperatives:

➤ *We must establish the empirical foundation for trauma-informed evaluation.* Claims about retraumatization in research settings (both those asserting widespread harm and those dismissing such concerns) currently lack robust empirical grounding. The field requires immediate rigorous investigation into the actual rates, severity, and effects of E&R-related retraumatization. We need to identify which evaluation approaches, designs, and evaluator behaviors pose the greatest risks, and we must develop evidence-based protocols for trauma-sensitive practice.

➤ *We must bridge the knowing–doing gap.* Many evaluators likely employ trauma-sensitive practices intuitively, yet most remain unconscious of how their approaches align with established trauma-informed frameworks. The field needs systematic documentation of current practices, assessment of their effectiveness, and development of explicit trauma-informed evaluation competencies. We can no longer rely on good intentions when evidence-based frameworks exist.

➤ *We must center participant voice and experience.* Evaluation participants themselves must become partners in defining what trauma-informed evaluation looks like. We need participatory research that explores how individuals with trauma histories experience different evaluation approaches, what practices feel empowering versus retraumatizing, and how evaluation processes can be designed to actively support healing and growth rather than simply avoiding harm.

➤ *We must transform evaluation education and practice standards.* Trauma-informed evaluation cannot remain the domain of specialized scholars; it must become fundamental to evaluation competency. This requires integrating trauma-informed principles into evaluation training programs, developing practice standards and ethical guidelines, and creating accountability mechanisms that ensure trauma-informed approaches become standard rather than exceptional.

➤ *We must expand beyond mental health settings.* Although Bosk's pioneering work in mental health contexts provides crucial foundation, trauma-informed evaluation principles apply wherever human experience is being studied, which is everywhere. The field must develop frameworks for trauma-informed approaches across all evaluation contexts.

This transformation requires courage from evaluation scholars, practitioners, and institutions. It demands that we acknowledge how traditional evaluation practices may have caused harm, that we invest in developing new competencies, and that we prioritize participant well-being alongside methodological rigor. Most importantly, it requires that we recognize trauma-informed evaluation not as an additional burden but as an ethical imperative and a pathway to more valid, meaningful, and transformative evaluation practice.

The foundation exists. The frameworks are available. The moral case is clear. What we need now is the collective will to act. The people we serve (those who trust us with their stories, their time, and their hopes for change) deserve nothing less than our complete commitment to practices that honor their humanity and support their healing. The time for trauma-informed evaluation is not tomorrow or next year. The time is now.

CHAPTER 4 ACTIVITY

Read and analyze any peer-reviewed study or evaluation report involving a population you assume would have trauma(s). You might choose an article from Appendix A, an article cited in this chapter, or one you find on your own. As you read, take notes on these questions:

- Are any of SAMHSA's Six Principles explicitly mentioned or implicitly addressed? If so, which ones? How were they addressed?
- What could the researchers have done differently to make the study more intentionally trauma-informed?
- Do you see any evidence that study participants might have been at risk of retraumatization? What did that look like? Be careful to distinguish retraumatization from triggering or remembering, as we discussed in Chapter 1.
- Conversely, is there reason to think participation may have benefited participants?
- What else did you notice?

CHAPTER 5

TIER's Congruence with Evaluation Approaches

Let's get theory-ous.

WHAT YOU'LL LEARN

Now that you have a better understanding of the Six Principles, we show how they align with some evaluation theories and approaches. This book is not meant to be a theory-heavy work; however, we do think it necessary to cover the landscape of evaluation theories and address where we see TIER fitting in. We encourage you to reflect on your past, current, and future studies and think about what you could do differently to make your study more trauma-informed, regardless of your chosen approach.

Understanding theory isn't just an academic exercise; it's the foundation that makes our trauma-informed work both intentional and effective. When we understand where TIER fits within evaluation theory, we can apply it more strategically, defend our methodological choices, and explain to stakeholders why trauma-informed approaches lead to better, more valid results. More fundamentally, we think theory is important because when we begin to infuse our thinking with theories that have been developed by other scholars and ourselves, we begin to think more critically rather than just acting out of habit or instinct. Our hope is that by jump-starting this conversation, the whole field can start having a more meaningful discussion about trauma and how it relates to existing modes of evaluation practice.

What Is Theory?

What do we mean when we talk about **theory**? In common speech, we might use the word to connote general academic thinking and writing about a topic. This might include how evaluation relates to other fields, how one might understand evaluation, or how one might or ought to practice evaluation. Throughout evaluation scholarship, terms like *theory*, *model*, *approach*, and *lens* are used in both colloquial and technical registers—sometimes interchangeably in everyday discourse, sometimes with more specific meanings in technical use. We follow the field's practice of using both registers as context requires while being explicit about our technical definitions when precision matters. Here, though, we want to be clear. Like many other evaluation "theories" in the colloquial sense, TIER functions as a **lens**[1]—a way of viewing and enhancing any existing evaluation approach through the Six Principles of Trauma-Informed Care.

In the context of the evaluation field, Smith (2010) emphasizes that the terms *theory* and *model* are used interchangeably. He considers theories to cover "explanations of underlying fundamental issues such as the nature of evaluation purpose, valuing, evidence, use, and so on" (p. 384). In the technical register, Smith considers models "more or less coherent resolutions of theoretical issues that provide a compatible set of prescriptions for how to conduct an evaluation" (p. 384), which can operate on the level of ideology, operational strategy, and intervention.

Using Smith's framework, we can examine TIER across these three levels to understand both its theoretical foundations and practical applications. TIER functions as a trauma-informed lens, a way of viewing and enhancing any existing evaluation approach or method through the Six Principles of Trauma-Informed Care. Many other evaluation "theories" in the colloquial sense would be more accurately characterized as lenses as well, and we encourage recognition of this distinction throughout the field.

As an ideology, we build TIER on the foundational beliefs that considering issues of trauma in evaluation practice makes good sense for the following reasons:

1. Attending to issues of trauma will lead to better, more valid results due to greater trust and transparency with participants and stakeholders.
2. We have a moral imperative to do better due to the historical and continuing injustices perpetrated at the hands of the scientific community.

[1]Throughout this book, we use *lens* to describe TIER because it modifies how you see and practice evaluation rather than replacing your chosen methodology entirely. Think of it as trauma-informed glasses you put on, regardless of whether you're doing experimental, participatory, or utilization-focused evaluation. The lens helps you ask different questions, notice different dynamics, and make different choices within whatever approach you're already using.

As an operational strategy, we seek to provide a concrete (and, far as possible, evidence-based) set of basic behaviors, attitudes, and postures directed toward making evaluation practice more trauma-informed. As an intervention, we reject the notion that evaluators can be completely neutral. In fact, we consider it impossible for the evaluator to not affect the very thing they are studying. In psychology, this is known as the **Hawthorne effect:** "the effect on the behavior of individuals of knowing that they are being observed or are taking part in research" (APA Dictionary of Psychology, 2026). If we assume that we are changing the very communities in which we operate, we should seek to position ourselves as agents of positive change. Specifically, by employing TIER, we hope that our research efforts, rather than simply being neutral or benign, will contribute to the healing of trauma.

To sum it up, while we may refer to it as a theory or approach, TIER is a trauma-informed lens that can be superimposed on existing evaluation approaches and methodologies, operating as an intervention for reducing individual and collective trauma. Unlike comprehensive evaluation theories that prescribe specific methods, TIER provides principles and perspectives that enhance whatever approach an evaluator chooses to employ, based on the beliefs that attending to trauma will lead to more just and valid results and that we have a moral imperative to do so because of the need to both rectify and prevent injustice and harm.

How TIER Fits

Now that we have established what a theory/model is and how TIER functions as a lens, let us consider how TIER fits into the vast world of research and evaluation approaches. We examine TIER through three complementary frameworks that help position it within evaluation scholarship and show how it enhances existing methodologies.

TIER and the Evaluation Theory Tree

The **evaluation theory tree** (Christie & Alkin, 2012) has become one of the most influential frameworks for understanding and categorizing evaluation approaches in our field (and itself exemplifies the field's practice of mixing theories, approaches, models, and lenses under the umbrella term *theory*). This taxonomy organizes evaluation theories into three main branches based on their primary emphasis: methods, use, or values. Understanding where TIER fits within this dominant framework helps establish its legitimacy and shows how it relates to established evaluation scholarship.

When considering this influential taxonomy, we situate the TIER lens with other value-driven theorists such as Donna Mertens, Jennifer Greene, and Goldie MacDonald. For such theorists, methods and use take a backseat to the way the evaluation itself is conducted to promote outcomes that advance justice or democracy. The TIER lens enhances these value-driven approaches by providing specific attention to trauma's influence on evaluation processes. We also tip our hats to the work of Guba and Lincoln (1989), who, in their groundbreaking book *Fourth Generation Evaluation*, distilled a serious evaluation process that takes values and valuing seriously while also leveraging a constructivist frame to explain variations in those very value sets. Such nuanced considerations of the values of all involved at all levels are of utmost importance and are certainly at the root of all evaluation approaches that hope to advance equity through practice, approaches that the TIER lens can strengthen.

Connecting TIER to Equity and Decolonization

Advancing **equity** means addressing "issues that are inherently complex and underpinned by social norms, biases, and privilege, all of which are internalized at the individual, organizational, and systemic level—perpetuating advantages for some and disadvantages for others" (Dean-Coffey, 2018, p. 527). Like decolonizing evaluation approaches, TIER challenges dominant knowledge systems that have historically excluded and harmed marginalized communities. Both decolonizing and trauma-informed approaches recognize that traditional evaluation methods can perpetuate colonial practices that retraumatize communities. TIER specifically addresses how evaluation processes themselves can either contribute to healing or compound historical and ongoing trauma. Our guest authors explore these connections between trauma-informed practice and equitable evaluation in depth in Chapter 6.

TIER in the Evaluation Garden

Building on this foundation, we can examine how TIER fits within contemporary evaluation frameworks. Montrosse-Moorhead, Schröter, and Becho (2024) offer a nuanced view of how evaluation approaches overlap and complement each other. They view each model as a collection of different elements that all contribute to an approach, including approaches to values, valuing, activism for social justice, context, promoting use, engagement in the evaluation process, depth of engagement in the evaluation process, and power dynamics in making decisions.

TIER is closely related to other approaches that score high on the activism, power dynamics, and context petals of the evaluation garden. Examples of such approaches would be Made in Africa, nation-to-nation evaluation, transformative participatory evaluation, and fourth-generation evaluation (Montrosse-Moorhead et al., 2024, p. 5). Figure 5.1 visualizes these petals and levels, and Table 5.1 breaks down how TIER fits in the evaluation garden on each dimension, using the level descriptions from Montrosse-Moorhead and colleagues (2024) to define our stance on each dimension.

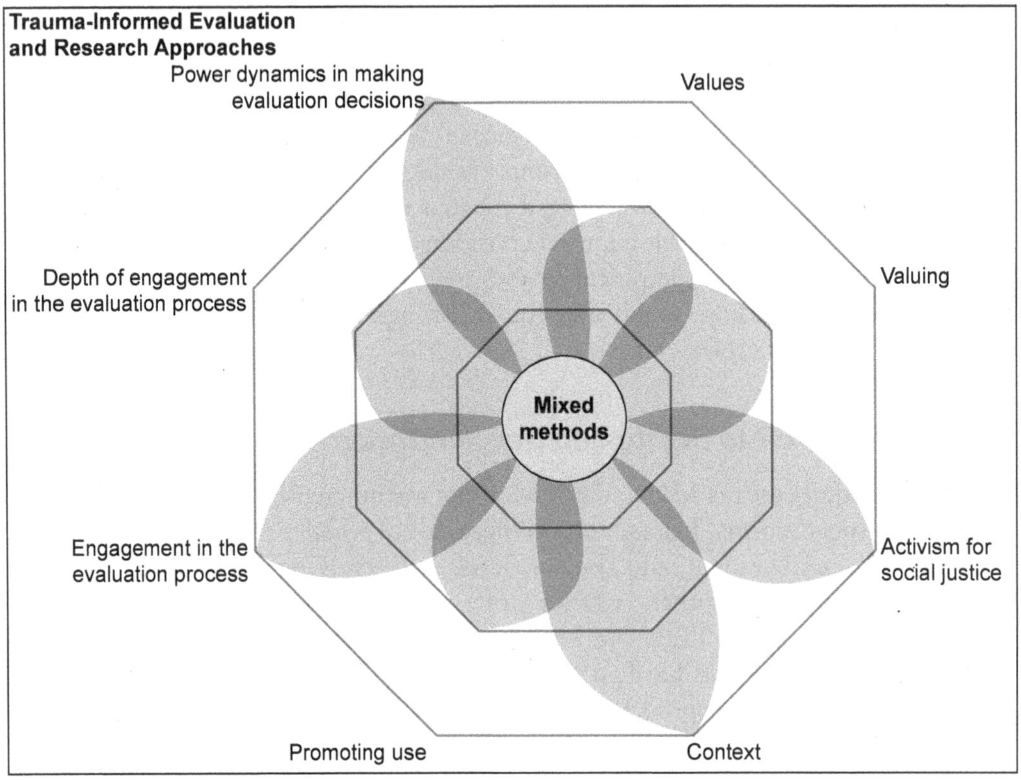

FIGURE 5.1. TIER's petals of the evaluation garden.

What does this all mean in practical terms? The frameworks we've just examined show that TIER isn't creating something entirely new—it's making visible and intentional what the best evaluation approaches already do partially. For example, empowerment evaluation already emphasizes participant voice and collaborative decision making, which aligns with TIER's principles of empowerment and collaboration. What TIER adds is explicit attention to how trauma affects these processes and concrete strategies for enhancing safety and healing. Rather than choosing between theoretical sophistication and practical application, TIER helps us achieve both.

Building on Established Approaches

Despite there being many models advancing equity, decolonization,[2] and empowerment (which we see as going hand in hand addressing trauma), few examine how

[2]Hopson, Kirkhart, and Bledsoe (2009) define *decolonizing evaluation* as "locating it within Indigenous cultural specificities, preferences and practices. It means recognizing and critically interrogating Eurocentric knowledge systems and standards of inquiry that have historically been imposed upon Indigenous cultures in Africa, Asia and the Americas" (p. 62).

TABLE 5.1. Evaluation Petals of TIER

Dimension	Description	Dimension level	TIER's approach
Values	Beliefs, attitudes, and ideas about what is of value, good, important, etc. Values guide what happens at each stage.	*Level 2:* Values are important, but the approach doesn't play an active role in surfacing them.	Values of the marginalized and traumatized should be surfaced and centralized. How to do this depends on other evaluation approaches employed.
Valuing	An evaluation approach's guidance for evaluators includes a process of determining the merit, worth, or significance of something.	*Level 2:* Valuing is important, but the approach doesn't explain how.	Evaluators should employ strong valuing approaches, guarding against the default application of the values of those in power.
Activism for social justice	The extent to which evaluators are to act in support of a cause as the primary purpose of evaluation.	*Level 3:* Activism for justice frame is used and positions the evaluation as a driver of or tool for social change.	Minimizing trauma and fostering resilience are justice issues that must be attended to during the evaluation process.
Context	Extent to which evaluations attend to their surrounding cultural, historical, and/or political contexts or systems.	*Level 3:* Considers attending to and integrating context essential and includes processes for doing so.	Context drives what constitutes trauma and/or resilience. It changes the perceptions of participants and can render the evaluators' actions as helpful or harmful.
Promoting use	An evaluation approach may guide evaluators to facilitate use. This could be of evaluation findings, or of knowledge.	*Level 2:* Use is important, but the evaluation does not play an active role in promoting its use.	Creating a trauma-informed evaluation process will be beneficial for evaluation use. We are not prescriptive as to how to facilitate use.
Engagement in the evaluation process	Who is involved in evaluation planning, interpretation, reporting, and decision making.	*Level 3:* A variety of groups make decisions, including those with and without formal power.	Involvement of those at the bottom of the power structure is essential for minimizing retraumatization and maximizing resilience.
Depth of engagement in the evaluation process	The extent to which different groups of people are engaged throughout an evaluation and in what roles.	*Level 2:* Those involved are consulted in some or all evaluation phases.	Consultation of traumatized groups happens at all stages. However, certain groups may not have the emotional resources or privileges (including physical and emotional safety) to participate.
Power dynamics in making evaluation decisions	Who is engaged in decision making and how.	*Level 3:* Collaborative, inclusionary decision making involving a broad range of engaged groups.	Powerlessness is a core result of trauma. We advocate direct decision making by those affected by trauma and oppression.

Note. Adapted from Montrose-Moorhead et al. (2024).

they address trauma in an in-depth way. Often, trauma considerations remain implicit or are limited to specialized mental health contexts. Our goal is to provide evaluators with concrete tools for assessing and enhancing their trauma-informed practice across any evaluation context.

To demonstrate how the TIER lens works in practice, we can examine how existing evaluation approaches already incorporate (or could better incorporate) SAMHSA's Six Principles of Trauma-Informed Care. This analysis reveals both the strengths and gaps in current methodologies, showing where trauma-informed enhancements would be most valuable.

By systematically examining approaches through this lens, we can move beyond theoretical positioning to practical guidance. The following assessment shows how different evaluation methodologies align with trauma-informed principles and where there are opportunities for strengthening their capacity to promote healing rather than harm.

Approaches and the Six Principles

In this section, we examine several dominant and emerging evaluation approaches and methodologies, applying a rating that reflects how each of them might include, even inadvertently, one or more of SAMHSA's Six Principles of Trauma-Informed Care. This is not meant to be an exhaustive list of evaluation approaches, as that is beyond the scope of this book. While any critique that we have missed a major or emerging theory of importance may be fair, the central goal of this section is to teach researchers and evaluators to critically examine approaches from a trauma-informed perspective, allowing space for modifications as necessary. Additionally, some of these approaches refer to specific types of research design (such as **randomized controlled trials** [RCTs]) rather than holistic evaluation approaches. Regardless, underlying the application of all of these is an evaluative intent.

Table 5.2 suggests a wide range of applicability of the Principles, from low to high, depending on the type of evaluation one is employing. We selected these evaluation approaches using maximum variation sampling to demonstrate the full range of how SAMHSA's Six Principles appear across different methodologies, from approaches that align well with trauma-informed practice to those that currently show little alignment.

Informal/Nonsystematic Approaches

Informal evaluation is a core feature of human cognition, and possibly of other nonhuman entities with complex cognition (Scriven, 2013). Essentially, any cognition that involves making a judgment or a decision contains an evaluative aspect. For the most part, that this happens on a subconscious level is of no harm. For instance, when one decides to eat oatmeal rather than toast, an underlying

TABLE 5.2. How the Six Principles Show Up in Other Approaches

	SAMHSA'S Principles of Trauma-Informed Care					
Approach	**Safety**	**Trustworthiness and Transparency**	**Peer Support**	**Collaboration and Mutuality**	**Empowerment, Voice, and Choice**	**Cultural, Historical, and Gender Issues**
Informal/nonsystematic	Low	Low	Low	Low	Low	Low
Single-criterion econometrics	Low	Medium	Low	Low	Low	Low
Theory driven	Low	Medium	Low	Low	Low	Low
Utilization focused	Medium	Medium	Medium	Medium	Medium	Medium
Empowerment	High	High	High	High	High	Medium
Transformative social justice oriented	High	High	High	High	High	High
Consumer oriented	Low	High	Low	Low	Low	Low
RCTs/experiments[a]	Medium	Medium	Low	Low	Medium	Medium

[a]The history of human experimentation and randomized controlled trials (RCTs) is littered with horrible abuses of disadvantaged people and populations. Therefore, some may be confused by the relatively high rating here. This is due to the institution of human subjects review boards that are now standard practice in research with people. We consider this a significant safeguard but still more needs to be done to improve IRBs' trauma sensitivity.

evaluation is taking place: One has decided that based on certain reasons that one would be "better" or "more preferable" than another. Oftentimes, one may not know exactly why one has made this decision.

However, informal evaluation often takes place in situations with more import. For instance, consider a person running their own nonprofit organization, perhaps providing coats to children in need. This individual may not conduct any formal evaluation process or needs assessment. Instead, they use the emotional response of those with whom they work to gauge the results of their work. They sense a positive emotional response in themselves and in their recipients whenever they give out a coat.

Such an example may seem innocent enough, but consider other situations in which informal evaluation processes are conducted. For instance, a city or other municipality may implement a new policy without any sort of formal evaluation process, potentially leading to outcomes that are detrimental to people with low influence and voice. This could also be the case with evaluations that are based on opaque or poorly established criteria, including prejudices or primal sentiments. Take for instance drug policy, which is often evaluated by broad swathes of the society based on what may seem prudent, moral, or fair when in fact there is plenty of evidence that supports policy changes that may be contrary to what some consider common sense. From our perspective, this sort of informal evaluation, which is done either tacitly or informally, is perhaps the worst approach of all when it comes to important matters that affect the lives of real people. It is not hard to imagine how ad hoc evaluations can and do result in the perpetuation of trauma. In our estimation, this lack of systematicity and process constitutes a significant risk to the safety of people affected by decisions based on them as well as a breach of trustworthiness and transparency.

So how might TIER principles be applied to informal evaluation? This is difficult, as systematically including TIER principles would automatically render it a more formal evaluation (which we would of course support!). However, in contexts where quick informal evaluation is necessary, we would advise proponents of TIER to ask the following questions:

- Whose voice is being left out of this process?
- What unintended effects might come about because of this decision?
- What historical contexts might we be overlooking here?
- What potential harm might this decision cause to vulnerable community members?

As informal evaluation is based heavily on personal intuition, the best one might be able to do here is develop one's own sense of justice and equity, infusing the decisions with such an ethic.

Single-Criterion Economic Evaluation

Economic evaluations that rely on a single criterion and are focused on an economic indicator such as cost or efficiency, such as **return on investment**[3] **(ROI)** and **cost analysis,**[4] are older evaluation methods largely coming from economics and financial accounting (Stufflebeam & Coryn, 2014). With the rise of neoliberalism in the 20th century, we saw a philosophical and political bend toward valuing growth and profit as the chief indicator of progress. (Consider the singular focus on the stock market when assessing the health of the economy according to electoral prospects of an incumbent president.) A business focus on profit as sole evaluative criterion should be of significant concern to those who care about justice in general. Likewise, a nonprofit organization could be overly focused on cashflow, using their

[3]Defined in Phillips and Phillips (2019) as "the ultimate measure of accountability that answers the question: Is there economic value added to the organization for investing in programs, processes, initiatives, and performance improvement solutions?" (p. 2). ROI is "used to evaluation the efficiency or profitability of an investment or to compare the efficiency of a number of investments" (p. 2).

[4]Scriven (1991) defines *cost analysis* as the "practical process of calculating the costs of something" (p. 105). While cost analysis and other single-criterion econometric evaluation methods fall short of being trauma-informed as standalone methods, we strongly endorse their use in the broader suite of evaluation methods. Indeed, Scriven often bemoaned the exclusion of cost-inclusive evaluation methods in the basic evaluation toolkit (Yates & Persaud, 2024).

own economic interests as the barometer for success. But how many have been traumatized in the name of profit—or by the nonprofit industrial complex?

These approaches could be aligned with TIER by turning away from cost or profit as the sole criterion for judging a business or social endeavor. Enterprises that do not take into account their effect on their communities may be optimizing for their bottom line in the short term but are likely poisoning the well for future generations. To make such approaches more aligned with TIER, we suggest that those employing economic evaluation methods broaden their evaluative frame, asking themselves the following questions:

- Beyond cost or revenue, what are the effects I would want this to have on real people?
- How would I know if what we are doing is hurting people?
- What outcomes would make me feel proud about what we do for people?
- Are we listening to people for reasons other than just maximizing profit?

Systematic Approaches

While the two prior approaches are unlikely to be used in isolation by any professional evaluator, we now enter the realm of common and accepted evaluation practices. Indeed, many people think **theory-driven evaluation** *is* evaluation without realizing it is just one in a whole menagerie of approaches. Highly **systematic approaches** to evaluation, such as Scriven's (2015) **consumer-oriented evaluation** and traditional experimental evaluation are also widely used in fields such as medical research and product evaluation. Many also attempt to apply these in human services evaluation as well.

Essentially, theory-driven evaluation is based on the premise that if one can articulate a **logic model** or a **theory of change** and then measure the inputs, outputs, and outcomes, one may be in a good position not only to evaluate but also to describe how the **evaluand** (the object of evaluation, e.g., a program, product, organization, or policy) operates mechanistically. Normally, this is based on inputs from those in power, being derived from the program directors' or the funders' design of the program. The greatest risk with this form of evaluation is one that is common to many other forms: the risk of defining success in accordance with the views of the powerful.

These risks are also present with consumer-oriented evaluation. Although there is high transparency, as one can follow the reasoning and conclusions of the evaluator from beginning to end, there is a risk of success being defined solely by the evaluator or by those in power, leading to the deficiencies in other areas.

Experimental evaluations, including RCTs—which are widely used in biomedical research—or the large-scale economic evaluations run by the likes of the JPAL Poverty Action Lab, have the benefit of heavy oversight and scrutiny of IRBs.

As it is often categorized as formal research, there is heavy emphasis on safety. However, a focus on issues of equity, justice, and historical issues may be lost.

For those employing these systematic approaches, the following questions may help steer the evaluation toward design and execution decisions that are more in alignment with TIER:

- Whose values am I prioritizing—those in power (funders, program managers) or those the program is meant to serve?
- Beyond IRB review, have I shared my evaluation design, instruments, and protocols with community members for their input?
- What specific steps am I taking to ensure psychological safety for all of my participants at all stages of this evaluation?
- What steps do I have in place in case a participant shows signs of distress or a mental health crisis?

High-Engagement and Justice-Oriented Approaches

What we are calling here **high-engagement approaches** such as **empowerment evaluation** and **utilization-focused evaluation** (UFE) begin to receive higher marks in terms of trauma sensitivity. Although not explicitly designed to minimize trauma, the participatory nature of these approaches with an emphasis on engagement with the stakeholder adds some safeguards, especially in the case of empowerment evaluation. While UFE is a significant step forward, the focus on use over other factors could be a deficiency leading to the evaluation being co-opted by the powerful. Other highly engagement-oriented models such as empowerment, **transformative evaluation**, or **culturally responsive evaluation and assessment** (CREA) all are naturally more trauma-informed, as they focus the evaluation on those with less power. For such evaluation approaches, wearing the TIER lens may reduce the need for major shifts in practice.

Practitioners of these approaches may want to ask themselves these questions in their quest to align better with TIER practices:

- If I am working toward justice and equity, do I include trauma under the umbrella of injustices that must be rectified?
- Am I excluding participants in the name of not doing harm? Is this impulse based in fear or likely and legitimate harm that would come from their involvement?
- How am I creating space for people to participate in ways that feel safe to them, even if it's different from my preferred methods?
- What specific steps am I taking to build trust before asking for vulnerable community members' time and stories?

A Good Approach Does Not Always Mean a Trauma-Informed Approach

To illustrate the need for intentionality in integrating TIER, we provide an example of a principles-based approach that ignores trauma but seeks to provide healing. In 2010, Tom Wolff authored a book called *The Power of Collaborative Solutions: Six Principles and Effective Tools for Building Healthy Communities*, which promotes building healthy communities through cooperation and collaboration. Wolff defines cooperation as exchanging information, modifying activities, and sharing resources for mutual benefit and to achieve a common purpose (Wolff, 2010). This is like SAMHSA's Principle of Collaboration and Mutuality. Both take cooperation and require exchanging information, co-creating activities, and focusing on mutual benefits. Wolff then explains that collaboration goes beyond cooperation in that it enhances the capacity of another for mutual benefit and to achieve a common purpose by sharing risks, resources, responsibilities, and rewards (Wolff, 2010).

It sounds wonderfully trauma-informed, doesn't it? Except, there is not a single mention of the role that collective and historical traumas would play in a group's capacity to build healing communities as well as the trauma-informed approaches that may help them heal and build capacity.

This is the case with many methods and approaches. We use Wolff's work simply to illustrate that empowering, participatory approaches—as great as they may seem—are not necessarily trauma-informed, even if they emphasize (by design, not by intent) some of the Six Principles. Now, imagine how transformative Wolff's framework could be if it were also trauma-informed. Building healthy communities requires healing, and to heal from collective and historical trauma, the traumas need to be recognized and acknowledged. Many social psychologists engaged in this kind of work know that trauma is an issue, and some have modified the approach to include TIER practices.

Restorative and Transformative Justice in Evaluation Practices

We bring one more thing to TIER: **justice**. In the **restorative justice** paradigm, Evans and Vaandering (2022) define justice as "the reciprocal pursuit of what everyone needs for their individual and collective well-being" (p. 51). That sounds like what Wolff's framework is striving for, doesn't it? And like what developmental, empowerment, and transformative evaluation approaches strive for. In fact, this definition of justice sounds like the goal of many programs and initiatives that we research and evaluate.

The findings and recommendations of a trauma-informed study have the potential to bring justice, or lead to justice being done, in a program or community.

Ginwright (2016) sees healing justice as an antidote to the hopelessness caused by structural/collective trauma. To heal from trauma, one needs justice, but not the punitive, vengeful justice wielded like a weapon in most European-based legal systems. **Healing justice** includes mindfulness and somatic practices; conversations; restorative and healing circles; contemplative practices such as meditation; faith-based teachings and gatherings; cultural and indigenous practices, such as drumming circles and sweat lodges; and activist art, such as murals, Theater of the Oppressed, and music. Communities of color frequently learn about and adopt **transformative[5] justice**, which "works for safety, justice, and healing, without relying on state systems" (Turner, 2020, p. 299). Its primary goal is the safety and healing of people who have experienced the trauma of violence of all kinds. The second goal is accountability and transformation of those who caused the harm, interrupting the cycle of violence and preventing further acts (Turner, 2020). Yoder (2005) reminds us,

> without an experience of justice, deliberate acts of harm often become chosen traumas, a shared traumatic event that is chosen to be kept alive through generations and becomes an integral part of a group's identity. Chosen traumas are characterized by an obsessive sense of being wronged by the other and by a sense of entitlement. (p. 29)

Restorative and transformative justice practices can be integrated into a study to discover how an individual or community defines justice and what they need to move forward and heal, and we will see an example of this later in the book. For now, keep in mind that TIER can be a step forward on the path toward healing justice.

WRAP-UP

By structuring and designing E&R in ways for people to reflect on and remember their stories and experiences and to reconnect with others and break the isolation, we have the potential to facilitate healing justice for individuals and communities. We need to practice listening deeply and asking questions that allow people to move through the pain into a place of hope for the future. A researcher or evaluator has a role in helping people break their silence and move through the pain of trauma by validating and acknowledging their people's experiences, responding

[5] Whereas restorative justice seeks to return the victim to their initial state before the harm occurred, transformative justice is a series of practices and philosophies designed to create change in social systems. Mostly, they are alternatives to criminal justice in cases of interpersonal violence or are used for dealing with socioeconomic issues in societies transitioning away from conflict or repression (*https://library.skagit.edu/justice*).

with care and empathy, and integrating resilience and justice practices into our approaches.

In alignment with Reid and colleagues' (2020) observations regarding the divide between theory and practice, Picciotto (2021) emphasizes the chasm between the lofty ideals that initially characterized the field of evaluation and the current landscape where evaluation predominantly serves as a commercial enterprise. He asserts that this disparity forms the root of discontent within much of the evaluation community today. The dissonance between an evaluator's perceived role and practical realities generates distressing emotions, especially if the researcher or evaluator is frustrated that they cannot provide participants with the appropriate assistance (Huff, 2023; Ledoux, 2015). We hope that TIER as a lens will mitigate and alleviate some of the tension we feel between theory and practice and that TIER can be helpful in choosing an approach or methodology that is maximally tailored to the context and can integrate the Six Principles of Trauma-Informed Care—an approach that has the potential to facilitate justice and healing.

CHAPTER 5 REFLECTION QUESTIONS

1. We mentioned a lot of different evaluation approaches in this chapter. How aware are you of them? If you already do evaluation, do you know which ones you tend to use? Are there any approaches that you wish to explore more deeply with a TIER lens?

2. Consider the theories or approaches that you work with frequently. Examine them to see where any of the Six Principles might be present or missing. Now, what would it take to make that approach *intentionally* more trauma-informed? Draw it in your journal or discuss with colleagues. Based on what you know right now, can you start looking at your work through the TIER lens?

CHAPTER 6

Equity-Focused and Trauma-Informed Evaluation and Research

MELANIE WARD, RUCHA LONDHE, and KATRINA BLEDSOE

What is equity? And what does it have to do with trauma?

WHAT YOU'LL LEARN

We might assume that because we're designing trauma-informed studies addressing the Six Principles that our studies are also just and equitable. Wrong. In this chapter, our guest authors, Melanie Ward, Rucha Londhe, and Katrina Bledsoe, help us connect concepts of equity with trauma-informed principles, adding a deeper dimension to TIER and further connecting TIER with CREA and other approaches that purposely seek to empower participants to be the change they wish to see. While assessing disparities across program outcomes is critical to understanding progress toward equity, centering equity within evaluation processes themselves can help attend to the historical, cultural, and contextual factors that create and perpetuate disparities and trauma over time. In this chapter, we provide a brief overview of what we think it means to be equity focused in TIER and why vigilance is needed in the work.

Introduction

Equity means that everyone, of every background, has a fair opportunity to achieve optimal outcomes (Jones, 2014). Advancing equity typically means reducing or eliminating **disparities**, or differences in outcomes that affect communities who have faced systematic marginalization, discrimination, and/or traumatization. Evaluation and measurement approaches to address equity typically involve assessing and reporting on changes or reductions in disparities or gaps associated with the implementation of a program, strategy, or policy.

Inequities persist in part due to systematic forms of oppression ingrained in societal institutions that create and reinforce disparities and gaps in health, education, employment, and other outcomes. Racism, sexism, heterosexism, ableism, ageism, classism, and other identity-based forms of prejudice and oppression contribute to systems of power that regularly discriminate against stigmatized and marginalized populations. These systems of power serve to create and reinforce values, narratives, and assumptions that continue to uphold structures, systems, and policies that are both inequitable and traumatizing.

Centering Equity through Equitable Evaluation Processes

Traditional approaches to evaluation are rooted in paradigms about knowledge creation that have historically privileged certain forms of knowledge, truths, or ways of knowing and marginalized others (de Sousa Santos, 2014). Academic and scientific institutions and those formally trained to operate within them have been historically positioned as centers of knowledge creation and have thus defined what legitimate knowledge is, who may produce it, and what is considered truth (Mertens, Hall, & Wilson, 2025). These traditions have largely privileged the most powerful societal ideologies and positionalities (e.g., white, male, heterosexual, nondisabled) to shape research agendas, public discourse, and ultimately, the narratives that define social problems. Communities facing the greatest inequities have historically been the subjects of E&R studies and often have endured scrutiny, observation, exploration, and testing for the sake of a greater society from which they often are excluded. However, members of these communities have rich experiential, professional, cultural, and personal knowledge that can help fill gaps in our understanding of societal problems and improve programs designed to address them. Without incorporating this knowledge, traditional evaluation approaches run the risk of perpetuating or exacerbating disparities by driving decision making based, at best, on partial truths and, at worst, on complete inaccuracies (Chicago Beyond, 2018).

Centering equity in E&R requires approaches that address legacies of systemic oppression, challenge predominant narratives of what's considered standard and traditional, and eliminate power dynamics within the study process. In addition to supporting equitable outcomes, centering equity also means supporting equitable processes. To illustrate this concept, we draw from Camara Jones's (2014) commentary on health equity and power. Jones defines health equity as "the assurance of conditions for optimal health for all people," which requires "valuing all individuals and populations equally, recognizing and rectifying historical injustices, and providing resources according to need" (p. S74). Furthermore, those involved in this process must engage in "active input, constant vigilance, and continuous correction" to explicitly address inequities embedded within the evaluation process (Jones, 2014).

Similarly, the Equitable Evaluation Initiative (EEI; 2024) defines *equity* as both means and ends. *Equity as means* refers to "working toward outcomes in ways that model dignity, justice, and love without re-creating harm in our structures, strategies, and working relationships" (p. 2). *Equity as ends* refers to "the absence of avoidable or remediable differences among groups of people, whether those groups are defined socially, economically, demographically or geographically" (p. 2).

An equity-centered evaluation approach challenges singular or predominant forms of knowledge and evidence. Namely, it requires all involved to challenge deeply held beliefs, or orthodoxies, that can stand in the way of implementing equitable evaluation principles. Participant or community-driven approaches to evaluation processes (see more later in the chapter) offer opportunities to challenge these orthodoxies by expanding the evaluation team's understanding of the systemic drivers of inequity and facilitating evaluation processes that are responsive to cultural values (EEI, 2024). Integrating the knowledge and perspectives of communities who experience inequities throughout the evaluation process can help evaluators examine and challenge predominant narratives and ideologies that reinforce societal inequities and work toward new understandings.

Equity- and Trauma-Informed Approaches

This orientation to equity is particularly appropriate for trauma-informed E&R approaches due to the effects of cultural, racial-ethnic, group, and generational trauma on marginalized communities. A trauma-informed approach acknowledges the role that trauma may play in one's life or in the experiences of a community with a shared culture or identity. Without incorporating a trauma-informed lens, evaluators and researchers may not properly ensure the physical and psychological safety and trust necessary to engage with and clearly understand the experiences of communities served by a program or policy. Additionally, understanding how one's own trauma can influence the work is critical, as we discuss in Part II.

Intersection of Equity- and Trauma-Informed Approaches

Trauma does not occur in a vacuum; it occurs within the context of intersectional identities of the person: race/ethnicity, class, ability, gender identity and expression, first language, sexual orientation, religion, immigration status, and so on. All experiences of discrimination and oppression, direct or indirect, based on social identities cause trauma. For research studies and programs to demonstrate an understanding of trauma and mitigate the hardship caused by trauma, it is essential to address the trauma brought on by the experience of systematic oppression and

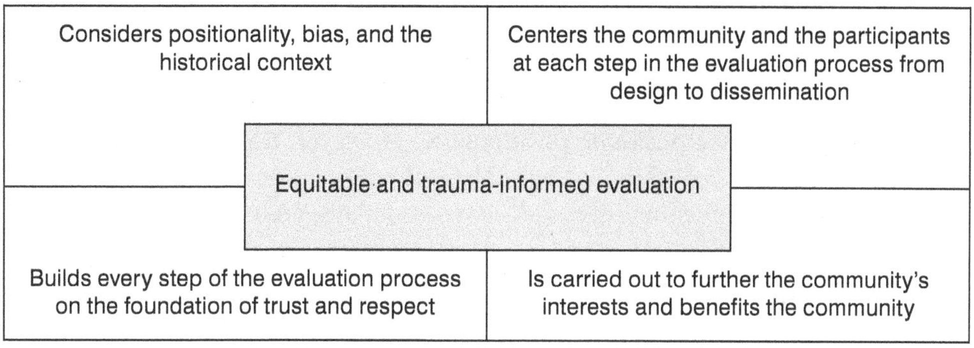

FIGURE 6.1. Equitable and trauma-informed evaluation concepts.

injustice. Recognizing the signs of trauma in individuals and communities becomes an essential element while establishing relationships, whether in a therapeutic or a research environment. This intersection begins with a complete acknowledgment and integration of knowledge about the root causes of trauma, using a culturally responsive lens, and implementing measures to resist retraumatization.

Assuring conditions to advance equity and address trauma within the evaluative process therefore involves including specific concepts and well-planned strategies to implement equity-centered, trauma-informed evaluation practices such as (1) understanding and addressing issues of positionality and bias; (2) community-engagement approaches; (3) building trust and respect; and (4) consistent, accurate, and appropriate data collection methods (see Figure 6.1).

Implementing an Equity-Centered, Trauma-Informed Equitable Evaluation

Being equity centered in a trauma-informed evaluation requires us to dig deeper into the Six Principles and expand on them. Here, we include positionality and bias, historical context, community engagement, and data disaggregation.

Positionality and Bias

Positionality is often defined as our understanding of ourselves, who we are, and what we bring to our research (Ladson-Billings, 2000). It is how we view, value, and approach situations based on our physical and social background and social standing, our experiences (or lack thereof), our upbringing and training, and our outlook on life. A key aspect in being able to implement an equity-centered, trauma-informed research agenda is understanding how positionality influences our view of trauma. This is particularly true not only in how we view it but also in how we respond to it and interact with others who experience trauma.

In general, however, research has not consistently addressed trauma, nor has it considered how researchers will recognize its influence. Trauma is often thought to be monolithic in the research paradigm, and much of that perspective is based on a positivist and postpositivist positionality. However, trauma is dynamic and uniquely experienced. Within an equitable evaluative framework, we understand that an individual's positionality and views about research determine how they define trauma, what they consider "credible" traumatic experiences, and how they conduct research.

To that end, positionality and bias are linked in that one's positionality is shaped by one's beliefs, values, and background. Bias is introduced when our beliefs and prejudices or monolithic beliefs influence and/or determine how we design, conduct, and analyze the results (Thomas & Campbell, 2020). Bias can influence the way that trauma is defined and addressed, particularly for those who are most affected but often least consulted. For instance, in an evaluation of substance use disorders (SUDs), not understanding the underlying factors behind the SUD and the accompanying trauma, our biases of what we believe SUDs are caused by, and by extension how to prevent and treat them might influence the kinds of research questions asked, our perspective on what should be developed as a strategy to address SUDs, how the data should be analyzed, and the like.

It is arguable that positionality in research is a combination of understanding where one might be in terms of axiology (values), ontology (the belief in what is considered truth), epistemology (in what way we can know what is truth), and methodology (the methods we can use to be able to know truth) (Mertens & Wilson, 2025). It is this perspective that addresses the way we will approach the research paradigm. It also helps us situate our perspective of how we will do the research and how we might understand and react to our own trauma and to that of those who are the focus of the research. An equitable evaluation approach posits that there are multiple perspectives and experiences that are true and that these may affect people in different ways. Thus, there is no one dominant or normative experience of trauma. The approach challenges us to curtail our biases about what is knowable and the experiences that accompany it.

Historical Context

Understanding historical context will often shape why and how certain systems, cultures, and experiences are in place (Caldwell & Bledsoe, 2019). It is rare that situations happen in a vacuum; these are often illustrative of a particular perspective. In many cases trauma has been long-standing and legacy (e.g., historical legacy). To truly understand how trauma occurs, researchers must look back at historical context and ask questions such as what are the root causes of the trauma? In what way has trauma continued and evolved over time? What did the situation and subsequent trauma morph into? Additionally, how has the situation and trauma been addressed over time, if at all? Without an understanding of how the situation occurred as well as the changes that are needed, it is difficult to conduct research with an eye that is both empathetic and sympathetic to the community. The research process itself will fail to explore deep issues that may help to provide what we like to refer to as a "kaleidoscope of understanding": From different angles, different understandings of the problem emerge, as well as what one can do to address it.

Community Engagement at Each Step

Community engagement principles acknowledge that communities most affected by programs, policies, and systems are not often involved in knowledge creation, change-making efforts, or decision-making processes. Community engagement has been defined as "the process of working collaboratively with groups of people affiliated by geographic proximity, special interest, or similar situations to address issues affecting their well-being" (CDC, 1997, p. 11).

Community-engaged research is research that listens to, collaborates with, and incorporates ideas, thoughts, and insights from people and communities most affected by a particular program, initiative, or policy. Organizations that work on research that often affects policies are increasingly including and working with community members and others with lived experience as partners and experts. In doing so, there is much more likelihood of engaging in an authentic and real way with those most affected, particularly on issues that are trauma based and influenced.

Equity-focused trauma-informed research places a strong emphasis on understanding and addressing the disproportionate impacts of trauma on marginalized and vulnerable communities. Community engagement in such research is critical to ensuring that the voices and experiences of these communities are central to the research process. By centering the voices and experiences of those most affected by trauma and inequity, who have not conventionally had opportunities to inform the programs and services they receive, researchers can contribute to more equitable practices and policies that address systemic injustices and promote healing and resilience.

Community engagement in an equity- and trauma-informed evaluation includes co-creation of the research with those individuals with lived experience. This involves the engagement of lived expertise in the various evaluation processes including, but not limited to, framing social issues and outcomes, generating research questions, collecting and analyzing data, disseminating findings, and making decisions. Lived experience refers to knowledge based on perspective, personal identities, and history beyond one's professional or educational experience and comes from people who are directly affected by social issues and strategies designed to address them.

We expand on SAMHSA's Six Principles that are foundational to ensuring authentic community engagement in equity-focused trauma-informed research: (1) collaboration and mutuality, (2) peer support, (3) empowerment, (4) trust and transparency, (5) physical and emotional safety, (6) informed consent and confidentiality, and (7) avoiding retraumatization.

Collaboration and Mutuality

Equity-focused trauma-informed research begins with recognizing the expertise and knowledge held within the community itself. It involves establishing collaborative partnerships where community members are seen as equal partners in the research process. Collaboration ensures that research questions, methodologies, and approaches are co-designed with community members. This mutual decision-making process helps to ensure that the research is culturally responsive, relevant, and respectful of community norms, values, and experiences. By fostering collaborative relationships based on mutual respect, trust can be built. This trust is essential for engaging community members who may be hesitant or skeptical due to historical or systemic injustices and traumas.

Peer Support

Peer support involves including individuals with lived experience of trauma as co-researchers, advisors, or peer mentors. Peer support provides validation and solidarity to participants by acknowledging their experiences and emotions. This validation is crucial in creating a safe and supportive environment where participants feel understood, valued, and supported, free from (re)traumatization by the research process. This sharing promotes empowerment and agency among participants. This includes, but is not limited to, piloting data collection instruments and methods with partners with lived experience. Engaging participants at the outset of the research can help address trauma up front, as well as better understand how communities will react to the research.

Empowerment

Equity-focused trauma-informed research seeks to empower communities by amplifying their voices and agency in decision-making processes. This includes empowering participants to define their needs, priorities, and desired outcomes from the research as well as having respect for traumatic experiences. Empowered communities are better equipped to advocate for policy changes and systemic improvements based on research findings. Equity-focused trauma-informed research supports these efforts by providing evidence and narratives that can drive meaningful policy reform and community-level interventions.

Trust and Transparency

Building trust and respect begins with a solid foundation of an individual relationship. Data collection should not be a transactional activity. Data collectors need to take the time to build rapport, put participants at ease, and pause to allow participants time to process their thoughts and feelings. Demonstration of empathy, a genuine interest in the participant's story, and a safe environment go a long way in building this initial rapport. Researchers also need to be honest with themselves in relationship to their own possible past traumas. Being transparent about the research and one's connection to it goes a long way in establishing that foundational trusting relationship.

Physical and Emotional Safety

Safety considerations while implementing trauma-informed equitable data collection include a wide range from a calming, nonchaotic, secure physical environment to giving the participants the desired emotional space and from using positive, respectful language to offering trauma training to data collectors and others engaged in the research enterprise.

In addition to SAMHSA's Six Principles, equity-centered trauma-informed research calls for additional considerations, which are summarized here but expanded on throughout the book.

Informed Consent and Confidentiality

Informed consent is a process that ensures a participant fully understands the research and what is being asked of them prior to consenting (Thomas & Campbell, 2020). It ensures participants are choosing to take part in research of their own free will, without undue pressure or coercion. The initial consent conversation is *not* to persuade someone to participate; it is to let them know what the study is about and figure out whether they want to participate. Reminding participants that their participation is voluntary and using an ongoing, iterative consent process is essential to building trust. It is also essential to ensure that participants are empowered to make participation choices and can withdraw at any stage in the study.

Resisting Retraumatization

Establishing a trusting relationship with participants helps in resisting retraumatization. Providing empathy and sympathy and being aware of and sensitive to participants' emotions and experiences help not only establish a strong relationship with the participants but also foster trust and respect in that relationship. Active nonjudgmental listening, respecting autonomy, and making research findings available to research participants sustain a transparent relationship.

Data Disaggregation

Sharing evaluation results with the community members is as important as collecting those data. Furthermore, what is crucial is the consistent and accurate disaggregated analysis of data across the various dimensions of intersectionality such as race/ethnicity, sex, gender, and ability. Equitable data analysis follows two processes: (1) structural/functional and (2) substantive. **Structural/functional analysis** seeks to analyze the data sources and data collection methods and opportunities for the influence of biases, both implicit and/or explicit. On the other hand, **substantive analyses** are conducted to better understand the "why" behind the data, the context that provides additional details about the data. Finally, trauma-informed and equitable analysis engages the very participants who are most affected in the process of meaning making and gaining insight into the collected data.

WRAP-UP

The integration of equity-focused and trauma-informed approaches within E&R represents a significant paradigm shift toward more just and effective practices. By centering equity within E&R processes, we acknowledge and actively address the systemic disparities perpetuated by historical and ongoing forms of oppression. This approach requires challenging traditional norms that prioritize certain forms of knowledge over others and actively engaging communities that have been marginalized and traumatized.

Community engagement, then, emerges as a pivotal strategy in this transformative process, ensuring that those most affected by social programs and policies are not only heard but actively engaged in shaping research agendas and interpreting findings. Collaboration and Mutuality foster relationships based on respect and shared decision making, and Peer Support validates and empowers individuals with lived experience of trauma. Empowerment becomes a cornerstone, allowing communities to advocate for meaningful policy changes grounded in their realities and needs. Building trust and respect throughout the E&R process is fundamental to mitigating trauma. Informed consent, confidentiality, and ensuring physical and emotional safety are essential practices that uphold ethical standards and promote a supportive research environment. Moreover, employing consistent, accurate, and trauma-informed methods ensures that diverse perspectives and intersectional identities are fully represented. This approach not only validates the experiences of marginalized communities but also provides insights that are crucial for developing interventions that are responsive and effective and can potentially mitigate past trauma.

Equity-focused trauma-informed approaches to E&R are a recent development and are what we believe to be a natural continuation of the evolution of research as the field becomes more aware of and sensitive to the harm E&R have done—and continue to do—to individuals and communities. Contemporary evaluation theory has evolved to embrace the inherent complexities of evaluators, acknowledging their unique identities, intersectionalities, values, biases, and life experiences that they bring into the evaluation process. This recognition extends to acknowledging the significance of the evaluator's capacity for compassion and empathy within the evaluation context and for the role of the researcher to change from that of an expert to a collaborator (Elliott, Bjelajac, Fallot, Markoff, & Reed 2005; Huff, 2023). Many agencies—especially governmental agencies—seek experts to track only service deliverables and desired outcomes, thus eliminating even the possibility that evaluators and researchers take a more active role to alleviate suffering and address the root causes of inequities and injustices (Ahrens et al., 2023).

In essence, an equity-centered, trauma-informed approach in evaluation research embodies a commitment to social justice, accountability, and the ethical imperative of ensuring all voices are heard and valued. By embracing these principles, we move closer to achieving equitable outcomes and fostering resilience in communities affected by systemic inequities and trauma.

CASE STUDY 6.1 Cultural Adaptation of Trauma-Informed Research Practices

RACHAEL JACKSON

When conducting trauma-informed research, it is critical for evaluators and researchers to consider the cultural issues that could influence the way we understand and interact with survivors of trauma. Although the physiological response to trauma is the same across cultures, the experiences that cause trauma, the interpretations of trauma and its symptoms, and the way people talk about trauma vary greatly by culture. At NORC (National Opinion Research Center, University of Chicago), when we research populations at heightened risk of trauma, we include questions about the interaction between trauma and culture in our formative/scoping assessments and discuss these issues with local field interviewers to ensure we are doing our best to use culturally appropriate trauma-informed practices and language.

In 2021, NORC worked with a local data collection firm, Kantar, to study the prevalence of commercial sexual exploitation of children (CSEC) in Kenya. Given that the NORC team was made up of primarily Western researchers without lived experience of CSEC, we employed two practices to ensure we considered the micro- and macrocultures that affected the study respondents. First, we conducted a series of focus-group discussions with teens in the sex trade in each of the study regions to learn about their microculture. We learned that many focus-group participants did not consider themselves to be "victims" or "survivors" of CSEC. Several youths reported coming from backgrounds of poverty that they considered more traumatic than their current situation and trading sex for money helped them to get out of poverty. They also tended use employment language to describe their situations. Those who worked under a pimp were part of a "company," and those who worked alone were "self-employed." Although most teens had experienced traumatic situations while engaged in the sex trade, they did not consider the "work" to be traumatic.

To be trauma-informed, we must avoid putting unwanted labels on people. So, given these findings, we removed all references to CSEC, "victims," and "survivors" from the informed consent and survey forms. However, given that CSEC is a serious crime by both local and international standards, we did not want to legitimize their harmful experiences by calling it "work." Therefore, we wrote the survey so that the first time we talked about CSEC, we defined the concept for them and asked participants what term *they* preferred to describe it. We then programmed the survey to fill in every place that would have used the term *CSEC* with the term that was more familiar to the respondent. For example, many teens referred to their CSEC experiences using a phrase that translates roughly to "the hustle." So, we might ask a question like this: *About how long has it been since you last did any kind of sex trade or "the hustle," whether voluntary or involuntary?*

In this study, it was also important to consider the macrocultural issues that might affect respondents' survey engagement, so during data collection training, we talked at length with field interviewers (who were all Kenyan) to ensure we were using the right language to talk about trauma and distress. We hired a local consultant to present a training module on culture and trauma. In this module, the consultant presented the findings of a paper that reported cultural terminology related to distress in Kenya. He then facilitated a discussion among the field interviewers to determine whether the reported terminology was commonly used in their communities, whether some terminology differed between tribes, and whether any of the survey questions or trauma content management strategies seemed to come from a Western perspective that did not feel right to the data collectors.

Based on the interviewers' feedback, we revised the survey instrument to ensure it was using culturally appropriate language and developed "cheat sheets" of trauma-informed and culturally appropriate phrases interviewers could use to help respondents manage any trauma responses they might have. For example, the term *thinking too much* (*kufikiria sana*) is a way to describe grief, stress, and depression. So, if field interviewers noticed a respondent getting distressed about the content of the survey, they could check in with them by saying,

> "I know that talking about hard things that have happened can make us think too much. The most important thing for us today is that you feel okay with the things that you choose to share. I just want to check in to see how you're doing."

Through our formative discussions with people with lived experience and in-depth conversations with data collectors, we were able to design a trauma-informed study that was culturally appropriate at both a micro and macro levels. We focused on identifying language that could make both respondents and data collectors feel comfortable talking about the difficult topic of CSEC.

CASE STUDY 6.1. REFLECTION QUESTIONS

1. Why is it important to center equity when conducting trauma-informed research?
2. How might participants in your study/evaluation think about their experiences? How do the micro- and macrocultures of which they are a part influence their outlook on these experiences?
3. What training or other resources can be provided to field staff to ensure they understand and can interact respectfully with people from different cultural backgrounds?
4. How can we design studies—from sampling through results dissemination—to engage communities and be culturally appropriate and informed? What can facilitate using this approach? What are some of the barriers?

CASE STUDY 6.2 Mandatory Reporting

Erika Keaveney

Research projects working with vulnerable populations are confronted with the possibility of learning about situations or behaviors that are subject to mandatory reporting laws. Researchers face an inherent tension when studying these topics or populations, as mandated reporting negates respondent confidentiality, which is essential to both data accuracy and the ethical conduct of human subject research. This tension must be addressed through the following steps: (1) understanding what mandatory reporting requirements exist, (2) establishing procedures for adhering to such requirements across the research life cycle, and (3) clearly disclosing any and all limits to confidentiality during the consent/assent process to enable respondents to make informed decisions on what they share with the research team.

In the U.S. context, researchers whose projects face a heightened risk of child or elder abuse disclosures, for example, can conduct state statute searches at *ChildWelfare.gov* and *mandatedreporter.com*. Although most states limit mandated reporters to social workers, counselors, educators, medical professionals, and law enforcement, 11 states require faculty and staff at institutes of higher learning to report child abuse, and 18 states require reporting by *any* person—regardless of profession. In addition, several states require mandated reporters to disclose known or suspected cases to their institution, regardless of where and how they learn about the case.

Some states have also adopted "*Tarasoff* statutes," which require mental health professionals to report serious threats of physical violence against any reasonably identifiable victim. Although existing case law has not extended such statutes to researchers and evaluators, mandated reporters engaged in E&R may be obligated to report such threats uncovered during data collection with a separate institution. Studies engaging mental health professionals in data collection should therefore take steps to understand the obligations of such professionals to report (Google keyword searches such as Tarasoff+[state] should yield relevant legislation).

In contrast to domestic guidance, there are no international compilations of mandatory reporting requirements by topic or location. Thus, the impetus is on the research team to conduct a thorough review of policies and regulations for foreign jurisdictions via national legislation portals/databases and targeted Google searches. Keyword searches should be conducted in the language(s) of government and include an exhaustive list of keywords on relevant topics (e.g., "Child Rights Act"+[country],labor+law+[country],"Labor Act"+[country], "Human Trafficking"+law+[country], etc.). In addition, research teams should consult with local research firms and legal advisors to ensure full compliance with laws and policies directed at protecting vulnerable individuals in the designated country. Local ethical review boards may also be able to provide guidance on mandatory reporting requirements (see the U.S. Department of Health and Human Services' International IRB database at *www.hhs.gov/ohrp/international*).

It is important to note that lack of *legal* obligation to report does not exempt researchers from an *ethical* obligation. Uncovering child abuse or credible threats of harm to oneself or others must be handled with the utmost care and will generally require the intervention and support of experienced professionals. Research teams should thus comprehensively describe plans for engaging qualified professionals, organizations, and agencies, along with referral procedures and logistics in their IRB protocol. As always, any limits to confidentiality—whether mandated or not—must be fully disclosed to study participants during the consent process.

CASE STUDY 6.2. REFLECTION QUESTIONS

1. How might disclosure of mandatory reporting requirements affect study participants' willingness to share sensitive information with the research team? How can mandatory reporting live alongside the Principle of Trust and Transparency, especially with marginalized populations?
2. What can researchers and evaluators do to ensure complete and accurate data on sensitive topics in the face of high refusal rates?
3. Under what circumstances might a formal report of abuse actually *increase* risk to the victim? What can researchers do to better understand and navigate unforeseen risks associated with making a report?
4. Do you think it is ethical for researchers to engage mandated reporters as field interviewers? Why or why not?

PART III

Doing TIER

At last, what you've been waiting for. The first chapter in this part focuses on you again—how to *be* a trauma-informed researcher and evaluator. Much of what you read here may already sound familiar, but we'll go even deeper. In Chapter 8, we focus on how you can design and frame your study using trauma-informed principles. The following two chapters describe trauma-informed approaches to surveys (Chapter 9), interviews, and focus groups (Chapter 10), followed by suggestions for analysis and reporting (Chapter 11). This part is where your knowledge of trauma and research methods all come together. Because we do not (and cannot possibly) address every method for collecting/analyzing data, we encourage readers to transfer and modify what they learn in this section and apply your learning to other data collection methods as applicable.

CHAPTER 7

Being a Trauma-Informed Researcher and Evaluator

Evaluators are enlightened beings who sometimes talk with their mouths full, make embarrassing statements, and forget to close the garage door. We all need a little help sometimes.

WHAT YOU'LL LEARN

In this chapter, we discuss what it means to *be* a trauma-informed researcher or evaluator. Simply learning about the Four (or Five) R's and Six Principles is not enough. As we've said, the work starts inside each of us. We start by explaining **resilience** and how practicing **empathy**, vulnerability, and openness while incorporating **resilience practices** (like breathing breaks) can make us and those around us more resilient, less triggered and anxious, and more open. We consider what healing from trauma requires and what our roles might be in that process. We point you toward resources for practices that will help you build resilience and promote healing, starting right now.

A Trauma-Informed Practice: Box Breathing

Please don't skip this activity. Take a minute to slowly scan your body, from your toes to your head, noticing any areas of tension or discomfort. When you are ready, inhale for four counts, hold for four counts, exhale for four counts, and hold for four counts. Do this five times. Now, scan your body again. Notice if anything changed as you breathed. Do you feel more centered or calm? Do any parts of your body feel less tense?

We also invite you to pause and take a moment to reflect on how resilient you are—how resilient your study participants are. You are still here. They are still here. We may be broken and injured to various degrees, but we are still here.

As one trauma counselor says to her clients, "WOW! Look at all you've done despite what happened to you!" We are still here because humans are resilient. As evaluators and researchers, we are in a position of power to facilitate and promote resilience—our own, our clients, and our participants. Yes—it *is* our job. By wearing the trauma-informed lens, we can reach that high-hanging fruit and do good.

What Is Resilience?

Resilience at the individual level "describes the quality needed to survive extreme conditions yet retain the capacity to find a way back to expressing the defining quality of being and the essence of purpose" (Lederach & Lederach, 2010, p. 68). Resilience is also described as adaptability, resourcefulness, a capacity to face and negotiate risky situations (Lederach & Lederach, 2010), and the ability to sit in discomfort and **self-regulate**, interrupting the brain's instinct to fight, flee, or freeze. Self-regulation is the ability to "monitor behavior and adjust it to meet the expectations of the environment. . . . It involves reflection and the ability to use self-comforting strategies to keep internal arousal at a manageable level" (Craig, 2017, p. 63).

Resilience at the community level describes "the capacity to forge solidarity, to sustain hope and purpose, and to adapt and negotiate creatively with the challenges presented" (Lederach & Lederach, 2010, p. 69). Menakem (2017) believes that, like trauma, resilience can be passed on from generation to generation, as it is both intrinsic and learned. It can be manifested both individually and collectively and is more about *being* than doing, just like *being* a trauma-informed researcher and evaluator.

Decades ago, we thought that the brain was not capable of healing itself. Now we know that is not always true—the brain is resilient and capable of healing itself[1] (from some injuries) by rewiring neural pathways when environments and experiences provide a safe counternarrative to trauma. The brain's ability to heal is called **neuroplasticity**, and one thing that promotes neuroplasticity is sustained contact and connections with people who care, set appropriate boundaries, and show genuine interest (Craig, 2017; Mears, 2012). Trauma-informed researchers and evaluators can create the kinds of connections that promote neuroplasticity and resilience if we take the time to connect with our participants.

Protective and Compensatory Experiences

We feel it is important to call attention to the protective factors that promote a child's resilience. These are known as **PACEs (protective and compensatory experiences)**, and they are the antidote to ACEs. Even though many children experience

[1]We know that some progressive diseases like Alzheimer's and others are currently incurable and that conditions in the brain prevent it from being able to heal.

adversity, they usually also have some PACES in their lives, and those protective and compensatory relational experiences lead to emotional regulation and resilience. Hays-Grudo and Morris (2020, p. 23) list these relational factors:

- Unconditional love from a parent (or another primary caregiver such as a grandparent serving in a parental role)
- Having a best friend
- Volunteering in the community
- Being part of a social group
- Having the support of an adult outside of the family (e.g., coach, mentor)

Resources we identify as PACEs include the following:

- Living in a clean and safe home with enough food
- Having the resources and opportunities to learn (good school, other educational experiences)
- Having an engaging hobby and/or an artistic, creative, or intellectual pursuit
- Being part of organized sports or having regular physical activity (or both)
- Being part of a family with routines and fair, consistent rules

For many children, protective factors occur at school or within other organizations or systems (Masten & Motti-Stefanidi, 2020), and we talk more about this in Chapter 12.

Because any study involving human, social services, criminal/juvenile justice agencies, educational institutions (all levels), and health-related organizations—to name a few—means studying trauma-affected people and populations, we believe that being ignorant of ACEs and other kinds of trauma, including our own, is irresponsible, unethical, and potentially retraumatizing. The prevalence of ACEs alone—not including collective traumas—justifies our call for TIER to become a universal precaution and best practice.

Healing Trauma Wounds

Ginwright (2016) explains that healing is an "explicit process of restoring individuals and communities back to optimal health" (p. 38). This assumes that humans were once in optimal health, perhaps before chattel slavery and colonization. There is no timeline for how long recovery might take, as it varies by individual and community. Levins Morales (1998) tells us that "recovery from trauma requires creating and telling another story about the experience of violence and the nature of the participants, a story powerful enough to restore a sense of our own humanity to the abused" (p. 15). For example, communities that come together to share their stories after a tragedy set the community up to move from tragedy to healing (Mears, 2012). Healing from historical injuries, such as genocide, slavery, and or gender discrimination, takes time and often requires some kind of restorative justice process, such as Truth and Reconciliation Commissions. Racial healing in part requires racial socialization whereby people of color come to know their strengths, understand the world in which they live, and position themselves to thrive through continual education (DeGruy & Leary, 2005). Healing involves building self-esteem and taking control of the inner world. It means understanding the debilitating effects that cortisol and adrenaline and other hormones related to toxic stress have on the body. It involves understanding the importance of regular exercise and a healthy diet.

That said, healing individuals and communities from trauma takes more than self-care and awareness of the harms. It also takes more than resiliency practices because we can be resilient and still repeat the behaviors we learned and embodied because of trauma. Healing takes a conscious awareness along with therapeutic, somatic, and spiritual processes to bring the embodied trauma to the surface and rid the body of its poison. All trauma, be it recent or historical, needs to be metabolized and healed. That is why people can't simply "get over it."

Healing trauma involves recognizing, accepting, and moving through pain—which is what Menakem (2017) refers to as **clean pain**. It often means facing what you don't want to face—what you have been reflexively avoiding or fleeing. By deciding to walk into that pain, and being willing to experience the pain fully, one can move through it—metabolize it and put an end to it. "In the process, you also grow, create more room in your nervous system for flow and coherence, and build your capacity for further growth" (Menakem, 2017, p. 165).

Partridge (2010, pp. 56–57) explains how researchers and evaluators working with native peoples and other traumatized communities provide opportunities for healing:

- *Reflection:* Research and evaluation, particularly qualitative methods, provide opportunities for people to reflect on their stories and lives, perhaps see the destructive forces at work, and find healthier ways to move forward.
- *Remembering:* This involves breaking the silence with others and sharing experiences so people do not feel alone. Remembering with others creates connection.
- *Resolving:* This involves working through the spiritual, emotional, and physical and mental wounds of the trauma. Ceremonies, rituals, and interactions with community members play a large role in this.
- *Reconnecting:* This occurs when traumatized individuals move away from their isolation and become actively involved in their communities.

Partridge (2010) explains the structure of the healing process, which "must have a beginning and an end. All the theories say so. We soon realized that we needed to go into this not just getting people to talk about their losses but helping them discover that talking about them would produce a gain" (p. 57) This last point speaks directly to the historical and sometimes present tendency for evaluators and researchers to extract information for their own benefit and ignore the needs of the community. TIER includes helping participants form connections between their stories and their future by making it clear what they have to gain. Mears (2012) offers some ways that evaluators and researchers can support trauma recovery and healing:

- Promote a sense of safety, support and flexibility.
- Promote calming. "When a person appears to be lost in emotion or panic, it helps to provide a compassionate, grounded presence" (p. 162).
- Promote a sense of self and collective efficacy. Help participants gain a sense of control and believe there is opportunity for positive outcomes. Commit to sharing positive outcomes of the study with participants—if you can.
- Promote connection with you, with others in the study, with the program or organization, and with the community.
- Promote hope. "Optimism is associated with positive outcomes and is a powerful tool for reducing the likelihood of negative psychological effects following a trauma" (p. 162).
- Provide immediate access to support (counselors, social workers) after engaging with participants.

Recognizing Our Window of Tolerance

In Chapter 1, we introduced the window of tolerance (WoT), a concept developed by Dr. Dan Siegel (2009). Remember, when we are regulated, or calm, information flows through our cerebral cortex and our executive functioning is high. In this state of being, our WoT is wide open, as we are in the "zone where our nervous system is relaxed, calm, alert, engaged" (Graham, 2010, p. 2). We are balanced, safe, and in a state of homeostasis where we can remain present in the moment. With our WoT wide open, we can take in or tolerate what is happening around us and remain in our "higher brain." There, we can recover quickly from stressors and regain our energy. If our bodies can remain relaxed, we are then able to focus our attention on what our participants are saying and feeling. Figure 7.1 provides us with a visual to imagine what our WoT looks like open. The squiggly line represents the stressors we have, but even so, our WoT remains open.

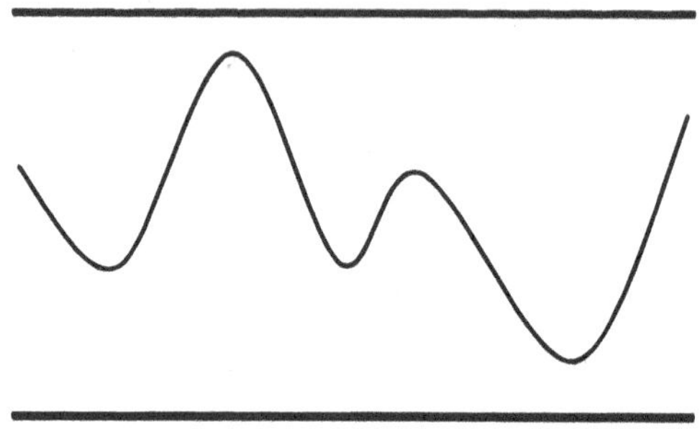

FIGURE 7.1. Open window of tolerance.

Awareness of our own triggers and trauma responses and the ability to interrupt them in the moment with self-regulating practices have a direct bearing on our ability to sit with participants and clients in painful and stressful situations. We need to understand and recognize our own triggers because hearing the stories of trauma-affected participants or clients may cause our WoT to close if we have similar stories, experiences, or feelings. Our WoT closes when our amygdala has been activated, the hijack of the cerebral cortex by the lower brain has begun, and our executive function is going offline. Our muscles tighten up, our breathing becomes shallow, or we hold our breath, and our focus has turned from our participants' stories to our own stories, memories, and feelings now coursing through our brains and bodies (see Figure 7.2). We are no longer present with our participants, which means we are no longer hearing them because we are lost in our own trauma story. And a transcript cannot capture the nuances of expression, tone, and body language.

Take a moment to reflect on the following questions about our WoT when it closes:

- What happens to the validity of our research when our WoT closes?
- Do we lose valuable information while we are managing our own trauma responses?
- What happens to our interactions in the moment with the participant(s) across from us?
- Can we listen attentively?
- Can we respond with empathy?

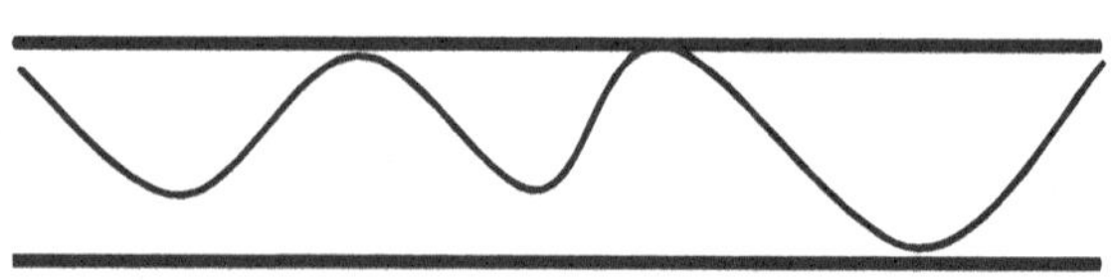

FIGURE 7.2. Closing window of tolerance.

A closing WoT does not mean the interaction is over. It means it is time for you to self-regulate and do resilience practices. Does that mean pausing, taking a break, or inviting participants to stand and stretch? How about getting some water or taking some deep breaths? Yes to some or all of the above. That is why developing and normalizing a regular resilience practice routine is so important. Raising awareness about our WoTs—knowing what it feels like when they are open and when they are closing and understanding what causes them to close—is critical to our ability to stay present and regulated when we are collecting and analyzing data, especially when we are interacting with other humans in real time. Likewise, you need to keep an eye on your study participants and look for any signs that their WoT may be closing. This leads us to the next question:

What Is a Trauma-Informed Researcher and Evaluator?

Being a trauma-informed researcher and evaluator requires us to take a holistic, human-centered approach to our work. The ability to feel and communicate empathy is foundational and essential to being a trauma-informed researcher or evaluator. Empathy can be defined as "vicariously feeling with a suffering person" (Jones, Bodie, & Hughes, 2016, p. 5), or "the ability to sense other people's emotions, coupled with the ability to imagine what someone else might be thinking or feeling" (*Greater Good Magazine*, n.d., para. 1). Brené Brown (2012b) says, "[e]mpathy is connection; it's a ladder out of the shame hole" (p. 81). Empathy is so important when working with trauma-affected populations that Coll, Sawyer, Scholl, and Hauser (2019) recommended empathy development for staff who provided therapeutic residential care to struggling teens—something that may be needed for researchers and evaluators as well, given that for some of us, being empathetic does not come naturally.

Empathy grounds TIER by challenging traditional practices calling for emotional distance or "objectivity." Instead, TIER embraces relating to participants as fellow human beings, not as distant human subjects. (We would love research to use the term *research with and by human beings* instead of *human subject research* to intentionally reposition evaluators and researchers.) Being a trauma-informed researcher or evaluator means we may have to reenvision, redefine, or expand on some of the rules and procedures that IRBs require and that professors teach us in graduate school. We have noticed a shift in IRB language toward acknowledging trauma but, as in the literature, it's a superficial nod. Brown (2012b) reflects this notion:

> Very early in our training, we are taught that a cool distance and inaccessibility contribute to prestige, and that if you are too relatable, your credentials come into question. While being called pedantic is an insult in most settings, in the Ivory Tower we're taught to wear the pedantic label like a suit of armor. (p. 12)

What Brown described is what we are striving to change. And we have models for the kind of change we need. Judy Atkinson (2002), an aboriginal Australian researcher, shares the indigenous philosophy of ***dadirri*** that guides her approach to life and how she conducts her research:

> Listening to one another is an Australian aboriginal gift. The principles and functions of the *dadirri* are: a knowledge and consideration of community and the diversity and unique nature that each individual brings to community; ways of relating and acting within a community; a non-intrusive observation, or quietly aware watching; a deep listening and hearing with more than the ears; a reflective non-judgmental consideration of what is being seen and heard; and, having learnt from the listening, a purposeful plan to act, with actions informed by learning, wisdom, and the informed responsibility that comes with knowledge. (p. 16)

Atkinson's research on transgenerational trauma was grounded by *dadirri*, which then shaped the dialectic between the researcher and the researched.

> "I will listen to you, share with you, as you listen to me, share with me. Our shared experiences are different but in the inner deep listening to, and quiet, still awareness of each other, we learn how to grow together." . . . *Dadirri* listens and knows; witnesses, feels, empathizes in the pain under the anger, and, if the anger is accompanied by action, seeks to understand the thoughts and feelings behind the action. *Dadirri* then seeks to find the source of that pain in knowledge-building for a deepening understanding of the more complete story of the person. (p. 18)

Brummer and Thorsborn (2021) add the following:

> when this exchange of experience happens in life-enriching and restorative ways, it can be a dance between a speaker connecting with a listener and a listener connecting with a speaker. We can use honest expression to connect someone with what is alive in them at any given moment. We use empathy as a way of hearing what is alive in them. Sometimes, when others are struggling to use language to engage with us, we may use our questioning skills to find our way to their heart and what is alive there. (p. 138)

Let's pause here. Have we ever heard words like those above in our research courses—even those grounded in critical theory? Maybe. If we were lucky. But probably not.

Being trauma-informed also means being vulnerable—something many of us are very uncomfortable being. Being vulnerable may involve sharing our own feelings or experiences with participants and stakeholders, which builds trust and connection (Atkinson, 2002; Brown, 2012b; Thorsborne & Brummer, 2021). Vulnerability requires researchers to sit in uncertainty, to take risks, and to expose themselves emotionally. (If this is making you anxious, take a deep breath. Or five). Vulnerability terrifies most traditional researchers and evaluators who want to avoid it out of fear the research will go sideways or be invalidated, as Brené Brown describes. But expressing empathy for trauma-affected study participants and clients promotes resilience and healing for everyone, which is TIER's end game. No one is asking researchers and evaluators to be therapists. But we are asking that we strive to become authentic, genuinely caring, empathetic, and trauma-informed human beings who happen to do E&R. How we interact with participants and clients can play a part in helping them break the cycles of violence (acting in and acting out) and take a step forward on their healing journey.

Instead of remaining neutral and detached, there is a growing sentiment that we must fundamentally redefine our perception of E&R, viewing it as a *service* to our fellow human beings (Bledsoe, 2021) and not an analytical exercise. This paradigm shift toward emphasizing love and service "means that the heart of the evaluator grounds the work" (Bledsoe, 2021, p. 17). Grounding our efforts in compassion and care necessitates that we invest time in building relationships, actively listening to individuals, striving to understand their experiences, and providing assistance where needed (Widdershoven, 2018). Bledsoe's (2021) proposition acknowledges that the evolution of evaluation centers on embracing our shared humanity, vulnerability, and capacity for love, care, and grace, even in the face of personal risk to one's livelihood or well-being.

Holding Safe and Brave Spaces

Ensuring that you and your participants are physically, emotionally, spiritually, and mentally safe is essential to being a trauma-informed researcher and evaluator. Your ability to create and hold safe spaces, or what some call brave spaces, is reliant on your self-awareness, your ability to regulate in the moment, and your ability to keep your WoT open. Let's start with defining safe and brave spaces.

A **safe space** is typically defined as an environment where individuals feel physically and emotionally secure and where they are free from judgment, harassment, and discrimination. In a safe space, individuals feel comfortable expressing themselves and sharing their experiences. A safe space is undoubtedly essential for building trust and establishing a sense of community among teams.

On the other hand, a **brave space** is where individuals feel encouraged to speak up and share their perspectives, even when they might be outside the norm, uncomfortable, or challenging. In a brave space, individuals are expected to speak freely, confront their biases, challenge their assumptions, and engage in constructive dialogue. A brave space is where individuals feel empowered to take risks, make mistakes, and learn from one another (Stubbs, 2023).

What then does it mean for a researcher or evaluator to hold safe and brave space? The answer to that question is twofold. First, study participants should be invited to determine what kind of space is safe for them. Second, we need to create and maintain that safe and brave space even when there is tension, pain, or conflict during the participant encounter. To do this, we need to keep our WoT open, be present, be empathetic, and be self-regulated. The second we lose ourselves to a stress response or trigger, we jeopardize the space. Case Study 7.1 by Evelyn Cruz describes her awareness of how grief was affecting her and what she did to move through it.

CASE STUDY 7.1 Wisdom of the Heart: Working through Grief toward Health Equity during the COVID and Racism Pandemics

EVELYN CRUZ

It was the summer of 2020, and I was attending a work-related equity training, when I suddenly started to experience all kinds of physical discomfort and a torrent of emotions—frustration, irritation, impatience. . . . As the Director for Program Planning and Evaluation at Centro Hispano of Dane County in Madison, Wisconsin, I design and implement strategies toward mental health and well-being equity. Throughout my 20-year career in public health, I have attended, created, and facilitated many events similar to this equity training, seeking to bring awareness to the history of racism in the United States and how it affects our well-being. I have worked toward systems change by centering the voices of those most affected, facilitating spaces for trust building. Despite all this emotionally charged work, I had never experienced these feelings with such intensity.

So, I turned inward to understand them. The murder of George Floyd was a significant and traumatic event in the middle of the worldwide COVID crisis. The murder—which we all witnessed through social media and news coverage—left me in shock and disbelief at the inhumanity it represented. Many of us who identify and/or who the world sees as Black, Indigenous, and People of Color (BIPOC) experienced grief tied to this murder—a murder that was one of countless others, the product of a racism crisis. We were also experiencing COVID as grief. Many BIPOC were disproportionately at risk and affected by COVID. Thus, I began to understand that I was experiencing the trauma and grief of dual pandemics.

The Kübler-Ross (1969) grief cycle helped me better understand my physical discomfort and the swirl of emotions. During the equity training, the grief over losses through COVID and the images of George Floyd's murder left no room to discuss racist microaggressions and daily forms of oppression on an intellectual level. I am all too familiar with them from my own life. Table 7.1 lists stages of grief after the Kübler-Ross cycle and a description of how my own processing of Floyd's murder reflected these stages from left to right.

As I made sense of my feelings, I envisioned and hoped for a different way to train, teach, and evaluate that did not assume participants are unaware of or had neutral or no feelings about the training topic and current events. Instead, I dreamed of shifting to an approach that acknowledges and honors our emotions and shared humanity by centering our grief. Making transparent the emotions in grief—the wisdom of the heart—allows us to be our full self, and step into our full humanity. This supports our healing path.

We all navigate and are influenced by systems, policies, ideologies, and power hierarchies, but our experiences are different based on our positionality within them.

TABLE 7.1. Stages of Grief, Based on the Kübler-Ross (1969) Grief Cycle

Shock and denial	Pain and guilt	Anger and bargaining	Depression	The upward turn	Reconstruction and working through	Acceptance and hope
"A state of disbelief and numbed feelings."	"Feeling that the loss is unbearable and that you're making other people's lives harder because of your feelings and needs."	"Lashing out or telling God or a higher power that you'll do anything they ask if they'll only grant you relief from these feelings or this situation."	"This may be a period of isolation and loneliness during which you process and reflect on the loss."	"At this point, the stages of grief like anger and pain have died down, and you're left in a more calm and relaxed state."	"You can begin to put pieces of your life back together and move forward."	"This is a very gradual acceptance of the new way of life and a feeling of possibility for the future."
"After the murder of George Floyd in combination with a worldwide pandemic, I felt numb in the face of all the suffering and lack of resources and systemic barriers to address them."	"I felt pain seeing the murder of George Floyd. I experienced fear for my Black friends and family. Seeing the impact of COVID in our community and the lack of resources to address the needs."	"I felt a lot of frustration, impatience, and anxiety because I didn't understand my swirl of emotions."	"I spent a lot of time reflecting. The required social isolation during COVID made my times of solitude easier."	"Processing allowed me to understand how all these feelings are part of a grieving process and allowed me to relax into feeling them, normalizing my experience."	"I shifted my work toward healing strategies and strengths-based evaluation narratives."	"I have found joy and hope in the new work strategies and transformative evaluation to support a holistic and strengths-based narrative about our community, centering our humanity."

Therefore, experiences of oppression or trauma affect us differently. If we tap into these experiences intentionally, grief can open us to think, train, evaluate, and communicate about racism, oppression, and other trauma-inducing experiences in ways that avoid defensiveness and judgment. Allowing our full range of emotions and feelings can enable us to stay open and curious, to learn and change, and honor our collective humanity.

Grief is personal and grief is healing. I present as a brown woman and belong to a family of varied phenotypes. English is my second language. I am an immigrant. I also have citizenship, am college-educated, and have a job with fringe benefits that allow me financial safety and security. I also have a support system of family, friends, and professional connections that make me feel emotionally safe and connected. My experience of grief was affected heavily by being a person of color. Like most people, I felt shocked at the murder of George Floyd. But I also felt fear for the brown and Black people in my family and circle of friends. I also felt anxious a lot of the time, not knowing what to expect, and not understanding my uncomfortable feelings. Understanding how all these feelings are part of a grieving process allowed me to relax into feeling them, normalizing my experience, and reducing my anxiety. I was able to reconnect with more ease and joy with family, friends, and the support system helping me to again feel emotionally safe and connected.

Leaning into the intense emotions I felt during the summer of 2020 and understanding them as part of grieving and healing has allowed me to step into my work in a new way—as my full self, honoring the wisdom of my heart and my full humanity. I shifted from trying to change systems toward personal and community healing.

In equity and social justice work, we may focus on addressing the ideologies and systems that leave vulnerable people outside the system. I leave that work to those who have the emotional space to do it. The dual pandemics gave me a motivator to focus my professional work. In my grieving stage of acceptance and hope, I see the possibility for community healing by supporting personal and community resiliency and elevating the wisdom, assets, and strengths of our communities of color. Healing ourselves and our communities requires us to have the ability to come into spaces in our full humanity, as our full selves, and honor the wisdom of our hearts.

I wish there were more spaces for intentional and personal grief work in professional settings, including public health, education, and anti-racist and equity training, such as the one I participated in.

CASE STUDY 7.1. REFLECTION QUESTIONS

Before going on, please take whatever time you need for a breathing and movement break and to sit with any emotions that might have come up for you while reading Evelyn's story. When you are ready, reflect on these questions in your journal or with a safe person.

1. Did you experience the murder or George Floyd and COVID as dual pandemics? Why or why not? How do you think your positionality shaped your perception of the events of the summer of 2020?
2. How were you affected in your situation? How did you respond to the pandemic(s)? What emotion(s) did you feel at the time? How did they affect your work?
3. Evelyn knew what she needed to do to move through the grief she was feeling. What would you do, or what did you do? What might you still need to do to center yourself again?
4. How can you take Evelyn's experience and apply it to your own life and work moving forward?

In TIER, we invite everyone to be physically, mentally, and emotionally present in the space and to support each other as they feel their feelings. An important aspect of holding space is managing judgment while you are present. The person who is holding space helps set the tone for a kind, curious, and judgment-free interaction where the other person can be vulnerable (Kahn, 2020). For a researcher or evaluator to hold safe and brave space, they need to be adept at curtailing judgmental thoughts and regulating their own responses when they hear something painful, disturbing, or triggering (or something they disagree with or are offended by). More than withholding judgment and being curious, holding brave space involves seeing all people as worthy and relational (Evans & Vaandering, 2022) and focusing on them without being led astray and distracted by our internal thoughts and reactions. It means doing *research with and by human beings.*

Relationships Matter

Once we look at study participants as people and not subjects, we can focus on building relationships. This does not mean becoming "BFFs," but it does mean that we take time to form genuine connections with our participants before diving into data collection. This is where restorative justice theory is helpful. At the heart of restorative justice is the indigenous-based understanding that everyone and everything is interconnected and because we are all connected, we work in good ways. To better understand how we can work in good ways, we use the relationship and power matrix to see how power influences relationships. For decades, this matrix has been used in the restorative justice communities to help practitioners, researchers, and academics move from positions of *power over* to *power with.* The matrix has evolved since its inception as the field continues learning and growing. Evans and Vaandering's (2022) iteration of the matrix in Figure 7.3 helps us reflect on how we use our power as researchers and evaluators, and how striving toward *power with* interactions facilitates safe and brave spaces.

Let's walk through the matrix, starting in the lower right quadrant. Researchers and evaluators frequently approach participants from a position of *power over,* given the nature of the work, the advanced educational degrees, and the perception of "expertise." When nonprofit organizations and public agencies attempt to do things *for* people, seeing them as objects of need (lower right quadrant), they are exerting *power over* people. For those we deem unworthy, unqualified, too risky, or too traumatized, we simply ignore and exclude from our studies (lower left quadrant). We can do that when we have power to decide who gets into our samples and who does not. Additionally, when we assume participants are too fragile to tell their stories and fail to offer them opportunities to tell them, we are in this quadrant. Researchers and evaluators (and our clients) are likely to see participants as people to be managed while we do things *to* them (upper left quadrant). Our fields have a long history of using "human subjects" to extract information and then leaving them no better off than they were before.

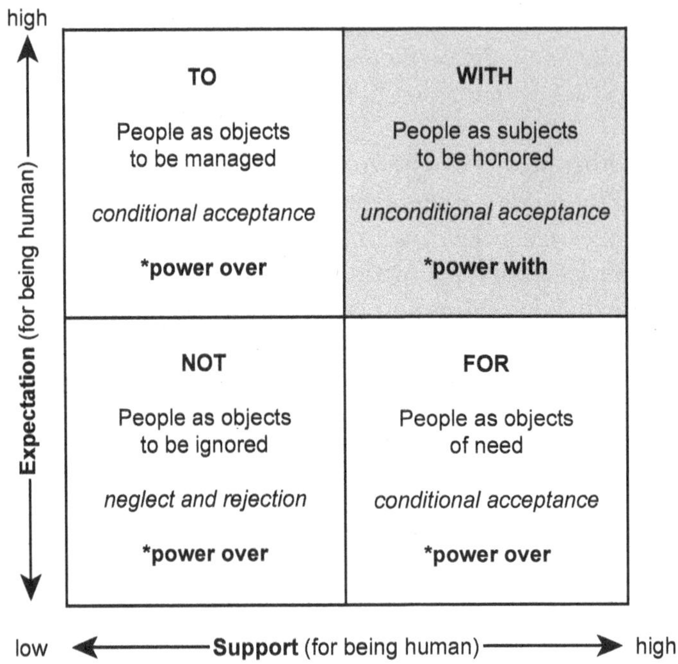

FIGURE 7.3. Relationship and power matrix. From Evans and Vaandering (2016). Reproduced with permission from Skyhorse Publishing.

However, TIER allows us opportunities to redistribute power and engage *with* people. When we believe that people are truly deserving of being honored for who they are; that they have inherent worth; and that we, researchers and evaluators, are also humans, and we can then create a safe space of unconditional acceptance and share power (upper right quadrant). We intentionally shift power dynamics to create a sense of togetherness, belonging, and gratitude. As we've already said, it may mean that we too become vulnerable as a pathway toward building trust and trustworthiness (Brown, 2012b). It means that we give ourselves permission to break the "rules" and have a personal or emotional response. It means that we take time to express care and empathy for someone who has just shared something painful with us. It means we decenter ourselves and our need to extract information and instead focus on what our participants are saying, feeling, and experiencing. Sometimes when we are asking people to share difficult stories with us, we need to step into the brave space, hold it, and offer support so our participants can deal with whatever comes up for them. This is how we facilitate healing and resilience.

At the AEA annual conference in 2023, Donna Mertens concluded her talk on transformative evaluation by saying that sometimes she hugs her participants or cries with them. If the esteemed scholar-evaluator Donna Mertens can be genuinely human during the course of her work, *so can you*. Donna's empathetic response did not invalidate her study. She simply took a moment to be a compassionate, caring, human being when someone was in pain. And she did this *while* collecting data. She sat in the pain with an open, caring heart and offered compassion, comfort, and empathy. Although some in the audience gasped audibly, many applauded her.

Mindfulness and Resilience

Research shows that people who practice mindfulness are more capable and willing to express empathy and that mindfulness helps us not react or judge while we attend to the needs of others (Jones et al., 2016). We stand on such research when we advocate that evaluators and researchers develop mindfulness, meditation, and other resilience practices. Vulnerability, empathy, and deep listening can help us promote connection, belonging, resilience, and healing *while* collecting data. Data collected through genuine storytelling is often richer in detail and more valid than data collected in other, less personal methods. We give concrete examples of trauma-informed and empathetic responses in upcoming chapters on data collection.

How and what we communicate, verbally and nonverbally, determines how well we build connection and trust—the core of good relationships. Trauma-informed communication involves more than not judging what trauma stories someone shares with us; it requires active **acknowledgment**. We speak with our words and our bodies and facial expressions. Take a moment and reflect on the language you generally use and ask yourself, Do I convey openness and vulnerability so I will build trust and connection, or do I convey distance, or worse, arrogance? Do I acknowledge what participants said, or do I just move on to the next question?

Incorporating Resilience Practices

We started this chapter asking you to pause and breathe. Breathing deeply is the easiest and most accessible way to self-regulate and calm down. We refer to practices that activate the parasympathetic nervous system (PNS) as resilience practices. Reesma Menakem (2017) provides his readers with numerous resilience practices throughout his book *My Grandmother's Hands*, and there are more websites, books, videos, podcasts, and healing practitioners than we can list that can help you develop your own resilience routine. Boyes-Watson and Pranis (2020, p. 16) state, "We need practices to build habits of living from the core self." These practices are not woo-woo—they help us take control of our minds, brains, and bodies. Graham (2010) reminds us that when we are triggered, we may need to reopen our WoT as soon as possible using resilience practices right in the moment. Here, we explain the importance of resilience practices, why we need to employ them, and give you some examples.

Self-care practices, mindful moments, meditation, breath work, yoga, and exercise help build our capacity to tolerate discomfort so we can examine, process, and metabolize what may come up when we are triggered. Simple gestures like putting your hand on your heart and breathing goodness, safety, trust, and ease into the heart can calm and ground us. Craig (2017) suggests interventions directed at regulating the brain and stomach, such as "patterned rhythmic activities like walking, dancing, singing, and meditative breathing [which] allow a return to a calmer cognitive state, where problem solving and higher order thinking can occur" (pp. 7–8).

Menakem (2017) tells us that to access and move through trauma pain and memories, one must be quiet and calm and center the body because that's where trauma lives. What helps us calm down and counter negative effects of cortisol and adrenaline is another hormone called oxytocin, which allows us to reengage our cerebral cortex (Graham, 2010). Our brains can release oxytocin when we feel safe, connected, and have a sense of belonging. As we discussed in Chapter 6, the cerebral cortex is also where we process our emotions by thinking about them. By tapping into positive emotions, memories, or feelings like gratitude, kindness, or compassion at a time when we are also upset, we can rewire the neural firing pattern of the negative emotion. This requires not only awareness of the emotion but the ability to sit with it with interest and curiosity and not let it overtake us (Graham, 2010). Creating new neural pathways through positive connection with others enhances our ability to stay in the present, not be controlled by trauma memories, and develop new coping mechanisms. The key is to put space—what Pema Chödrön (2009) calls a "mindful gap"—between the stimulus and the patterned response/feeling. In that mindful gap, one can breathe and begin to integrate the positive calming feeling of breath with the stimulus, thus rewiring the brain over time. This is why integrating grounding and mindfulness practices into our work with clients and participants is essential.

It is also important that researchers and evaluators incorporate self-reflection so that we can examine our approaches to our work, how it affects us and others, and what feelings come up that may need to be metabolized. Guided imagery and mindfulness techniques help people learn how to "objectively observe their internal and external experiences—how they feel, what bodily sensations they are aware of, and what they are thinking about" (Craig, 2017, p.77). Learning to distinguish between oneself and one's feelings is an important step in helping achieve emotional regulation.

WRAP-UP

Being trauma-informed requires us to know ourselves, our traumas, our triggers, and our resilience practices intimately. We have to get good at recognizing when we are triggered and what we can do about it. We are leaders who need to create and hold safe and brave spaces, muster the courage to know when we and/or our participants are having stress responses, and feel comfortable inviting them to join you in self-regulating resilience practices. Of course, this also means we have to get comfortable with these practices ourselves before we can bring them into our work with others. It might seem a little weird or woo-woo to some. And it would be OK to laugh about it. But remember—we are striving to normalize trauma-informed practices so that someday we are all caring for ourselves and others during the course of a study—without it being scary or weird.

CHAPTER 7 REFLECTION QUESTIONS

1. How does the concept of mutual sharing that Judy Atkinson describes as *dadirri* make you feel? How does *dadirri* fit or not fit with how you've been taught?
2. Think of a time when someone expressed genuine empathy for you. How did they do it? What did it feel like to receive empathy?
3. Now think of a time when you expressed genuine empathy for someone else. How did you do it? What did it feel like to give empathy?

CHAPTER 7 RESILIENCE ACTIVITY

Find a quiet place where you can get comfortable and won't be disturbed for a few minutes. Sit and take five deep breaths in through your nose, holding for a count of four and exhaling through your mouth to a count of six. Notice how you feel with each breath. Notice but don't engage with the thoughts that come and go in your mind. Just watch them come in and out of your mind. Return to normal breathing and just sit quietly. See what comes up for you. Approach your thoughts or feelings with interest and curiosity but don't get caught up in them. It's like this: "Oh—well, that was interesting! I wonder where that thought came from?" When your mind wanders, come back to the breath. When you are ready to open your eyes, journal your thoughts and feelings about what we talked about in this chapter so you can reflect on your E&R practice. See what comes up for you. Consider developing this exercise as a regular practice.

CHAPTER 8

Designing and Framing TIER

Evaluation is a lot like herding cats, but the cats are all afraid you'll judge them, so they hide under beds, even more than they usually do. Now to decide which cats to pursue . . .

WHAT YOU'LL LEARN

In this chapter, we challenge you to think about who the "right" team is, who the "right" funders are, and who the "right" partners could be for your study projects. We assert that how you frame your evaluation or research study is essential for paving the way to include trauma-informed practices. Then, we encourage you to frame your study in values that will inform your choice of method/approach. We emphasize grounding your design in values that allow you, your team, and your community to make sound and appropriate judgments about a program's effectiveness and integrity. Although we don't tell you how to convene and frame a study, we give you many things to think about and hope that you and all involved will carefully consider and discuss the issues we bring up here.

Power and the Purse: Issues of Power, Oppression, and Funding

An evaluator or researcher might think that being trauma-informed centers on how we collect data. Indeed, as we have noted before, the bulk of evaluation literature focuses on doing no harm during the data collection process to avoid retraumatizing participants. However, the implications of researchers' actions with traumatized individuals and communities must be considered from day one. In fact, the design of a study often starts even before an evaluator is hired. That is, the funders often dictate the terms and set out some of the basic parameters of study design in their request for proposals, demonstrating their power of influence. The language they use and the constraints they set often dictate real design limits, which may or may not be beneficial to traumatized groups of stakeholders. Considering that most funders, especially governments, are not even remotely trauma-informed, limiting our ability to integrate TIER is more common than not.

While some of us believe we are indeed agents of good and that we promote equity in and through the work we do, these sentiments may cover a darker reality. Beyond just the practicalities of avoiding discomfort for participants, clients, and researchers alike, there are deep issues of (in)justice when it comes to the economic, corporate, and neocolonial interests at the heart of the nonprofit industrial complex. It is a system from which many evaluators benefit, perhaps not always to the benefit of the people we would ultimately hope to serve. Market forces are commanding, and these forces shape our values, not the other way around, unfortunately.

The nonprofit industrial complex is powerful and drives evaluators to operate in ways that may ultimately not be ethical or beneficial to those whom we would like to think we are serving. Ahrens and colleagues (2023) assert that the neoliberalism that has defined the current sources of funding in evaluation leads to the definition of success as it aligns with the goals and objectives of the funders and at the hands of researchers who are usually not well versed in the context they seek to evaluate. They assert that this leads to the increased marginalization of communities through deficit-based conceptions held by evaluators and their clients. Unfortunately, the meritocratic system of awarding evaluation contracts is tilted toward the already powerful, systematically placing the flow of capital in the hands of the already privileged. This also influences whose values are used to deliver judgment and determines whose evaluative questions are asked.

We have been guilty of participating in these systems ourselves. Both of us have been involved in evaluations where midway through the project, we walk into a hornets' nest of bad blood between traumatized communities and the questionable motives of funders and grantees.

Having lived in this tension, our experience has led us to believe that these are dynamics that every evaluator should take seriously and that striving for *power with* is critical to a trauma-informed approach. While we all would like to live in a world where evaluation would be a simple comparison of weighing the "plain facts" or determining "what the data say," that is simply not the case. An evaluator being insensitive to the dynamics of historical and ongoing trauma can do real harm to the claims, outcomes, and conclusions of an evaluation—and to its participants. A perception that the evaluator or funder is out of tune or out of step with the community can lead even the most methodologically air-tight of projects to come to naught, all because of optics. We cannot wish these dynamics away.

Trauma-Informed Convening

So, what is an evaluator or researcher to do? We hope that we can offer some practical advice for contracting and convening in at least trauma-neutral ways, and hopefully in ways that promote resilience.

The Right Team for the Job: Confronting Cultural, Historical, and Gender Issues

The first step in trauma-informed convening must involve serious self-reflection. As we said in Chapter 7, an evaluator or researcher must be open to the possibility that they are not the right person for the job. We developed a series of questions in Table 8.1 to help make this determination. We know that there are no easy answers and no simple heuristic. However, when one honestly considers these questions, one should be able to arrive at a wise and reasonable answer. Any one of your answers may or may not be disqualifying, but we challenge you to have honest conversations with yourself and others to determine whether you are the right person for the job before the start of any contract. However, if your answers indeed lead you to step back from a proposal or contract, the appropriate remedy may be instead to expand your team to include more people with a wider range of backgrounds and experience, including lived experience. Take a look at Table 8.1, reflecting on our questions and our possible considerations. We hope that these will guide your decision making and leave you with greater confidence in yourself and your team's ability to handle your evaluation participants with care.

As you can see, there are a dizzying number of factors to consider before even starting an evaluation with traumatized groups. As stated before, a reasonable step for rounding out deficiencies in an evaluator's own experiences and perspectives may be in building a well-rounded team. Chapter 6 emphasized that including others from the groups involved can go a long way toward building trust and avoiding pitfalls of mistrust and retraumatization.

However, we have some concerns. First, there is a history of those in power gaining access to those with less privilege for exploitative purposes, including **trauma porn** (see Chapter 11). Second, evaluators must guard against the impulse for tokenism, which is the symbolic inclusion of people of a disadvantaged background for the purpose of gaining favor or credibility. Unfortunately, such tokenism can ultimately do more harm than good and cause moral injury to the individuals that we tokenize.

How can we then avoid these problems? What sets tokenism apart from inclusion? We suggest that the answer here is true and meaningful partnership. Shared leadership is different from tokenism in that it offers real decision-making power and agency to our partners. Rather than a symbolic involvement, real partnership involves ceding some control. It may involve some discomfort, knowing that

TABLE 8.1. Reflection Questions before Beginning an Evaluation

Category	Question	Possible considerations
Identity	"What are the dimensions of my identity that may interact with the identities of others involved in this project?" "Are there situations in which my identity could cause serious disturbances or discomfort in others?" "Am I a part of a group that represents historical traumas or historical oppression to stakeholders?"	In most cases, belonging to a particular group will not preclude an evaluator from working on that project. However, one should acknowledge the challenges that may arise and seek to head them off by making sure the team is well balanced to maximize psychological safety for participants. In some cases, identity *may* be grounds for limiting contact with participants (e.g., a male evaluator with women in a domestic violence shelter). Don't let ego get in the way of sound judgment here.
Internal prejudices, biases, and insecurities	"Do I have unspoken, unconscious, or conscious bias against the groups involved in this project?" "Is there a chance I might reveal these prejudices in a damaging/retraumatizing way to the people I'm working with?" "Are there blind spots in my views, experiences, and judgments?"	Internal biases are often difficult for us to recognize in ourselves. A frank discussion with a trusted friend, team member, or therapist may help expose and process any biases, recognized or not. Beyond eliminating bias (which may not be entirely possible), one must be ready to graciously accept correction in situations where prejudices may be exposed.
Past trauma	"Are there traumas in my own past that I have not addressed?" "Am I capable of not making my experience and my trauma the center of this project, instead centering the experience of key stakeholders?"	Evaluators should do the necessary work to ensure that their own trauma reactions do not put the project in jeopardy. Working with a therapist to process past traumas is a great way to ensure adverse reactions do not hijack interactions with participants. If you are not confident in this, make sure your team can cover your weaknesses.
Training and competence	"Do I have the requisite training and expertise to identify the key issues at hand in this evaluation as it pertains to the historical traumas experienced by the stakeholders?"	There are plenty of resources (including this one!) for building competence in working with traumatized populations. Evaluators may look for online courses in mental health first aid, trauma response identification, and more. And as always, build a good team with diverse skillsets.
Tact and skill	"Even if I have all the right content knowledge, do I have the skills and tact to have sensitive conversations?"	This may not come naturally to everyone. If you don't have a basic level of confidence and comfort, make sure others on your team do.

you may not be calling all the shots anymore. This is the equity-focused trauma-informed approach described in Chapter 6.

We must also balance the considerations of identity with the expertise needed for the study. We do this by finding partners with deep expertise that are also representative of the populations we are working with. Simply including someone on the team because of their identity without regard to their requisite skills is not the answer. We may have to cast a broader net to find true experts, but they are out there for sure! It may also cost us a little more money to do so. But also remember: A person's background and lived experience are also strong contributors to expertise.

The Right Funders for the Job: Avoiding Corporate Reputation Laundering

In addition to thinking about the integrity of the evaluation team, it is also important to vet the funders of the study, as they will have ultimate control over the product, the parameters, and the distribution of the final product. We must ensure that we are partnering with funders who are open to hearing our opinions; willing to engage in trauma-informed evaluation practices (or learn about them if they do not know); and not simply working to save face or engage in **corporate reputation laundering**, the practice of using evaluation or research to improve public perception without genuine commitment to addressing underlying problems or harm. Yes, perhaps if you are a funder reading this, it resonates. But the painful fact is that some research and evaluation is done to "prove" what funders want to show, not what really is—especially when it comes to racial inequities.

Evaluators who allow themselves to become compromised in such a way risk being co-opted, operating as de facto public relations operatives rather than independent evaluators. This undermines both the integrity of the evaluation and its potential to create meaningful change for traumatized communities.

Assessing Funder Integrity

How do we avoid such situations? Below is a list of suggested questions to ask yourself when considering a funder's integrity:

1. What is this funder's history with traumatized populations? If there is a questionable or blatantly negative history with traumatized populations, is there credible evidence that the organization has sufficiently made repairs, or is in the process of such repairs?
2. Is there any evidence of an attempt at **corporate reputation laundering** through evaluation or research?

3. Is there any evidence of internal knowledge of, or at least openness to, trauma-informed evaluation practices?
4. Is there evidence that the funders are willing to accept your influence, or is it their way or the highway?
5. Are the funders on a tight deadline that limits the ability of the evaluator to build real relationships with stakeholders, especially those in the community being studied?

If an organization follows standard evaluation contracting practices without considering these factors, many of these questions will raise red flags for the trauma-informed evaluator. These questions are valuable to consider before deciding whether to respond to a request for proposals. It is encouraging when we see funders who are willing to try innovative methods, allow ample time for community engagement, and share decision-making authority in their evaluation processes.

Systemic Constraints and Bureaucratic Challenges

Beyond individual funder intentions, evaluators often work within bureaucratic systems that can constrain trauma-informed practices in both direct and indirect ways. Indirectly, the pace of funding cycles, political attention spans, and review processes can place significant pressures on evaluators and limit their ability to implement TIER principles effectively. More directly, many governmental and nongovernmental agencies require preestablished evaluation frameworks that may not align with trauma-informed approaches.

For example, evaluators working with the Organisation for Economic Co-operation and Development (OECD) must employ the Development Assistance Committee Criteria (2019). Many other frameworks are required by various nongovernmental agencies and governmental departments. Although these frameworks are not inherently incompatible with TIER, evaluators need to consider how to adapt and enhance them to meet trauma-informed standards while satisfying institutional requirements.

Advocating for Change

This matters because a funder's priorities and objectives (which often respond to political, social, financial, and other environmental factors) can significantly constrain both the process and outcomes of an evaluation. Just as the slightest difference in a rocket's trajectory at launch can cause it to miss the moon entirely, small compromises in evaluation design can lead to significantly different outcomes for the communities we serve.

We acknowledge that implementing TIER principles requires more resources than traditional evaluation approaches. Building authentic relationships, ensuring adequate compensation, conducting thorough stakeholder engagement, and maintaining trauma-informed practices throughout the evaluation process all demand additional time, funding, and expertise. However, we argue that these upfront investments often prevent costly mistakes, reduce the risk of community backlash that can derail projects, and ultimately lead to more valid and useful findings. The cost of doing evaluation poorly (in terms of wasted resources, damaged relationships, and potential harm to traumatized communities) often far exceeds the additional investment required for trauma-informed practices.

Funders often have much more latitude than they lead evaluators to believe. We should advocate from the outset for adequate time and resources to engage with traumatized populations in respectful and healing ways. This means learning how to have difficult but necessary conversations with those who fund our work. If a funder claims to want an equity-focused study but refuses to allow adequate time for community engagement or funding to appropriately compensate participants, they may simply be checking boxes rather than facilitating genuine change in communities, similar to what many organizations did with diversity, equity, and inclusion initiatives.

As trauma-informed evaluators, we have a responsibility to push back against systems and funders that would compromise our ability to do no harm and promote healing in our evaluation practice.

The Right Partners for the Job: Including the Community

As we emphasized in Chapter 6, equity-focused TIER focuses on community engagement and engaging the right stakeholder groups in the right ways. This takes time and money. When considering whom to involve and how, we must consider aspects of adequate compensation, meaningful participation, and safety.

Adequate compensation means that if we are expecting trauma-affected people to give us their thoughts, time, and input, we (and our funders) should be willing to compensate them for it. Some have argued that paying participants, or compensating them with gift cards, could amount to coercion. We think that this is a convenient excuse and that most people would appreciate some gesture of compensation for their time, especially if they have a choice about the kind of compensation they receive.

When Martha interviewed victim/survivors of domestic violence, she and the funder discussed a variety of ways to compensate the women for their time and contributions. They decided to offer them choices of gift cards, some for groceries, some for clothes, and some for whatever they wanted. There are online platforms that make this process easy. The women appreciated being empowered to choose compensation based on what they needed most at the time. Please don't assume that everyone loves Starbucks gift cards.

The Right Approach for the Job: Ensuring Safety

We also need to engage with traumatized stakeholders in a way that is safe, both emotionally and physically. As of late, emotional safety has taken a front seat. Although it is good that people are becoming more aware of trauma and traumatic stress, we are still seeing practices that reinforce avoidance and fragility, which in fact are core PTSD symptoms. When we as communities avoid tough topics or conversations in the name of safety, the message we are sending is twofold: (1) Words can be irreparably damaging and harmful and (2) people who are traumatized are damaged and cannot recover (see our discussion on hypersensitivity/avoidance).

Although they may be coming from a place of good intentions and sensitivity, these limiting beliefs are not trauma-informed. These ideas are effectively disempowering and operate to keep people stuck. So, from our perspective, trauma-informed convening is *not* avoiding difficult conversations or excluding people. If trauma-affected people are not at the table, we risk misunderstanding them and doing more harm. In our experience, safety looks like this:

- Expressing confidence in people's ability to tell tough stories and have hard conversations
- Pushing through and managing our own discomfort when hearing these stories (self-regulating in the moment)
- Creating space for the participants to decide whether to engage in a conversation
- Creating space for participants to give us feedback on how/when/where/in what manner we ask difficult questions
- Communicating and believing in the healing power of sharing

The one caveat we have here is that there may be situations in which sharing one's story, or even being approached, may do real physical harm or cause significant distress to people. Consider the example of people in conflict or war-torn regions, where associating with people from a certain background (e.g., a white American evaluator) could mean very real risk of physical harm or even death (Cohen, 2012). Weiss (2025) points out that situations of ongoing traumatic circumstances, suffering, or extreme power imbalances may also complicate participation for people:

> Members of these communities with ongoing suffering and instability may not be receiving sufficient psychosocial support, may be prone to have higher hopes for research, may be likelier to feel like they are at a disadvantaged end of a power differential with the researcher, and may also be burnt out from interviews by other researchers, aid organizations, or journalists. For example, participants in political violence research may hope that the research will draw attention to a conflict or crisis and lead to the end of the conflict or crisis. (p. 10)

Weiss makes clear that evaluators and researchers in such circumstances have a higher bar to meet in terms of providing significant support, such as on-site counseling, if the decision is made to move forward with the study.

Outside of these trying circumstances, we must ask ourselves if our decision to exclude trauma-affected people is truly about our participants' safety or, rather, our own discomfort. If it is the latter, perhaps we are the ones who need to be excluded from the process. In fact, research has demonstrated that participation in evaluation activities can be a very positive experience, even for those who have experienced the very worst of traumas. For instance, Campbell, Adams, Wasco, Ahrens, and Sefl (2010) report that in a study of female rape victims, 88 out of 92 women expressed that participating in the process was positive (p. 69). Weiss (2025), in a scoping review of trauma-affected participants' perception of engaging in research, found that "a majority of participants—including those who experienced distress during the research—report being glad that they participated or chose to complete their participation" (p. 20). This is a call to do our own personal work, include others, or get out of the way.

So, how do we approach our community partners and invite their collaboration? We suggest the following steps:

1. Identify any severe safety issues. For instance, is the evaluation taking place in an area of significant violent conflict, such as a war-torn area, or gang activity? If so, excluding certain groups may be warranted.
2. Once basic safety is assessed, evaluators should conduct inventories of stakeholder groups' readiness for involvement (Andrews, Pepler, & Motz, 2019).
3. Invite involvement. If the main concerns are simply emotional discomfort, participants should be allowed to decide whether to participate.
4. Make agreements. Participants should be given information about what it would mean to participate. Evaluators should expect to make amendments to their plans to accommodate the needs of stakeholders.

There is one more thing to consider during this phase of a study, and that is ensuring that values and ethics are agreed on and lived into so that no one is traumatized, especially the evaluator or researcher. The following case study teaches a valuable lesson.

CASE STUDY 8.1 Ethical Riders in Your Contract

STEPHANIE EVERGREEN

Toward the end of a project, my client told me, "We met as a group and have decided we'd like the dashboard's graphs to be red if the metric is trending bad and green if the metric is trending in the right direction." The client is asking for a change that would make the work inaccessible to people who are red–green colorblind! What do you do? Just do it because they are paying you? Push back? I pushed back. Here's what I said:

> "I strongly advise against this. You told me during our initial conversations that a key tenet of your [name-drop-worthy] foundation is equity. Choosing red/green makes you inequitable. Like I recommended in my initial sketches of the dashboard, let's use orange and blue instead. Need another reason? Your logo is red. So assigning red to the bad data would conflate 'bad' with *you*. Don't do this. You hired me to give you the best possible advice and that's my advice."

They pushed back on my pushback. *They told me to do it anyway.* And that's when I wish I could've quit the project because now we were consigned to create something I would never be able to share. What good is having a name-drop-worthy client if you're so embarrassed by them that you'd never drop the name?

I was venting about this on a call with my students when one of them asked me, "Could you put ethical riders in your contract?" Yes! Of course I can. You can put anything you want in your contract. (Granted your prospective client may retreat from the engagement—but you'd have your dignity intact.)

Inclusion riders are a way for people with privilege to open up space for those who have been traditionally overlooked. Employment contracts can contain morality clauses that say you can be fired with cause for engaging in acts that damage the company's image or reputation.

With these specific models already laid out for us, I'm curious about what it could look like to apply the same idea more broadly so that I'm not committed to begrudgingly making this inaccessible dashboard. The integrity of aligning our work to our values is too important to give up just because it sounds like it'll be hard. As is so often the case, we often learn we have boundaries after they've been violated.

Note. Adapted from Evergreen (2023).

CASE STUDY 8.1. REFLECTION QUESTIONS

We invite you to—if possible—discuss these questions with others.

1. What would you do—or what have you done—if your client asked you to do something that you know is inequitable or traumatizing? How would you push back? How would you handle the client's pushback?
2. Practice writing your own inclusion rider that clearly defines your commitment to equity-focused trauma-informed practices and what would happen if the client wanted you to violate your principles.

Framing the Evaluation

Building a team and forging relationships does not happen overnight. It takes time, dedication, and attention. But once that team has been built and relationships have been forged, the next step is the framing of an evaluation. We see the framing as consisting of several parts:

- Selecting the overarching approach to be used based on the study questions
- Selecting who will speak into the parameters, and how
- Setting the parameters for the study

Engaging Evaluation Theory and Frameworks and Selecting an Approach

The world of evaluation theory and approaches can be dizzying. Even the most seasoned evaluation scholars and professionals can get lost in the sea of acronyms, and new approaches are always emerging. We can get whiplash from the focus on utilization-focused evaluation shifting to one on empowerment- or transformative social justice–oriented practice. Yesterday's evaluation craze is now passé, or even worse, falls short in matters of equity and social justice. It can certainly feel hard to keep up.

We encourage you to look back at Chapter 3 on TIER-leaning evaluation approaches. As we will see in the next sections, the approach we select may have real implications for how we think about valuing, which is not inconsequential to trauma sensitivity. We recommend selecting an approach that is not only sensitive to issues of justice, oppression, and equity but also emphasizes a clear theory of valuing, as this will guard against the tacit yielding to the values of those in power.

The "J" Word: Judgment, Valuing, and Trauma

It's time for a word about **judgment**. It does not make us feel warm fuzzies. It may even seem to us to be counter to trauma-informed practice. We hear admonitions from every corner not to be judgmental. (Ironically, in a very meta way, this happens to be a judgment of judgment itself!)

However, we as humans cannot get away from judgment. Every time we make a decision, we are judging two or more options to determine which might be better. And when it comes to trauma-affected populations, making informed judgments is critical. When social scientists make determinations as to the efficacy of a trauma intervention (such as EMDR or trauma-focused cognitive-behavioral therapy), they are making judgments. And these matter greatly. We want to know about judgments of **relative merit**, such as therapy *X* works better than therapy *Y*. We may want to know **absolute merit**, like therapy *Z* reduces trauma symptoms by such and such amount. Failing to judge effectively would be to subject trauma-affected people to ineffective or even harmful treatment practices. Just think of the controversy around reparative or conversion therapy for LGBTQ+ people. It was the deployment of sound judgment that highlighted the damage that these harmful practices wrought.

When it comes to nonexperimental studies of social programs, we are judging. What is our judgment of the program in terms of its treatment of the end users? Was it worth the money we spent on it? Even if it was effective in moving the intended outcomes in the right direction, were unintended effects minimal and tolerable?

However, sound judgment is not like an equation, where the facts lead neatly to a conclusion. One cannot simply "look at the data" to judge the value of an intervention. Imagine, for instance, a universe in which conversion therapy in fact did "heal" a great number of LGBTQ+ people of their queerness. Would we then consider it a success? For most of us reading this book, likely not. For others, sadly, yes. What's the difference between the two groups? The difference lies in the values we apply to arrive at our judgments.

The Importance of Values

Evaluation at its core involves the application of values to make determinations about an object (i.e., a program, a therapist–client interaction, etc.). Whether we like it or not, we see the identification and application of **values** as core to what it is that evaluators are doing, and if one is not facilitating the judgment, one is not evaluating.[1] We caution against approaches that do not acknowledge the role of values and put them front and center. Why? Because if we don't, the risk of tacitly using the values of the powerful rather than the marginalized and traumatized is great. This may lead to judgments that are harmful and add to the burden of trauma.

Evaluators can guard against this by being clear about their judgments, how they arrived at them, and the source of **criteria.** Criteria should be sourced from the intended beneficiaries, not just the program managers or funders. This tacit co-opting by those in power is more likely in the case of some approaches than others.

Consider, for example, a theory-driven evaluation. Many are familiar with the use of logic models to evaluate programs. A logic model operates from two sole criteria: program fidelity and the desired/expected outcomes. Evaluations of this type are almost exclusively developed from the perspective of program managers who are looking for a specific set of outcomes. However, it leaves little room for the voice of the stakeholders to show up in terms of how success or failure is determined. The result could be an evaluation that is deemed a success when it, in fact, harms those involved. Or, conversely, it could result in the cancellation of a program that was enormously beneficial to service recipients; it's just that the beneficial outcomes were not detected by the logic model because they were unintended effects.

One example of this would be a library that happens to be a significant resource for people experiencing homelessness and mental illness. If that library's program theory does not recognize this service as core to the mission and funding gets cut, a community could see a gaping hole open in its social infrastructure, all because the values of the key beneficiaries were not identified. If one were instead to adopt an approach such as goal-free evaluation, or utilization-focused evaluation, and was sure to include all relevant stakeholders in determining the criteria of success for the library, such regrettable outcomes may be less likely to occur. Again, this is not to say that one must use a particular method. Rather, we ask that

[1] We consider the topics of values and criteria to be core concepts for everyone in the evaluation field. We would direct all of our readers to the work of Rebecca Teasdale (2021) for an accessible overview of the roles of values, valuing, and criteria in evaluation.

one do so with caution and make sure to pay specific attention to whose values are centered in the development of criteria.

Identifying and engaging values is essential to judgment and evaluation. While there is too much literature on value theory to cover here, it is important to gesture toward some significant scholarship on this issue. Sadler (1997) defines values as "descriptions or conditions that guide human action and are praise- or blameworthy" (p. 541). Schwartz (2012, p. 3) offers a detailed six-part value theory of the features that all values have in common. Although all six parts may be of interest to those wishing to go deeper into value theory, the most applicable to the conversation at hand are the first two points, which are relevant to much of our work:

1. "Values are beliefs linked inextricably to affect. When values are activated, they become infused with feeling. People for whom independence is an important value become aroused if their independence is threatened, despair when they are helpless to protect it, and are happy when they can enjoy it."

2. "Values refer to desirable goals that motivate action. People for whom social order, justice, and helpfulness are important values are motivated to pursue these goals."

It is not a new concept to ground a project or process in values. Restorative justice scholars and practitioners propose that humans share 10 common values: love, respect, inclusivity, generosity, courage, trust, sharing, empathy, humility, and honesty (Pranis, Stuart, & Wedge, 2013). It is not surprising that values are deeply personal and context dependent. They also have profound effects on the results of inquiry, both scientific and evaluative, as they drive what we find worthy of investigation, whose opinions we deem trustworthy, and the lenses through which we determine success. Schwandt and Gates (2021) give the example of various think tank institutions and how the underlying values behind their inquiry lead to vastly different findings regarding important socioeconomic issues such as abortion, climate change, tax policy, and drug regulations. The facts may be the same, but the conclusions, illuminated by their very different values, could not be more divergent.

So, as evaluators, how do we approach values in a way that advances the cause of trauma-affected people and communities? What would our study designs look like if we intentionally infused the 10 common values? From our perspective, values can be infused into a study in three different ways:

1. **Explicit infusion:** Values and their application are most transparent when they are explicated in the evaluation process from the get-go.
2. **Implicit infusion:** Values may be present and identifiable but not explicitly stated.
3. **Tacit/obscured infusion:** Values are hidden or not openly acknowledged.

The evaluators or funders may try to pass such an evaluation off as "objective" or value free.

We advocate for the first type—evaluation in which values are front and center. And whose values? We argue the values of those whom we are ultimately seeking to serve. In the design process, we can center values in a trauma-informed way by identifying the values of the funders, identifying the values of the stakeholders, identifying our own values, and identifying any conflicts between these. In doing so, our study can confront and manage any challenges that may arise from holding different values at the end of the evaluation, when judgments about a program and decisions about a way forward are to be made.

WRAP-UP

Once the right team, the right funders, and the right stakeholders have built a trusting, honest, and inclusive relationship and once the team of co-evaluators has identified the values they bring to the table, *then the fun can begin.* Will we use an exploratory and experimental arts-based approach that throws tried-and-true evaluation frameworks in the blender? Are we working toward an experimental approach that values a high level of scientific rigor? TIER is largely agnostic on these questions as long as these design decisions are done with care and critical thinking. *That's why we spent so much time talking about values and not so much about methods here. It's up to you. Just remember to always bring it back to the values.*

Case Study 8.2 provides an opportunity for you to integrate the importance of values for generating evaluative findings, along with the conflict that can occur between values—in this case, safety versus expediency.

CASE STUDY 8.2 Values in Action

AARON KATES

I was once contracted by a large national organization with dozens of local affiliates to conduct an evaluation of their policy for the protection of children and vulnerable adults. The policy had come under scrutiny because volunteers and administrators alike found the process for volunteer training and vetting to be onerous and time consuming.

As the evaluation unfolded, it became clear that much of what we were dealing with was a difference in core values between the leadership team and the implementers at the site level. Those in leadership were (rightly) concerned about the safety and welfare of those in the organization's care. Those at the local level cared about this too but were also experiencing the realities of mounting administrative burdens and volunteer shortages. This highlighted that those at the local level valued expediency in addition to safety.

Listening to the ground-level stakeholders and what they cared about, we identified some major problems with elevating only the leadership's value of safety at the expense of easy implementation. It turned out that many of the local affiliates were poorly adhering to the policy and creating their own workarounds. The desire to maximize the value of safety over all else, paradoxically, had led to compromised safety.

In the end, the organization was able to settle on a child protection policy that was just as thorough but had sanded off some of the redundancies and administrative pinch points. Now the organization reports much better adherence to the policy, which may not have happened had we only paid attention to the values of the leaders.

CHAPTER 8 REFLECTION QUESTIONS

Again, we invite you to discuss these questions with others to see what bubbles up.

1. What can evaluators and researchers do to make sure that the values centered and used to make judgments, draw distinctions, and make decisions in the evaluation process are not just those of the powerful?
2. What needs to happen during the evaluation design stage to prepare those who collect and analyze data to deal with trauma and trauma-affected people in resilience-building ways?
3. Consider potential research team members. Whom do you know? Whom do you need to know? What resources are available that can help you know who the "right" people are for various projects?
4. Imagine yourself speaking with a powerful funder. How do you envision a conversation about making their proposed study more trauma-informed? What values can you live into and perhaps introduce? Write out what you might say and practice saying it, so you are ready to speak truth to power.

CHAPTER 9

Making Surveys Trauma-Informed

Even if all you do is design and analyze surveys, you can still be trauma-informed. Really. Read on.

WHAT YOU'LL LEARN

People are surveyed all the time. But we are not talking about customer or website shopping satisfaction surveys. We are talking here about the surveys you will design for your research and evaluation projects.

We start this chapter with overall survey/questionnaire design considerations that should follow the same inclusive, careful design approaches to your study that we discussed in Chapter 8. We revisit the issue of informed consent introduced in Chapter 6, provide examples of ongoing consent and section introductions in surveys, and call attention to the importance of choosing your words carefully when developing questions. Much of what you learn in this chapter will also apply to designing and conducting interviews and focus groups and possibly other data collection methods. As always, we encourage you to spend time considering how to apply trauma theory and trauma-informed practices in your specific context.

For practice, we explore a highly insensitive survey to fully illustrate how seemingly innocuous questions can be degrading and offensive. As an activity, we give you opportunities to improve on that survey. We contrast the insensitive survey with an AEA member survey, used with permission that is not inherently trauma-informed but does take some of the principles into consideration, albeit inadvertently, because it is also addressing equity and inclusion (per Chapter 6). By comparing and analyzing these two surveys through a trauma-informed lens, we offer real-life examples of what to do and what not to do.

Introduction

So many people across various sectors—especially nonprofits—equate research and evaluation to surveys, perhaps because it is one of the most widely used—if not overused and poorly designed—methods for finding out what people are thinking about, what concerns them, and what they enjoy. Surveys misleadingly present as easy to design, which could be why many miss the mark.

To help you improve your ability to design trauma-informed surveys, we highly recommend Robinson and Leonard's book *Designing Quality Survey Questions* (2018), as they also do an excellent job of talking about special topics and sensitive questions in Chapter 6 of their book. We rely heavily on their work in this chapter.

Trauma-Informed Survey Design

Each day we are bombarded with surveys: online pop-ups, customer service experiences, political polls—you name it. It makes us tired. Worse yet, biased, offensive, or poorly constructed surveys can do real harm. Given the prevalence of survey fatigue that results in low response rates and the intrusive nature of many online survey practices, our first questions to you are *Why* do you want to do a survey? Is that the best method for your purpose? Do you really need it, and what do you do with the results?

Surveys are a tempting go-to because there are many advantages to using them:

1. Surveys offer the ability to generalize to a population and draw inferences based on a sample (when administered appropriately).
2. The cost and time requirements of surveys are significantly less than those attempting to interview or canvass an entire population.
3. Surveys can be conducted in a timely fashion.
4. Quantitative data collected through survey research can be statistically analyzed with a variety of readily available software packages.
5. Surveys can be replicated easily or adapted for various populations. (Rea & Parker, 2005, pp. 7–8)

However, it's too easy for organizations to say, "Let's just do a survey," without fully understanding the pros and cons as well as the importance of skillful design and a well-conceived evaluation question. Care needs to be taken from the outset to ensure the surveys have integrity *and* are trauma-informed.

Ongoing Informed Consent

There is a big difference between informed consent and ongoing informed consent. In standard research practice, informed consent is gathered at the beginning of the research process and is usually guided by an IRB. We think this is insufficient because people's comfort levels may vary greatly during the course of a study. The status quo informed consent is based heavily on legal risk reduction and does not live up to the highest standards of participant autonomy. Every survey should start by requesting the respondent's consent for gathering and using the information they give us and telling them how their responses will be used. Surveys under the purview of IRBs must present details about purpose, use, storage, and dissemination, often in terms that cause the eyes of respondents to glaze over and consent quickly just to get it over with. Trauma-informed ongoing consent is quite different, as it is grounded in the Six Principles and seeks to protect the participant in more and possibly different ways.

Ongoing informed consent is a trauma-informed approach that requires you to continue asking for permission periodically throughout the survey, not just at the beginning. Here, we provide some examples of things to consider and the language you might use in lieu of or in addition to your regular consent process, even if you think the survey is not about sensitive topics. Ongoing informed consent is a good practice to embed in any study. If your study requires IRB approval, you may have to take time to educate the IRB about this trauma-informed practice (and others); IRBs have acknowledged that trauma is "out there" but likely lack knowledge of specific trauma-informed practices.

Survey Introduction Examples

It doesn't matter if your survey is online, in the mail, in person, or on the telephone. You can integrate ongoing informed consent language throughout any type of survey. Here are some examples of how you might set up your introduction, with our comments in *italics*:

- "We believe your perspective is important and want to give you this opportunity to talk about . . . " (vs. "*We value your opinion.*")
- "Let me tell you who will see your responses." *Be transparent about what confidentiality and anonymity really mean and if mandatory reporting comes into play.*
- "This is what we plan to do with your information. And this is what we will *not* do with your information."
- We will not share your responses with anyone on the *team* (*assurance of confidentiality builds trust*). You may skip any question you do not wish to answer. Thank you for your honest sharing (*empowerment/voice/choice*). *While this language is also part of consent, it is a good trauma-informed practice to remind respondents of their options in longer surveys.*
- "Are there any questions I can answer for you before you start?" (vs. "*Do you have any questions?*") "If you do have questions any time during this survey," *explain how they can reach you—and be sure you have a way to respond!*

- "Do you have any concerns about this process or this study?" (*same—explain how they can reach you*).
- "You can change your mind at any time and opt out of this survey/study. I do not want you to feel any pressure to stay/continue if you are uncomfortable."
- "Are you ready to begin?" *Let respondents know how many questions there are and how long the survey might take.*
- "If you need a break at any time, please take one and come back to the survey when you are ready."

Of course, you will have your own language and style, but we hope you noticed that the language that we used was far more relational and casual than it was academic. By asking these kinds of questions at the beginning and talking like a regular person, not an academic, you build trust, you offer transparency, you show that you care (safety), and you empower the respondent to choose. In just the introduction to the survey, you can address a solid four of the Six Principles.

Asking to Participate

Next, we provide an example of your final request to participate in an online survey:

> "If you agree to participate, please select YES and begin the survey. If you choose not to participate, please select NO. You can choose to end the survey once you begin; however, *your partial responses before ending the survey may be included in some analyses.*"

This short paragraph offers choice and transparency. There is no implied shaming if the respondent chooses not to participate, and there is no penalty for quitting the survey. It was made clear that what people were willing to say up to any point may be included in the results (if that is your design), which acknowledges that a respondent could still contribute, even if they don't complete it. People who do not want any results included can decline to take the survey. The following case study provides more examples of real-life ongoing consent.

CASE STUDY 9.1 A Trauma-Informed Approach to Informed Consent Procedures

CARRIE FISHER and SOFÍA ALEJANDRA LADNER

At the Institute for Community Health, we often work with trauma-affected populations and have developed trauma-informed approaches to informed consent.

- *Choosing levels of confidentiality.* We know that participant control is a critical part of being trauma-informed and that choosing to share one's story can be either retraumatizing or empowering. Instead of paternalistically deciding to keep all data anonymous, we provide options for how participants want to share. Participants can (1) choose to be entirely de-identified so that their names and context clues to their identities will be removed; (2) choose to be entirely identified; or (3) decide on a case-by-case basis, where we check in with them about any quote that we want to include in a report. Participants also have the option to go "off the record," where they can talk through what they want to say and tell us how they want us to report it.

- *Consent is a dialogue.* During time-crunched research, there is always pressure to finish the informed consent process quickly. It is critical to resist that pressure and engage participants in authentic dialogue. One way is to ask the participant to explain what they understand about what will happen to the information they share. Another approach is to present choices, such as the confidentiality levels we describe above.

- *Opting in, not opting out of focus groups or interviews.* We have found it useful to ask participants to opt-in, not opt-out of an activity during the consent process. When we are doing virtual data collection, participants are given all the information about the study, and once the discussion is finished, a link to a new Zoom meeting is dropped in the chat. We tell participants that to participate, they need to click the new link. If they choose not to participate, they can leave the meeting without feeling pressured to join the new one. This looks a bit different in person where once the discussion on informed consent is finished, participants are then given a break. All people in the room are encouraged to stand up and enjoy the snacks offered at a side table. Researchers deliberately focus their attention away from the table, which makes it more comfortable for participants to leave the room inconspicuously and withdraw from the research if that is what they choose.

- *Congratulating colleagues for study withdrawals. When* a participant goes through the informed consent dialogue and then chooses not to participate, we congratulate each other because this means we successfully presented a genuine choice to participate!

- *Setting guidelines together.* In focus groups, the degree to which the experience feels supportive and empowering is determined by both the evaluator *and* the participants. As a trauma-informed practice, we set ground rules for the focus group conversations with participants (as opposed to telling them what they are), asking them, "What needs to happen in this group for you to feel safe sharing?" It's then easy to remind participants about our agreement during the conversation if needed.

- *Input into reporting.* Even with trauma-informed consent, participants rarely see the final report. This means that even though we strictly follow participants' wishes, they still haven't been able to see how their data were used. To improve this, we are sometimes able to host a collective analysis session as a follow-up to data collection. We recently did this with a group of people who are dually eligible for Medicare and Medicaid. After we conducted focus groups and performed a thematic analysis of the data, we invited participants to a feedback session. We then presented our findings and invited comments using a World Café facilitation style. This allowed us to refine and add to our results. Participants shared that they found this process very validating and empowering.

CASE STUDY 9.1.
REFLECTION QUESTIONS

1. What other ideas do you have for doing trauma-informed consent?
2. These procedures are described as being appropriate for trauma-affected populations; however, what other populations could you envision them being

useful for? At the Institute for Community Health, for example, we've found them to be useful when "studying up" or working with relatively powerful key informants who are reluctant to talk to us without assurances that they will have some control over their words. What other populations could this be helpful with?

3. What changes would you be interested in making in your own current procedures for ongoing informed consent?

Survey Length and Built-In Resilience Breaks

Keeping a narrow focus will help regulate instrument length. In most cases, shorter surveys encourage higher response rates and minimize the cognitive fatigue that can come with longer surveys (Robinson & Leonard, 2018). Cognitive overload or fatigue is always a potential risk, but trauma-affected people are even more susceptible to feelings of being overwhelmed or losing focus. Keeping your survey as short as possible will help keep your respondents engaged and may mitigate the anxiety that comes with feeling overwhelmed.

Martha recently received a survey request from a company wanting to test ideas about new product offerings. It was a quantitative survey that was supposed to take 15 minutes. However, around the 15-minute mark, the survey morphed into a very in-depth analysis of 12 product packages, presented in long tables that were difficult to manage on a mobile device. The company did increase the financial incentive to complete that section, but they did not offer an option to save and come back later. Although respondents like Martha may have returned when she had more time or was on her laptop with a larger screen, she was never given that option and then quit the survey. Then they asked for feedback, which was "wwwaaaaaayyyyyy tooooooooooo llllooooonnnnnnng."

We know that short surveys are not always what you need. So, during longer surveys, you should insert brief stretch, breathing, and bio breaks at regular intervals. If you are in person, model taking a break for your participants, which will make it safe for them to move, drink, breathe, or walk too. This holistic approach to survey research humanizes the process and facilitates connection based on the mutual needs of both surveyor and respondent. "You know what? We are just half-way through. Let's take five and come back to it." After the break, activate ongoing informed consent by asking, "How are you feeling? Would you like to continue now?"

If the survey is online and thus missing that direct human touch, you can still insert intentional breaks. This may look like "You are halfway through, so why don't you take a well-deserved break—walk around, stretch, get some water, and then come back in a few minutes." You may also offer the option of saving the responses and coming back later, although this option increases the risk that they might not return and complete the survey.

Consider offering a way for respondents to ask questions or voice concerns throughout the survey, and if you do this, develop a mechanism for answering questions or addressing concerns while maintaining respondent anonymity and confidentiality. Although you may not be able to answer the question in real time, you may be able to email/text the participant later, thanking them for asking and then addressing their question/concern. For example, a respondent may want to say, "Why are you asking about this when I thought this survey was about that?" (a sign of poor design for sure), or tell you, "I really don't understand what you are asking." Even the best survey question designers have a few clunkers, and unskilled survey designers have a lot of them. Think about this and get creative with your IT people and survey software designers. Find ways for your survey respondents to interact with you asynchronously. Remember, acknowledgment is very trauma-informed and healing, as it lets respondents know you heard them and care about them as humans, even if they opted out of the survey. "I hear you—thanks for calling this to my attention" "I got your question and wanted to respond" and "You're right, this question was confusing, wasn't it?" are powerful ways to acknowledge and connect with your respondent.

If a participant chooses not to continue, please do not ask them why. Trust that they quit for a reason. Honor them for what they gave you and thank them for what they contributed. You could, however, think about offering them the *choice* of giving you feedback or a reason for their leaving because you want to know if there is something you could have done differently. If so, do not make this a required question, but perhaps offer a pop-up that says, "I noticed that you're leaving the survey before you finished. Can we help you with something so that you can finish?" Again, you're "seeing" your respondent as a real person with a life that sometimes gets in the way. Of course, if they are triggered by something in your survey, you may not get a response. But if you do, take it seriously and try to address what the trigger was and revise it if you can.

Phases of Survey Design

Robinson and Leonard (2018) describe three major stages of survey design: (1) planning and predrafting, (2) developing questions, and (3) finalizing. Here we offer some trauma-informed considerations during each survey design phase.

Phase 1: Planning and Predrafting

During this stage, you will construct your research questions and purpose statement and determine whether a survey is the right data collection instrument to use. You will be clear about what surveys can measure and what they cannot. Finally, you will try to understand *who your respondents are* (Robinson & Leonard, 2018).

Community Engagement—Again!

The Six Principles come into play in this phase, particularly regarding understanding your potential respondents. We again emphasize that community engagement is essential to equity-focused trauma-informed research. Dr. Tasha Parker (2024) explained her approach below in an *AEA365* online post:

> My primary strategy for practicing equity and uplifting voices is directly involving the community in the evaluation work by partnering with community members, program implementers, and recipients of efforts and inviting them to participate as evaluation team members, liaisons, or reviewers. This has allowed me to gain invaluable insights into the cultural nuances and lived experiences that help shape the evaluations and provide a context that would likely have been missed. This collaborative and participatory approach has continued to enrich my findings and foster a sense of ownership and trust within the community.

Did you notice Dr. Parker's integration of the Six Principles? By purposely developing relationships with community members who will participate in the study, you open the door to people who can help you understand cultural nuances, language, communitywide traumas (such as crime, poverty, mass incarceration, police harassment and brutality, etc.), and potential triggers. You will have people to help you determine what to ask, how to ask it, and what to avoid. Parker's approach is *intentionally* culturally responsive, equitable, participatory, *and* trauma-informed. This approach builds trust, offers transparency, and pays attention to cultural, historical, and gender issues. It is empowering and done with care, making it safe and empowering for community members to engage with her and her evaluation team.

Identify Support Resources

When conducting research on sensitive topics, it is critical that you identify support resources that you and your respondents may access if you/they are triggered or experience stress responses. We don't recommend providing a sterilized list of 1-800 numbers and hotlines because they are unlikely to be used. Instead, provide real-time, in-person/online/phone support if possible or links and numbers to local resources. Community partners can help you find the best local resources. The more sensitive your survey or interview, the more attention you should pay to finding the appropriate way to support your participants and team.

Phase 2: Developing Questions

The next phase of survey design is developing your survey questions. When broaching sensitive subjects that may be associated with shame and stigma, think how to ask questions that help respondents feel that they are not alone. For example,

"Many people have experienced. . . . What was your experience?" Asking questions that break down isolation and connect respondents to others can help keep respondents present and regulated and feeling less judgment or shame. You may also need to redirect the focus by stating questions that allow people to think about others, such as "What would you say to a friend if they told you . . . ?"

Also, pay attention to your own language. Words can be used to heal or harm. Our casual discourse is full of violent and discriminatory phrases, some of which we may not be aware of. Common phrases like "That was the bomb!" or "The presenter totally killed it!" include violent language. Often, colloquial expressions have historical roots that are sexist, racist, and phobic. Some are obvious, but sometimes this language is more subtle or coded, leading us to commit microaggressions. What other words can you say instead? "That presenter was so powerful and effective!" "That was the best!" The more you practice nonviolent and nondiscriminatory language every day, the less likely you will be to use it in your conversations with team members and participants.

A known risk of surveys is the tendency for respondents to tell researchers what they think the researchers want to hear or present themselves in a better light than is really the case. This is called **social desirability bias.** To offset the problem of social desirability bias when asking sensitive questions, Robinson and Leonard (2018) suggest using closed-ended questions with a wide range of responses, which allow respondents to choose a response rather than construct one that may or not be accurate (p. 139). It is the survey designer's responsibility, in partnership with community members, to determine which type of question offers less risk to the respondents. Including quality control questions also helps mitigate this kind of bias (see Robinson & Leonard, 2025, pp. 135–137).

Have a Narrow Focus

Next, be clear about what questions you *need* to ask versus what questions you would *like* to ask. Stay close to your evaluation or research questions and avoid collecting unnecessary information. Some researchers may be tempted to "collect wide" while you have participants' engagement and attention, but that is extractive and exploitive and certainly not trauma-informed. If you think you may have questions in the future for a participant, then ask them for permission to contact them again at some point in the future. This permission to contact them, however, should not be mistaken for consent. Should you go back to the respondent, ask for ongoing informed consent again.

Break the Survey into Sections

Construct your survey in sections or groups, as opposed to creating a single big, long document. Provide a short introduction describing what respondents can expect for each group of questions and provide a rationale explaining *why* you are asking these questions. Sections also provide natural space and time for resting, movement breaks, and checking in with the respondent to see how they are feeling and if they want to continue. Here are some examples of section introductions with our notes in *italics*:

- "There are five sections in this survey. In this section, we will ask you six questions about yourself (*explaining what is ahead relieves anxiety*). We ask you these questions so that we can learn if and how different groups of people experience this service." (*You are developing trust by explaining why you are asking.*)

- "The next section has eight multiple-choice and two open-ended questions about your experience with your support team. If you would like to get some water, stretch, walk around a bit, click "Save" and come back in a few minutes if you can. Otherwise, please continue."

- "We only have five more questions for you and then you are done! We really appreciate sticking with us for a few more minutes (*honesty, acknowledging feelings, humor, gratitude*)."

- "In this section, you may find some of the questions a bit difficult to answer. We know you have gone through some difficult times, and some of the questions may bring up feelings or memories that are uncomfortable (*acknowledgment builds trust and safety—this shows you know something about them and their situation*). Feel free to skip any question for any reason. You may also save your survey and come back later, or you may choose to leave the survey (*choice*). We honor your choices and are grateful for your contributions to this study."

If your survey needs a statement like the last one, we recommend that you plan to offer postsurvey support as discussed previously. If you are interacting with the respondent in real time, pay very close attention to body language and behaviors. Ask if they are okay or if there is anything they need that you can help them with. Listen deeply if they want to talk something out. If you sense they need a break before continuing at any point, offer one, and model deep breathing, drinking water, and shaking out the hands and legs.

This means that you do it too! Doing resilience practices with your respondent creates a sense of trust, collaboration, and safety. You may also want to have counselors in a nearby or virtual room that respondents can debrief with or have a phone number to on-call counselors. (Of course, these supports will have to be included in the project budget, which you address in the contracting and design stages.)

Building In Ongoing Informed Consent

Ongoing informed consent includes closing each section introduction by asking, "Would you like to continue?" and if the answer is "no," providing options for returning to complete the survey later or opt out totally. When face-to-face, if a respondent conveys they are not okay to continue, respond with grace, gratitude, and empathy (and program your online survey to pop up and respond this way as well). Ask if there is anything you can do to support them or perhaps explore how you might identify and fill an unmet need.

Never use language that may shame a respondent who will not or cannot go on and never beg them or manipulate them because you want a completed survey. If they need to cry, hold a brave space for them. Sit in any discomfort, regulate your own responses, and see the human before you. You don't need to do anything other than just be there and keep your cool. This will send the message that they are fine and acceptable just as they are, even when they are in pain before another person.

If they cannot continue, be caring and grateful for the time and information they gave you. If compensation was promised, give it. If possible, follow up using appropriate channels in case that respondent needs additional support or would like to reengage with you. Again, working closely with the community will help you know what to do and who you can turn to for support.

Collecting Demographic Data

Collect only essential demographic information related to your purpose and disaggregate your responses during analysis, as discussed in Chapter 6. Demographic data labels can be inherently problematic given the rapidly changing language of identity. How does your study population identify themselves? Learn what descriptors your respondents use and use them, unless of course you are bound by traditional or government-required categories. Keep in mind that too many demographic questions may reduce anonymity and cause anxiety or opt-outs (Rea & Parker, 2005). If you are required to ask a plethora of demographic questions, include an "I choose not to answer" option if possible. Again, partnering with the community to be surveyed can provide insight into acceptable/preferred demographic descriptors as well as guidance on how data should be disaggregated and reported. Case Study 9.2 illustrates how tricky this can be.

CASE STUDY 9.2 Navigating Cultural Differences When Collecting Demographic Data

AARON KATES

I conduct a lot of my work with fairly conservative religious groups. I want to be inclusive to people of all gender identities when I collect demographic information, which can be a point of friction. I find that when I include categories such as nonbinary on my demographics response options, I get back a wide range of sarcastic, disgruntled, and unserious responses. It's apparent that I'm offending some of these people with my response options and I fear that it makes them skeptical of the whole process, which would harm the validity and utility of my results.

Lately, I have taken to just having a free response blank for gender. That way, people can enter whatever they want in an inclusive way, without creating issues for more conservative people. Responses can be easily categorized with a simple Excel formula once the survey is closed. This may feel like a cop out, but if everyone feels more comfortable, my survey is more respected by all, and my responses are therefore more valid. After all, surveys are about getting information in a sensitive manner—not about changing hearts and minds.

CASE STUDY 9.2. REFLECTION QUESTIONS

1. As you see in this case study, sensitivity can cut in multiple ways. What is inclusive to one group may offend another. In this case, Aaron offers a trick for sidestepping a hot-button culture war issue. Did he miss a chance to advocate for a position he feels strongly about?
2. Are there any ethical principles we might use to decide whether to sidestep controversial issues in a survey or qualitative protocol?
3. Stepping back, what role do you think evaluators play when it comes to persuasion? Does this change depend on the setting or situation (e.g., data collection vs. reporting; in the community vs. with funders)?

Require Answers Sparingly, If Ever

Finally, we recommend *never* forcing responses by requiring answers on online surveys unless it is absolutely necessary. (Government studies, which are rarely if ever trauma-informed, often require answers, and it will take time and advocacy to shift governments' thinking about those kinds of procedures.) That little red asterisk is annoying and sometimes enraging. Requiring answers violates the Six Principles, especially Safety and Empowerment/Voice/Choice. We realize that missing data could pose analysis issues, but that is for researchers and evaluators to deal with, not our respondents. We must appreciate a respondent's reason for not answering a question or not completing a survey. If certain information is indeed required, explain what is required and why and clearly delineate those from questions that are not required. Respect your respondents and appreciate their choices. Case Study 9.3 reflects Martha's experience completing a poorly designed survey.

CASE STUDY 9.3 Beyond Required Answers

MARTHA BROWN

I generally respond to surveys from organizations or businesses I am familiar with out of a sense of wanting to help them by providing honest feedback. A survey I was recently asked to take required every answer, which irritated me right off the bat. There wasn't a clear rationale for why every single question on the survey was required, other than the designer clicked the box labeled "require all answers." I could tell that the survey was made by someone untrained in survey design, probably because they were told to "do a survey." Okay, that happens a lot, so I'll take it.

Shortly after I began answering questions, I encountered a required, open-ended question that did not relate to my experience at all. I had nothing to say, so I attempted to skip the question but was confronted with the message, "An answer is required." Okay, so I typed NA, which had the question been closed, would have been an appropriate choice. But wait—it gets worse. This time, I was confronted with a pop-up saying that I had to type in *x* number of characters—and it was a high number! How could I do that when I had nothing to offer?!? Now I'm angry that someone is wasting my time. Who thought of requiring a number of characters—and why did someone think that character count was important? Or was this a default setting to their survey platform? I will never know. What I do know is that angering or overwhelming your survey respondents—or worse, triggering them—practically guarantees that they will quit the survey—which is exactly what I did.

CASE STUDY 9.3.
REFLECTION QUESTIONS

1. How would you have responded or reacted to a survey like this, especially if it were from an organization you cared about?
2. Would you have attempted to reach the survey designer and educate them? Would you let someone in the organization know how a poorly designed survey negatively affected their ability to get the feedback they were seeking?
3. What steps can you take when designing your trauma-informed survey to ensure the highest response rates and most honest responses possible?

Phase 3: Finalizing the Survey

Once you have drafted a survey with community input, it is time to pilot the survey with people who have lived experience with the survey topic. This could be willing friends or family members or community members you have been working with all along. It is important that you ask for specific feedback on language, vocabulary, readability, and the questions you've chosen. Words you may consider to be safe may be triggering to some people. Be prepared to reword some things.

Martha knows a woman who chose to use the term *assault* to describe what happened to her and her daughter. She did not say "rape," nor did she say "sexual assault." Although "assault" has several meanings and legally doesn't always refer directly to sexual violence, it was the word she *could* use to talk about what happened. We offer this example to show how some survivors of trauma may develop a code that allows them to speak about their experience in ways they can handle. This poses challenges for evaluators and researchers and may mean that as we interact with trauma-affected populations, we take time to discuss what words and language are most comfortable for that person. The answers are likely to change across individuals. If their chosen words could lead to confusion or be open to misinterpretation, have that sensitive conversation gently and with compassion or honor their words and note their meanings "in the margins." Then, do your best to use their language and words as you continue, despite your scripted protocol.

Conducting the Survey

Give the myriad options for how surveys are conducted, we invite you to make them work for your method. We believe that you can design surveys that don't require direct interaction with the respondents in ways that still promote connection and trust. It's all in how you set it up and in the language you use.

Make an Authentic Connection

If your survey is a synchronous interaction (i.e., you are together at the same time in some way), you *must* form a genuine, human connection before starting. As we've said before, this does not mean having a long personal conversation. It does mean acknowledging the gift of information and time this person is giving you and taking time to let them know *who you are*, not just what you do. Remember *didarri*?

Find something you might have in common to chat about. Relax, smile, and slow your pace. Questions like "How is your day going for you?" are more personal than the generic "How are you?" but you must also listen and respond appropriately to what the respondent tells you. For example, "Oh, it was going great until my kid fell off her bike and I had to deal with that." "Oh, I'm so sorry. Is she okay now?" (*empathy and concern*). Then, share something about your day, and if you have common experiences, let them know you can relate to how they are feeling, like "I fell off my bike last summer and got a concussion, so I know how that goes." Create a sense of "we're in this together."

Physical Comfort Matters

You may also ask respondents where they would like to be when they answer the questions, such as at a table, on a bench, standing, etc. Ensure that they know that you want them to be comfortable. For example, when some people get antsy or have limitations as to how long they can sit, they may want to stand. Tell them they are free to take care of themselves as needed and take a bio break if they need one. If you are in person, noise, room temperature, direct sun or wind, bad weather, lack of privacy, too many or not enough windows, closed spaces, and so on are all things to consider. *Know your respondents and anticipate their needs via community input.* Check out the Center for Victims of Torture at *cvt.org* and see how they use trauma-informed approaches at every level, including how they've designed the spaces in their treatment center. If you are online or on the phone, give your participants time to find a quiet, private place to speak with you, if they have one. If they are in noisy surroundings and with other people and/or children, be very patient and empathetic. Saying something like "I work from home, and trust me, I know what it's like when I'm in an online meeting and my dog decides to bark his head off at nothing" will help reduce any shame a respondent might be feeling about their surroundings. Remember that the respondent is still giving you their time despite the less-than-perfect environment, so be patient, compassionate, and flexible.

What about Purely Quantitative Research?

TIER practices can be more difficult to think about and apply for researchers and evaluators who are exclusively, or almost exclusively, quantitative analysts. If you don't interact with study participants and your computer is what you interact with the most, how can you apply the Six Principles? Quantitative surveys, many of which include Likert-type scales asking for strength of agreement or rating scales, are looking for numbers, not stories. Response choices are provided for a respondent, sometimes forcing them to choose a response that is "close" but not entirely accurate.

For some trauma-affected people, closed-ended questions can be less triggering, as they do not force people to tell the details of their experiences. For others, closed-ended questions may limit their ability to voice their true responses and cause frustration. It is important to understand this and be as sensitive to it as possible when deciding if your survey design relies 100% on closed-ended questions. Again, set your respondent up to succeed by letting them know the reality of your survey and go easy on requiring answers.

WRAP-UP

Collaborating with community members can help you design a quality survey and be trauma-informed. Know your respondents and take their experiences into consideration. Writing good-quality, nontriggering survey questions is a skill that takes time and practice. It is deceptively difficult. The sources we cited are excellent resources for learning good survey design techniques. Try to use appropriate humor, empathy, and connecting language throughout the survey, regardless of what format you are using. Surveys do not have to be dry and boring, just as they do not have to be triggering. With the right intention, even anonymous surveys can leave people feeling heard, valued, and respected. Those feelings lead to resiliency and healing.

CHAPTER 9 PRACTICE ACTIVITIES

In this section, we're first giving you our analysis of an actual survey introduction and then providing you with three activities to practice on your own.

Activity 9.1. An Example of Analyzing a Survey Invitation

AEA members received an invitation to participate in a survey from the American Evaluation Association. Even without the upfront intent to create a trauma-informed survey, we think that AEA did many things right. Executive Director Anisha Lewis gave us permission to use some of their survey questions as examples of equity-focused trauma-informed questions. Our comments are in *italics*. Feel free to add your own thoughts.

- "Hello, Martha." (*AEA used members' first names, which personalizes and humanizes the message. This may not always be possible, but when it is, do it.*)
- "There is still time to let your voice be heard. " (*vs. "to complete the survey." This language addresses Voice and has a relational tone.*)
- "As part of its strategic planning process, AEA is sponsoring a survey of its current and recent members to learn more about what individuals want most from the organization regarding services and leadership." (*Trust and Transparency—why they are conducting the survey and who they are sending it to, as well as saying that the purpose is to consider making changes based on the results.*)
- "Your participation in . . . will play an important role in helping set organizational priorities." (*Empowerment, Voice, and Choice—telling respondents that we hear them and take them seriously.*)
- "All responses to the survey will be used for reporting summary information across groups of respondents." (*While this works for AEA's audience, if you used this language with nonevaluators, respondents may not understand what this means. Know your audience and use their language.*)
- "Any open-ended responses you share will not be attributed to you by name." (*Confidentiality, trust, transparency—and again, pay attention to the vocabulary you use—it must match your audience.*)
- "If there are questions with which you are uncomfortable (*acknowledgment*), you may skip those and continue with the next survey item. (*AEA did not require answers.*) You may stop the survey at any time [and contact the person at AEA who can answer questions]." (*Provides a line of communication if there are issues or questions.*)
- "The survey will take you approximately 10–15 minutes to complete." (*Transparent, but an option to start and finish later would offer respondents more flexibility. Risk of cognitive fatigue is low with a 15-minute survey on this topic—as long as it really is just 15 minutes!*)
- "In appreciation for your time, a lottery was offered as a form of compensation." *We believe that all study participants should be compensated for their time and contributions and at the same time acknowledge that compensation may bias the sample and/or responses, as well as create an added expense. While many researchers use a lottery as a form of compensation, our jury is out on this practice, as we question the equity and fairness of providing a chance at winning a prize versus providing participants with compensation options and ensuring that all participants are compensated. Additionally, participants rarely have a say in how they are compensated. Yes, budgets do not always allow for this, but they should—an issue for Framing and Design!*

Activity 9.2. Survey during a Natural Disaster

Now it's your turn. Read the following scenario and consider the questions that follow:

> Several counties in a certain state experienced mass flooding due to climate change. Floods ruined the homes of high-, middle-, and low-income people alike. Property was lost, dams broke, and residents experienced trauma and toxic stress as the heavy rains continued week after week while they watched homes, trailers, RVs, apartments, and other structures disappear under the muddy, sewage-contaminated water. Roads were closed, making it taxing to get from place to place. People without relatives on dry land were left needing emergency shelter.
>
> Local authorities have asked you to conduct a survey of residents that would identify critical needs and determine the capacity of local resources in the community to provide immediate assistance. They need this information immediately to address the growing crisis, and you have very little time to implement, analyze, and report.

1. Alone or with your peers, identify all issues and strategies and quickly design and implement a trauma-informed survey that will help people get the help they need. What format(s) will you use (i.e., phone, in-person, mail, email, etc.)? Can you design and conduct your survey in the languages spoken in your community? To whom and how will you administer the survey? How quickly can you analyze the results? What will you do if you know certain populations in the community are underrepresented in the results?

2. How will you engage the community? Who will you work with throughout the process? Who will pilot the survey and provide fast feedback? Remember, people's needs are immediate and pressing, and you only have one chance at getting this right and getting quick results. How do you avoid sacrificing quality for speed?

3. Write some questions you think should be on this survey. Consider what is most important and how to ask the questions. What words will you choose? How long will your survey be? Put yourself in the shoes of a respondent and imagine how it would feel to answer the questions. Choose your questions, question type, and words with care to minimize triggering respondents who are already in crisis.

Activity 9.3. Practice Writing Trauma-Informed Survey Introductions

The following is an introduction to an in-person survey about homelessness conducted by the RAND Corporation between 1989 and 1995 (RAND, n.d.). We think the entire introduction is problematic and not the least bit trauma-informed.

> Now I have some questions about your physical and mental health, your use of programs and services, and your life experiences. The questions will take about an hour and a half. When we've finished, I'll pay you $10 for your time.
>
> This is a survey of people who sometimes don't have regular homes. We're asking about 1,500 other people in Los Angeles County the same questions. The information from this survey is intended to improve housing choices and other services for people who become homeless.
>
> You don't have to take part in this survey and can refuse to answer a question or stop the interview at any time. The survey information will be treated as confidential.

That is, nothing you tell us will be associated with you personally. Whether or not you participate in this survey will have no effect on any services you get from programs or agencies."

Now try rewriting the introduction to create more genuine connection and trust and to be more trauma-informed. Assume respondents have been voluntarily recruited, not coerced, have given consent, and generally know that they are sitting with you to take a survey about being unhoused. Look for opportunities to ask for ongoing informed consent.

Activity 9.4. Rewrite Your Own Questions

Dig out a survey you created at some point or search for one online. Analyze it wearing your trauma-informed lenses. What aspects do you think are equity focused and/or trauma-informed? What could be done differently? Rewrite anything you find that you feel can be improved, from the introduction, to transitions and sections, and of course, the actual questions.

CHAPTER 10

Trauma-Informed Interviews and Focus Groups

Did you really just ask me that?

WHAT YOU'LL LEARN

Much of what you learned about designing and administering trauma-informed surveys also applies to writing trauma-informed interviews and focus group protocols and asking those questions. You need community engagement in the design and throughout. You need to pilot protocols with people with lived experiences similar to those of your study sample. You need ongoing informed consent and to build in time for breaks. But unlike surveys that can be done impersonally online or on paper, interviews and focus groups require researchers and evaluators to be present with people, either face-to-face, on the phone, or in a videoconference.

We start this chapter with an example of what *not* to do so you can contrast a researcher-focused interview protocol with strategies to create protocols that are equity-focused and trauma-informed. We remind you that *being* trauma-informed is of utmost importance in these situations. We encourage you to consider your background and trauma history, your culture and class, your attitudes, your ability to show empathy and compassion, and your ability to create and hold safe and brave spaces. As we said earlier, you need to be the right person in the room, and if you are not, find someone who is.

Finally, we have three case studies in this chapter to help you apply the Principles in various contexts.

Interviewing Staff

Wear the trauma-informed lens when you are engaged in work that requires you to interview or survey program staff. Hatcher and colleagues (2020) learned this lesson when they were conducting research on a program designed to intervene and prevent men's intimate partner violence (IPV). Their evaluation participants and the people who worked with IPV survivors were themselves traumatized because they had also experienced the loss of coworkers and program participants to violence and murder. A manager said, "It's actually really shocking that we've had study participants who have died, been murdered, we've had an activist volunteer who was killed. You know, it's like life is really much more precarious, much more at risk" (Hatcher et al., 2020, p. 5). Remember that people who work with trauma-affected people may also be trauma affected.

Brené Brown (2012a) offers a tool on her website called the Engaged Feedback Checklist. Here are a few checklist items that apply specifically to how we might prepare ourselves to interview study participants:

- I'm ready to sit next to you rather than across from you.
- I'm ready to listen, ask questions, and accept that I may not fully understand the issue (and this may be the case when we are working with participants who are not like us).
- I can genuinely thank you for your efforts rather than criticize you for your failings.
- I can model vulnerability and openness that I [would like] to see from you.

Whatever form your empathetic expressions take, they must be authentic, unscripted, and real. Allowing yourself to be vulnerable can strengthen trust and create a sense of mutuality. Why not let someone know you or someone you love went through something similar, and that you "get it." Letting someone know what it feels like to be in their shoes helps them know they are not alone—and that in and of itself is healing.

Because we know that many survey and interview tools are not trauma-informed, Case Study 10.1 is an example of what NORC did to create trauma-informed interview tools.

CASE STUDY 10.1 Designing Trauma-Informed Interview Tools

ERIKA KEAVENEY

What questions are asked, and how, are among the most important considerations in designing trauma-informed research with at-risk populations. When researchers ask study participants to recall traumatic experiences, they are wading into a delicate situation that requires tact and grace. To minimize risk, it may be important to keep sensitive questions to a minimum and to also acknowledge that some questions may be triggering. We need to be ready to guide participants back to a calmer state (watch those WoT cues).

Researchers often try to capitalize on the fixed costs of fielding a study by adding items that are peripheral to the central research questions. Superfluous questions of a sensitive nature can increase the risk of psychological harm without a clearly justified benefit to the study population. For example, an evaluation of an aftercare program for survivors of sexual assault should not force respondents to relive their trauma by asking for a detailed recounting of the assault due to researcher curiosity. Instead, interview questions should focus on beneficiaries' experiences with the aftercare program and what could be improved to better support them going forward.

In many cases, however, sensitive items do address the central research questions. NORC's human-trafficking prevalence studies, for example, require going through a detailed list of indicators to establish whether the respondent is a trafficking victim, including indicators of physical and sexual violence, commercial sexual exploitation, bonded labor, and descent-based slavery. In our study on commercial sexual exploitation of children (CSEC) in coastal Kenya, it was important to understand the "push" and "pull" factors that drove children into CSEC in the first place to inform future prevention programming. Asking the children about the first time they engaged in a commercial sex act was highly triggering and elicited a trauma response in around 3% of study participants. Because of this, we took the time to prime respondents for the sensitive content ahead of time—not just during initial consent but throughout the entire interview. As sensitive content was introduced, we included scripts at the beginning of the survey module letting respondents know what was coming and reminding them of their right to "pass" on any question at any time for any reason.

Researchers can also consider capturing sensitive information indirectly. This could mean asking about peers rather than the respondents themselves or using strategies to elicit sensitive information anonymously such as self-administered surveys, list randomization, or randomized response. For the Kenya study, what qualified as a commercial "sex act" varied across governmental and intergovernmental agencies, meaning we had to ask about specific sex acts in order to estimate CSEC prevalence using both local and international definitions. Given the sensitive and intrusive nature of such questions, we used randomized response (referred to by field teams as "the dice game") to elicit information on respondents' engagement in qualifying sex acts while preserving their anonymity.

For the randomized response module, respondents were given a die and instructed to roll it before answering a question about a specific sex act (the interviewer could not see what number was rolled). If they rolled a one, they were instructed to answer yes to the statement, even if it was untrue; if they rolled a six, they were instructed to answer no, even if the statement was true; and if they rolled a two, three, four, or five, they were instructed to give a truthful response. Responses were tallied in accordance with the local and international definitional criteria, and data were transformed to back out the forced responses, thus yielding accurate aggregate summary statistics.

Finally, it is important to ensure the language of the instrument is appropriate for the study population. As a rule of thumb, surveys targeting adults in the United States should be written at an eighth-grade level, as indicated by the Flesch–Kincaid readability test (calculators are available for free online). For a survey NORC fielded with child laborers in rural Africa, we discovered that the "model" instrument required by the client was written at a high school level—despite being designed for children as young as five. It is also critical to ensure the language of the instrument is not inadvertently belittling or stigmatizing. Soliciting review and input from individuals with lived experience can help identify such issues. In the U.S. context, the CDC has published a guide on inclusive communication principles, as well as a list of preferred terms for marginalized groups and communities (available at *www.cdc.gov/healthcommunication*).

CASE STUDY 10.1. REFLECTION QUESTIONS

1. What are some ways researchers can ask direct, pointed questions about potentially traumatic events without making respondents mentally "relive" their traumas?
2. Do you think anonymous approaches to eliciting sensitive information are less stressful for respondents (vs. having to share information directly with another person)? Why or why not?
3. How might the inadvertent use of stigmatizing language or labels contribute to uncomfortable memories, triggering, or retraumatization? What can researchers do to ensure the language they use is not stigmatizing and reflects principles of inclusive communication?

Example of an Insensitive Interview

Sometimes, the best way to learn what to do is to learn what *not* to do. We found a non-trauma-informed interview protocol used with unhoused people (a trauma-affected population) in a study conducted by the RAND Corporation between 1989 and 1995 (RAND, n.d.) that is what Waapalaneexkweew (2018) referred to when speaking about research that does harm. We invite you to examine it online, as it is too long to include here, which is but one of the many things wrong with it. Go to *www.rand.org/health-care/surveys_tools/homelessness.html* and browse through it. It's a textbook case of cognitive overload, insensitivity, lack of empathy and connection, and shaming questions. We're calling attention to just a handful of items that are, well, just awful. We know you'll find more, but here is one:

> You told me that you spent nights in [a certain shelter] in the past 60 days. Now I would like to ask you about the specific nights you spent in these places. (HAND CALENDAR PAGES)

Given what you know about how trauma affects the brain, including memory and the ability to think chronologically as well as the mental health and SUDs that many unhoused people struggle with, what's wrong with this question?

The fact is that this question should not even be asked. Shelters have sign-in sheets and various ways to keep track of who is in their facility. Why not gather that data from the shelters instead of the respondent? We are curious about the purpose of this question and whether RAND understood that many unhoused people have mental health and substance use issues that may interfere with their ability to remember things that happened a few days ago, let alone 2 months ago.

It gets worse. On page 120 of the protocol, there is an observation checklist (go look at it) that asks the interviewer to check whether the respondents had strong body odor or outlandish dress, whether their behavior seemed bizarre or inappropriate, and whether the interviewer felt the respondent was lying (their words, not ours). Even though the participant might not see or hear that part of the protocol (and we advocate giving participants access to their own records!), the words used to describe a study participant were elitist, degrading, judgmental, and just plain gross.

At the end of the survey on page 124, there is a box for the interviewer that says, "If respondent has been selected for longitudinal study, *postpone payment* until after recontact information has been obtained."

It's hard to know where to begin to process this survey. We are particularly disturbed by withholding payment to an unhoused participant because they did not complete the entire interview. We wonder if anything good resulted from the survey and if any policy and programmatic changes were made that actually improved the lives of the unhoused. We offer this critique hoping that RAND will not sue us and instead learn and do better if they haven't already. Unfortunately, a protocol like this used to be the norm and unfortunately sometimes still is, especially in large research firms or government-funded studies. However, we can learn what not to do through examples like this one.

Being Trauma-Informed, Even When the Protocol Is Not

We understand many research and evaluation firms as well as graduate programs do not teach you how to humanize data collection. The above-referenced RAND instrument was most likely tested for reliability and validity, but if tested for trauma sensitivity, it would have failed. When you find yourself in situations like this, where you are handed a protocol and instructed to follow it, you have to be creative and find ways to minimize the harm that instrument is going to cause. This means that you must be present, caring, empathetic, and perhaps even apologetic for putting respondents through it. Do not ignore your critical role and what you bring to the interview. If you're stuck with a traumatizing study design, then *you must show up as your best trauma-informed self to mitigate the damage.* Or, if you have the courage, excuse yourself from the study, or push back (see Chapter 8). Moving forward with a study you know is harmful is likely to cause moral injury to you.

So, pretend you are an equity-focused trauma-informed researcher who has no choice but to use this protocol. You understand that the people you will speak with have experienced multiple traumas and are engaged daily in struggles to survive. They endure humiliation and violence on the streets. They are continually traumatized. You are not a clinician. You are also not a robot. You have to decide what kind of person you want to show up as—and hopefully that is not an "objective researcher-scientist" like this protocol required but as the equity-focused trauma-informed researcher that you are or that you are becoming. You create and hold a safe space that centers your interviewees, a space in which you can be fully present, a space that is physically and psychologically safe, and a space that is conducive to deep listening.

You are empathetic without being patronizing. Certainly, if you follow the script as written you know you will dehumanize and objectify your respondents. Despite the tool you were given, you look for and create ways to connect, ways to empathize, and ways to reassure and call attention to evidence of strength and resilience.

You prioritize building trust and connection. You acknowledge the pain they may be feeling, and you pay attention to their tone, expressions, and body language. You let them know these questions might be difficult, and you welcome them to ask for clarification or decide to skip a question. You might say that you're sorry for things that happened to them or for the awful questions you are required to ask them. You listen deeply and go slowly. You check in to see how they are doing and ask them if they need a break. You look for any stress responses, such as withdrawal, short or absent answers, fidgeting, agitation, emotional overwhelm, and loss of interest.

You tell them you are honored that they trusted you and felt safe enough to tell their story. Acknowledge that they took a step on their healing journey and that it took strength and courage to answer the questions.

Then, if you are holding their pain, you do some resilience practices before your next respondent comes in. You've built in 15–30 minutes between interviews so you can decompress. When it's time, you get up, approach the respondent with a smile, introduce yourself and ask them their name—which you will pronounce correctly—offer a handshake if they seem open to it or if culturally appropriate, and welcome them into the space. *You* are the key to mitigating harm when using harmful protocols.

Preventing Shaming

Shame often accompanies trauma, as trauma survivors will often place the blame for what happened on themselves, blame themselves for not preventing the trauma, or both. Brené Brown (2012b) has found that when people share their shame stories, their physical health improves and they show a decrease in stress hormones. Shame thrives on secrets and lives in the dark, but when someone shines a light on shame by talking with someone about it, shame loses its power (Brown, 2012b). If researchers and evaluators foster genuine, safe, and human connections with study participants, they may be gifted with someone's shame story or could sit with someone who is feeling shame when they tell their story. Perhaps this is the first time their story has been told.

No matter what study participants reveal, it is critical that we respond with care and empathy and not add to the shame. We do not want to be the person who winces, scrunches our face, or looks away. We especially do not want to increase the shame by sending the message that a particular story is unwelcome. We never want to end an interview or cut off a story because of our own discomfort, which can be humiliating for a participant. We want to be present, accepting, and empathetic, no matter what we just heard.

When we interview study participants, individually or in focus groups, we ask them to share their stories with us. The stories may be limited to a particular topic, but they are stories nonetheless: the story of their experience in a program, the story of the treatment they received, the story of how they implemented recommendations or engaged community members. Even quantitative data tell stories (and the evaluator or researcher often holds the power to decide what those stories are and how they are told). All stories require listeners.

Storytelling can be redemptive and freeing by bringing shame out of the darkness, and we want to set the conditions so that it is both. "When people begin to talk about their story, assume it, and reflect on it, [they] find meaning and significance in what they have lived through. . . . This is what allows us to go forward in life" (Cabrera, 2002, p. 10). Remember, honest expressions of empathy, compassion, and care mean a great deal to trauma survivors (Mears, 2012). Survivors of trauma can learn that "because of their experience they can be more than they were instead of less" (Mears, 2012, p. 207), which is an antidote to shame. We never want trauma and shame to define individuals and groups. Instead, we want to recognize and acknowledge their strength and resilience, knowing that trauma is just one part of who they are and what they've experienced.

Restorative justice scholar and practitioner Kay Pranis (2005) shares the importance of storytelling this way (the interjections are ours):

> Storytelling delivers information in a way that opens the listener [in this case, the researcher/evaluator]. When information is asserted or presented cognitively, we immediately engage in a screening device to determine whether we agree or disagree. We are primarily engaged mentally and begin thinking about how we will respond [or probe]. Storytelling employs a different kind of listening. The body relaxes, settles back, is more open and less anxious. We take in the story before screening the content. We are engaged emotionally as well as mentally. This different kind of listening allows information to be exchanged more thoroughly, leading to much greater understanding between people. (p. 39)

Let's break this down. First, when we listen to or read stories while we are in our heads, or cognitively engaged, we are limited by our biases, our judgments, our interpretations, and our purpose of the question. Our listening may be microscopic, picking up only on information we think matters to our study. But if we listen with our heads and our hearts and allow ourselves to imagine what our participants are thinking or feeling, we are listening deeply. We are actually getting better information. Judy Atkinson (2002) says, "Through the years we have listened to stories. In our Aboriginal way, we learn and listen from our earliest days. We could not live good and useful lives unless we listened. This was the normal way for us to learn—not by asking questions. We learnt by watching and listening, waiting, and then acting" (p. 9).

Listening versus Listening Deeply

How we listen can validate a participant's experience, offer hope, and provide a form of peer support. Empathetic responses naturally promote connectedness that encourages people to continue developing the sense of self-efficacy needed to heal and create positive change. This can happen whether you're working on a community level with coalitions, working with community members affected by a tragedy, or conducting an interview with individuals or in a focus group.

We need to provide the kindest possible environment for our participants by creating space for empathetic listening and responding (Mears, 2012) and then listen from our hearts and not just listen for answers to our questions. We call this **deep listening.** Listening deeply is a way to create a pathway toward healing and is a skill that can be learned. Here are a few deep listening skills you can practice:

- Prepare to be present and leave your concerns and agenda behind.
- Be attentive.
- Focus on listening, don't interrupt.
- Monitor your emotions, ground and regulate yourself. Find ways to disconnect from your internal reactions or triggers if you have them. (Breathe.)
- Demonstrate genuine interest both verbally and nonverbally.
- Avoid judgment or attempts to fix.
- Focus on the person's needs, expressions, and body language.
- Be careful not to overwhelm participants with too many questions.
- Listen for indications of strength, survivorship, and resilience *and affirm these.*
- "Be cautious about reframing another's story" (Center for Justice and Peacebuilding of Eastern Mennonite University, 2023, p. 83; Jones et al., 2016, p. 7).

As you see, listening deeply is very different from listening only to gather information. Deep listening requires connection, and "connection is the energy that is created between people when they feel seen, heard, and valued; when they can give and receive without judgment" (Brown, 2012b, p. 145). The antidote to trauma and shame is connection (Brown, 2012b; Mears, 2012).

Responding with Empathy

Picture yourself conducting an interview or focus group and someone tells you something that was really painful for them. What do you do? How does receiving that information feel? How is the storyteller feeling? How do you respond? Do you just go on to the next question on the protocol? We've heard the stories of some evaluators who were freaked out by the emotions of their respondent and just went on to the next question, so we know it happens.

Expressing empathy can take many forms—and for many of us, it takes practice. It could involve direct eye contact and the cessation of note taking, giving the storyteller our full attention. It might involve a gentle touch or gentle passing of tissues. When someone shares their story with us and is vulnerable, we might acknowledge them with an empathetic response, such as the following:

- "I understand. I have been in a similar situation."
- "I am really honored you shared that with me and that you trusted me with your story. Thank you."
- "I know it took a lot of courage for you to share that with me. I want to acknowledge how vulnerable and courageous you are."
- "That must have been very difficult or painful for you. I'm sorry that happened to you."
- "Do you mind if I ask you more about that or would you rather we move on?"

Expressing empathy might mean taking a pause and breathing together and asking participants what they need. And when everyone is calmer, you ask them if they are okay to continue. What you don't do is panic and unilaterally end the interview; worry that you have an incomplete interview if they can't continue; or just move on to the next question on the protocol, ignoring the emotions in the room.

After a particularly sensitive interview or focus group, you may need time and space to debrief and process anything that came up for you. Case Study 10.2 provides such an example.

CASE STUDY 10.2 Creation of the Interviewer Processing and Reflexivity Group within Wilder Research

NORA JOHNSON

In response to requests from interviewing staff, Wilder Research piloted an Interviewer Processing and Reflexivity Group. The group sought to offer interviewers a space to talk about their experiences engaging with respondents and the emotions that such interactions may evoke. The initial request arose from the convergence of several projects that covered sensitive or potentially traumatizing topics (including policing, suicide, and sex trafficking) that would all be collecting data around the same time.

From the beginning of the pandemic, interviewers were often conducting interviews in isolation, compared with conducting interviews in an office environment. This removed a critical aspect of interview processing and self-care that is built in when interviewers occupy the same space together. These shared spaces allowed for interviewers to decompress with one another after particularly difficult interviews in real time. This group was an attempt to formalize some of those previously informal supports. In addition, the ongoing collective traumas of the COVID pandemic and the murder of George Floyd in Minneapolis (and the subsequent protests outside the Foundation buildings) necessitated that additional supports be made available.

The pilot group consisted of weekly semistructured sessions for 5 weeks, led by two higher level research staff with expertise in trauma-informed research. Interviewers were encouraged to discuss any particularly difficult or memorable interviews they had and provide feedback, support, or insights to other interviewers. Once the short pilot was concluded, a full evaluation was conducted to measure the effects of the group. Given the sensitive nature of the subject and the fact that internal researchers known to respondents would be reviewing the data, the evaluation materials were sent through the Wilder Research IRB for review and approval. The pilot group leaders did not have access to the raw data or a list of individuals who participated in the pilot evaluation. In addition, all reports that came from the pilot were sent to all pilot evaluation participants (regardless of their participation in the evaluation) for review and approval before being more widely distributed.

The interviewer pilot evaluation generated several main findings.

- Participants of the pilot debriefing sessions appreciated having the space to talk about specific incidents and felt that their experiences were validated and normalized. In addition, they felt they were better positioned to advocate for more organizational support.
- Many interviewers who participated had experienced micro- or macroaggressions as part of their jobs. It was not uncommon for interviewers to experience racism, misogyny, and other threatening behaviors on occasion.
- Interviewers identified several structural issues that contributed to stress and burnout, including managing several high-stress or emotionally charged projects at the same time; working with aggressive project timelines that resulted from earlier project delays, leaving interviewers to then make up the time; interviewers not being consulted during study development and planning, especially including instrument development; and interviewers not being allowed time to debrief or seek supports due to project budget or time constraints.

CASE STUDY 10.2. REFLECTION QUESTIONS

1. Which of the Six Principles was key in this case study?
2. What do you take away from this case study? How might Wilder's experiences relate to your own workplace?
3. Given the findings of the Wilder study, what recommendations would you make for Wilder interviewers? What structural and procedural issues need to be addressed to make Wilder more trauma-informed?

Focus Groups and Circles

Designing and conducting trauma-informed surveys, interviews, and focus groups require similar approaches. However, when you are facilitating a group, there are some additional considerations. Some of your participants may be domineering, judgmental, angry/hostile, withdrawn, or nervous. It is important to set a welcoming, invitational, and relational tone from the moment you recruit participants until the end of the focus group. Try some trauma-informed practices like these:

- Convene the group by starting with some simple grounding or mindfulness practices.
- Use invitational language rather than directives, such as "If you so choose, we'd like you to . . ." or "We invite you to share. . . ."
- Hold your group in the most accessible, welcoming place you can find. Find out if anyone needs accommodations prior to the event and meet them.
- Be fun, welcoming, and down to earth. Dress and speak in ways that don't set you above or apart from your participants.
- Start with some fun icebreakers or other ways for people to get to know each other a bit. In some cases, they may know each other already and you will be the stranger. Share something personal about yourself.
- If you have time, lead the group in setting its norms or guidelines. If not, propose some guidelines and ask participants to affirm them. You can refer back to them if needed.
- Ask the group to avoid silencing behaviors when there are big emotions, like approaching the person, hugging, and so on. Although hugging may look like a comforting gesture, it's really a silencing gesture that conveys "Please stop crying. I'm not comfortable with your pain"—especially if the hug is initiated by a white person hearing the pain of a person of color. Instead of silencing behaviors, invite the group to sit in the moment and just hold space. Deep breathing is a great practice in these situations. Check in to see what people need, including taking a break so you, or someone in the group, can talk with the upset person privately.

Circles

Earlier in this book, we spoke about evaluation and research being a kind of justice, where everyone involved gets what they need for their collective well-being. **Restorative Justice Circles**, which are grounded in Indigenous traditions, are like containers or vessels that can hold whatever comes up because a Circle is bigger than the sum of its parts. Although the Circle is mostly practiced in Indigenous evaluations and restorative justice research (see Brown, 2018; Brown & Di Lallo,

2020), researchers and evaluators can learn the Circle process and use it in lieu of traditional focus groups. In Circle practice, all participants are invited to contribute to creating and holding safe and brave space. Case Study 10.3, by Elyse Fuerst, is a prime example of why in her situation, the Circle was a better choice than focus group.

CASE STUDY 10.3 Circle Did What a Focus Group Could Not

ELYSE FUERST

Sometimes, data collection occurs in the wake of tragedy or emotionally charged situations, leaving participants exhausted, guarded, skeptical about participating, and vulnerable to retraumatization. In the aftermath of racially motivated murders in a public space frequented by most people in a historically traumatized community, CCNY, Inc. and the Erie County Restorative Justice Coalition sought to understand the community's unmet needs. Evaluators recognized that historically, researchers who came into this community left a wake of trauma after identifying what was "wrong" and making no efforts to create substantive change. Given that knowledge, evaluators approached this work differently and more restoratively. Instead of using the traditional focus group method, we prioritized restorative practices, especially the Circle, to enhance participants' abilities to be active listeners, allow for self-expression, and foster stronger relationships, leaving participants empowered to respond to questions openly.

Trusted community-based organizations asked those affected to participate in a 2-hour focus group. We provided a catered meal during the first hour to allow time and space for building relationships. Everyone ate dinner together. This built a sense of community and broke down any power dynamics that existed between evaluators, Circle Keepers, and participants. Although participants came in guarded and unsure of what to expect, they left the dinner portion talkative and at ease. In the second hour, groups were created based on how participants were connected to the tragedy so that participants could validate others' feelings and experiences. Respected religious leaders from the community and mental health counselors provided spiritual and mental health support.

Instead of a facilitator leading a focus group, Circle Keepers kept the Circles. Circle Keepers differ from facilitators in that they are caretakers of the Circle process, ensuring everyone takes responsibility for making the Circle a welcoming safe place for open dialogue (Boyes-Watson & Pranis, 2020). Although both facilitators and Circle Keepers introduce questions and guide the group, Circle Keepers do not intervene or respond to participant comments. Instead, participants are empowered to do the work. Facilitators are often looked at as authority figures in focus groups. On the other hand, Circle Keepers are part of the group and intentionally behave in ways that mitigate perceived and real power differentials. Additionally, restorative justice and trauma-informed practices seek to establish safety, choice, collaboration, trust, and empowerment. Incorporating these practices and principles creates an environment where participants are more apt to provide honest and robust feedback.

Evaluators created a restorative Circle script to learn about the unmet needs of the participants. Circle Keepers invited the group to establish shared values and review the guidelines that served as the consensus-built Circle norms. Then, subsequent rounds included a check-in, five rounds of questions related to uncovering unmet needs, a check-out, and a closing round. At the end, participants received a $50 Visa gift card.

If the evaluators had chosen traditional and rigid focus group methodology, a space for healing and true understanding would not have been created. The team received feedback from participants that the first time they told their stories and felt heard was in the Circles. During the check-in and check-out, participants reported how they were feeling on a scale from 1 to 5 and spoke one word to describe how they were feeling. On average, participants came to the group feeling a 3.5, using descriptors such as "anxious," "tired," and "overwhelmed." Participants left the group feeling a 4.3, using descriptors such as "heard," "new beginning," and "hopeful."

Evaluators received invaluable insight into the experiences and needs of affected community members. Solutions to meeting unmet needs discussed by the participants reached far outside the scope of what evaluators had thought to ask. Participants felt safe to feed off one another's answers, allowing unique brainstorming to occur. Participants stated a need for more public benches, specifically gathering spaces outside of their churches so that they could gather, heal, grieve, and bond with their community. Committee members leading the support effort previously focused on financial, medical, and mental health support.

Restorative practices as a method of collecting data allowed for vulnerable participation and solutions that would allow community members to heal, grieve, and bond. This evaluation, then, empowered community members to take positive actions and went far beyond "do no harm" to "do good."

CASE STUDY 10.3. REFLECTION QUESTIONS

1. If Elyse had not insisted on the Circle and had been required to convene a traditional focus group, how do you think the results might have been different?
2. Why was the check-in and check-out process important to the evaluator and the group itself?
3. How did eating dinner together benefit the group? Do you think it was a factor in the groups' coming to consensus about what they needed?
4. Search for and watch a YouTube video of a restorative Circle process. Discuss how it differs from traditional focus groups. Assuming you were properly trained in Circle processes, under what conditions might you choose the Circle over a focus group?

Obviously, training is needed to learn the Circle process as well as to learn how to make studies (and people) more trauma-informed. Neither are mainstream (yet) in the evaluation and research worlds, and while reading this book is a huge step toward you becoming more trauma-informed, nothing is better than experiential learning with designing studies in real time. Case Study 10.4 illustrates how researchers at NORC were trained to be trauma-informed in the context in which they were conducting an international study.

CASE STUDY 10.4 Reframing Field Interviewer Thinking vis-à-vis Trauma-Risk Populations

KAREEM KYSIA

The frontline people for both rigorous and trauma-informed research are the qualitative and quantitative enumerators (local field staff for data collection) that we employ. In international research settings, sample sizes are often well into the thousands, and field staff easily reach 50 or more people. At NORC, we usually rely on a cadre of young adults with limited postsecondary education to conduct our data collection activities.

The importance of training in trauma-informed practices within this context cannot be overstated, especially when dealing with people in highly vulnerable situations. Some examples in NORC's prior work included helping field interviewers understand the physiological basis of trauma in the brain in contexts where mental health was highly stigmatized, overcoming victim blaming, and helping break down preconceived notions about what constitutes "human trafficking" (e.g., can a minor "consent" to commercial sex? [no]; are "beach boys" who are paid to have sex with older women victims of human trafficking? [yes]).

For a trafficking prevalence study in the Philippines with a sample size of over five thousand households, we employed over 60 enumerators across the country. During pretesting and piloting of the survey, it became apparent that enumerators had deeply ingrained biases that affected their ability to empathize with respondents and correctly identify situations that may constitute human trafficking. Most notably, enumerators (mostly female) had trouble understanding how trafficking survivors could stay with their exploiters and blamed the victim for not running away. They also felt survivors were partially responsible for getting into risky situations in the first place and had trouble differentiating between individuals who self-identified as survivors versus those who were classified as survivors using global indicators (regardless of self-reporting).

Following the short prepilot during which these issues were encountered, the training team brought enumerators in for a focused trauma-informed training session. This was the first trauma-informed training conducted by NORC's international team, and it was successful in educating enumerators on trauma, how it manifests, and how to deal with it in an interview setting as well as how personal bias can interfere with data collection and lead to retraumatization. Most importantly, a significant amount of classroom time was spent allowing enumerators to voice their concerns and biases in a safe environment. Actively talking through the issues was significantly more successful than simply presenting the issues in a didactic manner, without allowing participants to probe and voice their own opinions. For example, an active discussion around the parameters of consent in a trafficking situation allowed enumerators to not only understand the general rule (consent is not applicable in a trafficking situation) but also bring up real-life scenarios on consent to make the point even stronger. The training was well received by all staff, and anecdotal evidence from enumerator debriefings indicated that the lessons learned in the training were applied throughout data collection.

Following the Philippines study, trauma-informed training became mandatory for all NORC research projects engaging people in vulnerable situations—including the other NORC studies described in this anthology.

CASE STUDY 10.4. REFLECTION QUESTIONS

1. How can we identify different types of bias in local field staff and tailor training to address those issues?
2. What are some of the positive effects of applying a trauma-informed lens during training. For enumerators? For respondents?
3. What is the appropriate amount of time to dedicate to trauma-informed training given sometimes limited resources?
4. Given that trauma can manifest in different ways with different people in vulnerable situations, how important is it to tailor training efforts to the specific populations and subpopulations with which you are interacting?

WRAP-UP

Under traditional research and evaluation modalities, it is far too easy for interviewers and facilitators to harm study participants with insensitive questions and to also be harmed with compassion fatigue, burnout, and STS. Often the interviewers are not the same people who designed the study or protocol, which leaves interviewers and facilitators in the dust when it comes to entering the field with an insensitive instrument. We can and must do better.

A relaxed, safe, and trusting respondent will be more honest (making your findings more reliable) if they enjoy the research experience and, when possible, enjoy the time they spend with you. Interviews, focus groups, and Circles provide opportunities to connect, listen deeply, acknowledge people's challenges as well as their resilience, and honor your participants. Center yourself with the thought that you are receiving an incredible gift—someone willing to share their story with you. Listen and respond with care and respect. Slow down. Take breaks when needed. Acknowledge the person's humanity and your own. Show genuine gratitude for what you receive.

CHAPTER 10 REFLECTION QUESTIONS

If you are willing, turn the lens inward and consider these questions regarding how you show up to interviews and focus groups:

1. Where do you sit or stand? Are you standing over people or across from participants and clients? Are you able to sit next to participants and clients? Can you create opportunities for physical openness and vulnerability by sitting or standing with no barriers (desks, etc.) between you?
2. Check your posture. Are you relaxed, nonjudgmental, nonthreatening?
3. If it is culturally appropriate to do so, do you make eye contact? Do you know the cultural norms in your study context?
4. What is the proximity between you and your clients or participants? Are you too far away or too close?
5. What materials do you bring with you? A briefcase? Backpack? Fancy pens?
6. What is the background on your videoconferencing screen? What message does it send?
7. How do you dress? Are you looking "professional" in ways that set you above and apart from participants? What message does your choice of clothing send?
8. How would you describe your personality? Are you approachable? Are you reticent? Do you prefer to just get down to business, or do you take time to connect personally? Are you relaxed or tense?

9. Do you smile when you greet participants and clients? Is your facial expression one of openness, care, compassion, attention? Do you seem distracted? Are you watching the clock?

10. How are you listening to others? Are you constantly typing or writing? Can you record so you can listen deeply? *Hot tip:* People often wonder what we are writing, and that could generate mistrust/suspicion. Have a notetaker or use a recorder when possible so you can be fully present.

CHAPTER 11

Trauma-Informed Analysis and Reporting

It ain't over till it's over.

WHAT YOU'LL LEARN

The pitfalls of qualitative and quantitative data analysis could make a bad program look good or misrepresent the program's effect (or lack thereof) on certain populations or participants. Yes, those outliers matter, as do the voices that confront your findings. We must resist the urge to ignore negative outcomes in our reporting, and here we provide you with approaches to help you safeguard against the analysis and reporting pitfalls we describe. The words you choose in your report matter. The way you visualize your data also matters. To be trauma-informed during analysis and reporting, you need to involve the appropriate stakeholders and report findings in ways that make people *care* and spur them to *take action*. In other words, we want your work to help address the problem, not just describe it.

Introduction

It may seem unnecessary to talk about analysis and reporting in a book about trauma-informed research and evaluation. After all, the participants have gone home. At this point, there's nothing to worry about, right?

It is at this point, however, that our minds should be turning toward any potential negative outcomes because of the conclusions in our evaluation report. We may be tempted to go about reporting in a business-as-usual way, assuming that just by letting the "facts speak for themselves," we'll be doing our job. As we'll see, there are pitfalls to be avoided at every stage in the analysis process.

In this chapter, we talk about some common analysis and interpretation pitfalls, their connection to trauma sensitivity, and some safeguards we can take. Then we introduce you to some concepts in trauma-informed reporting.

Analysis

What does data analysis have to do with trauma? Well, resource use is important, and using scarce human and financial resources for ineffective programs can harm the interests of traumatized populations and does not help the broader cause of social justice and change. By making a program that bears bad fruit look good, we may just be inflating the ego and influence of the already powerful, like our funders. Dishonest or low-quality analysis practice may be covering up the pain and continuing trauma of those we seek to support. Let's dive in and see a few pitfalls and corresponding approaches to avoiding them.

Analysis Pitfall 1: The Wizard's Tower

Classic ideas of what a researcher is may cause people to imagine them as the wizard in the tower—a proverbial Saruman the Wise, gazing into his seeing stone with a supernatural and all-seeing perspective. As we've (hopefully) done our time, gotten a good education, and are employing sound trauma-informed social science methodology, we are the ones with the best view from our tower, right?

Stepping away from the silly metaphors, evaluators and researchers who do not include important stakeholders in the analysis, interpretation, and reporting are at risk of cutting out stakeholders at one of the most vulnerable times in the evaluation—when we are making judgments and drawing conclusions. This would transgress the principles of Collaboration and Mutuality, Trust and Transparency, and Safety. We must come down from our towers and engage the community throughout the entire study process. Remember all that talk about community engagement? An evaluator who draws their own conclusions from the data without checking in with stakeholders—including affected community members—risks doing damage. This is the most common assertion in the literature when it comes to analysis and reporting. Bosk (2023) states, "Asking clients how they make meaning of the presenting issues allows for the cultural perspective to be included in . . . the evaluation process" (p. 8). Additionally, she says, "Regular reports on evaluation activities and findings should be given at regular intervals. Infographics and other ways of sharing evaluation findings that are accessible should be used whenever possible" (p. 5). In this way, we are consistently checking our trauma-informed assumptions, interpretations, and findings as we go along.

Some evaluation models are very intentional about radical inclusion of stakeholders at the analysis stage. For instance, fourth-generation evaluation, or **constructivist evaluation** (Guba & Lincoln, 1989), includes a comprehensive process for stakeholder engagement throughout the evaluation. Specifically, we love their suggestion of using peer debriefing, negative case analysis, progressive subjectivity, and member checking to advance equity in analysis and reporting.

- **Peer debriefing** involves engaging with a neutral colleague to talk through hypotheses, conclusions, and interpretations, as well as processing any emotional reactions to events in the course of the evaluation.

- **Negative case analysis** is the "process of revising working hypotheses in the light of hindsight, with an eye toward developing and refining a given hypothesis (or set of them) until it accounts for all known cases" (Guba & Lincoln, 1989, pp. 237–238). They compare this to statistical tests in quantitative analysis in that the approach "provides confidence that the evaluator has tried and rejected all rival hypotheses save the appropriate one" (p. 238).

- **Progressive subjectivity** is "the process of monitoring the evaluator's . . . own developing construction" by way of documenting presuppositions. Along the way, they compare notes with stakeholders about conceptions. "If the inquirer 'finds' only what they expected to find, initially, or seems to become 'stuck' or 'frozen' on some intermediate construction, credibility suffers" (p. 238).

- **Member checking** may be a familiar concept for some readers who have studied qualitative research methods before. This is "the process of testing hypotheses, data, preliminary categories, and interpretations with members of the stakeholding groups from whom the original constructions were collected" (p. 239). Guba and Lincoln (1989) maintain that this is the premier method for maintaining trust and transparency with stakeholders. However, we caution readers that there are more ways—more accessible and equitable ways—to member-check than asking participants to read transcripts, summaries, or reports.

These techniques can go a long way toward helping us avoid getting comfortable in the wizard's tower. With humility as our leading value, we can guard against errors that can at best fail to paint an accurate picture or at worst cause people to draw conclusions that are damaging to traumatized populations.

Analysis Pitfall 2: The Central Tendency Goblin

Aside from leaning on one's own biased understanding, another challenge is the overreliance on measures of **central tendency** (such as means, medians, etc.) when analyzing quantitative data. This may sound wonky and a bit far off from the concerns of the trauma affected. However, there is a real concern that in the social sciences, the focus on the "average" or "typical" often excludes those in the margins. Consider the example of how many studies use the male body as the "default" in medical research (Plevkova et al., 2020), making the male body the standard for diagnoses and treatment while simultaneously excluding females and transgender people. This happens in qualitative as well as quantitative analysis.

In a similar way, when evaluators only report measures of central tendency, we are presenting the image of what response to an intervention may be for the "typical" participant. For quantitative analysis, we often focus on means and employ statistical tests that essentially look for generalization or differences in the typical. What is the problem with this? After all, we do care that an intervention is broadly effective or acceptable.

The problem is that not all our study participants fit the average, which requires us to look at subgroups to see who is fairing especially well or especially poorly. As you know by now, trauma-affected people often experience life and behave differently from "average" people (if there is such a thing). This practice transgresses the Principles of Safety and Cultural, Historical, and Gender Issues. Overlooking "outliers" results in ignoring people who are perhaps experiencing the lingering effects of a traumatic and unjust system. This could be because of a difference in ability to take advantage of program services, a difference in comprehension, or a difference in need.

Traumatic events and systems can cause many kinds of disparities, contributing to inequities in how effective a program is (or how harmful it is to a participant), and could contribute to even more trauma. The issue here concerns what we do with the people at the ends of the bell curve for whom the intervention does not work so well. What if an intervention has a significant effect for the mean but leaves a number at the margins worse off—even if that number of people is not "statistically significant"? Failing to look deeper into the margins causes moral injury to researchers who leave some in the dust for the sake of the majority.

In experimental research, this problem is known as **treatment effect heterogeneity**, which Imai and Ratkovic (2013) define as "the degree to which different treatments have differential causal effects on each unit. For example, ascertaining subpopulations for which a treatment is most beneficial (or harmful) is an important goal of many clinical trials" (p. 443). Smith (2022) highlights the pertinence of treatment effect heterogeneity for researchers concerned with equity:

> Programs that engender widely varying treatment effects among their participants may also increase inequality in outcomes in undesirable ways. Some programs may actually make some participants worse off. Learning that a program has a lot of idiosyncratic treatment effect heterogeneity, particularly when it suggests negative impacts for some participants, may provide a spur to program improvement via more attention to implementation fidelity, to the screening of applicants, or to participants' progress through the program. (p. 10)

In these cases, we suggest that quantitative analyses be used to identify those who have not fared well and explore their stories. Doing this could lead to identifying processes and systems that continue to traumatize certain groups of people.

The focus of this section has been on quantitative analysis, but the same issues can arise with qualitative research. Although normally attention is given to the predominant themes and narratives in qualitative data, we must give additional credence to the voices of dissent or dissatisfaction that we encounter. Even if it is the sole voice of pain, they should not be ignored. We should ask the questions, "What has gone wrong for this person in particular, and what could be done to level the playing field for them? How many more people like this are out there (or in our programs) that we don't know about?" We encourage employing the negative case analysis mentioned in Pitfall 1 (Guba & Lincoln, 1989).

Analysis Pitfall 3: Outcome Hacking

Those from the quantitative research world have likely heard of the concept of ***p*-hacking**. This refers to the practice of collecting many different indicators in a study and then testing the statistical significance of a wide range of associations and differences. Although this may sound reasonable, it can result in study findings appearing more significant than they are. If you test a hundred different associations, the chances of a false positive significance test go up, making the study findings seem more definitive and airtight (Head, Holman, Lanfear, Kahn, & Jennions, 2015).

Parallel to *p*-hacking, **outcome hacking** is a similar practice that happens when evaluators analyze data, categorizing it and slicing it many different ways to identify any plausible improvements that appear to have occurred. If this happens over a wide range of indicators, the chance of a false positive result is inflated. The risk is even greater when using data to which statistical tests are not being applied, as there is no associated significance value. Often, such results are taken to be fact. This pitfall could threaten the safety of those we seek to serve if they obscure real harms or an ineffective program.

How, then, can evaluators and researchers safeguard against outcome hacking? First, evaluators should use care when selecting indicators and deciding what tests they are going to conduct during the analysis stage. Rather than conducting scatter-shot data collection, the design stage should feature thoughtful and careful indicator selection, limiting it to data that directly relate to program outcomes that are aligned with the established values. Second, evaluators should report *all* associations and be careful about masking those that appear to be less favorable. Show it all, not just the favorable aspects! Third, evaluators should consider ways to preregister their studies. Although there are efforts in formal research fields to establish preregistration systems to counteract *p*-hacking, such a parallel system does not exist for program evaluations. One could remedy this by preregistering with another colleague or simply deciding beforehand what tests would be conducted and reported and include that in your report. At the very least, the evaluation team can hold one another accountable on this point.

When it comes to qualitative analysis, this means looking out for any reported negative consequences that participants raised and being sure to include them in your reports.

Reporting

When I (Aaron) was a teen, I took a family trip to Berlin, Germany, to visit my aunt and uncle. It was such a wonderful cross-cultural and linguistic immersion experience, about which somehow the press caught wind. "Local teen goes to Europe" was perhaps more newsworthy in the early 2000s than it is now. I don't remember much about that conversation with the reporter. I just remember eagerly anticipating my appearance in the newspaper.

When the day came, I had my dad drive me to the gas station to purchase a copy of the January 2, 2005, *Holland Sentinel.* Flipping through the pages with glee, I finally came to the story. There I was in the accompanying photo, grinning like the little bespectacled dweeb I was. I read with smugness the summary of my academic accomplishments and my recent international adventure. Then the article wrapped up with a nice juicy quote: "It wasn't as different as I thought it would be," I had told the reporter. "It was just like Michigan, except everyone speaks German."

Imagine my horror as I sat there. Of all the brilliant (or at least forgettable) things I'd uttered to that reporter, she chose *that*? I'm sure the reporter was a perfectly well-meaning person, I tried to tell myself. But I still couldn't believe it. My reputation thoroughly sullied, I'd never be able to run for public office.

Presenting and Depicting Traumatized Populations

This sad but true anecdote may seem silly. My first brush with infamy was relatively harmless. Turns out I underestimated my town's ability to move on from the cringy statements of a fifteen-and-a-half-year-old. But if such an innocent statement had mortified me, how much more must we guard the narratives of those with whom we're working?

Presenting and depicting traumatized populations can be a moment of heightened risk to emotional and physical safety but can also present an opportunity for evaluators to allow participants to exercise agency and choice. Risks to emotional and physical safety can include the following:

- Portraying groups in ways that are unflattering or promote stereotypes that can lead to increased emotional trauma or stigma.
- Portraying individuals in ways that are unflattering, emotionally damaging, or traumatizing, even if their exact identity is hidden.
- Carelessness in reporting, leading to someone's identity being disclosed. This could simply be embarrassing, or it could be physically dangerous.

So, what guidelines can we offer for reporting in trauma-informed ways? First, we recommend that evaluators use collaboration to meet the purposes of many of the SAMHSA Principles. Bosk (2023) advocates for a radical level of openness with participants, creating space in which they can disagree with, push back on, or offer different interpretations of the proposed study findings. We advocate that the evaluation team collaborate with affected populations in making meaning of data analysis and presenting findings in the report. This can help advance safety by offering opportunities for others to flag ways in which you may be insensitive in quotes or descriptions used. They can also flag safety concerns or privacy issues. Extra sets of eyes can also call attention to historical injustice and oppression having to do with representations and depictions you might not catch. Last, this will help build trust, empowerment, and collaboration with your participants.

The Danger of Trauma Porn

In one of Martha's workshops, a participant used the phrase **trauma porn**, which occurs when evaluators and researchers use the painful trauma story of any person for purposes that fail to dignify the individual, thereby serving to sadly "maintain the very structure of trauma and oppression it seeks to dismantle" (Gatwiri & Mapedzahama, 2022, p. 279). Gatwiri and Mapedzahama (2022) define Black trauma porn as a "performative racial project that utilizes the racial pain of Black people for the purposes of shocking people into an emotional response" (p. 278). The media use trauma porn frequently, especially if their motives are to further embed racial stereotypes and justify political platforms.

Other examples of trauma porn include when funders, clients, or researchers want to exploit and sensationalize people's trauma stories for their own benefits, such as fund-raising, marketing, or flag waving on websites or in annual reports. For example, commercials showing starving children of color covered with flies move some viewers to donate to the organization while reinforcing negative Western ideas of the world's poor at the same time (creating space for blaming them for their own poverty). The temptation to sensationalize stories is real, especially when funders apply pressure to or design studies to elicit sensational (and self-serving) stories. However, as trauma-informed researchers and evaluators, we have ways of consolidating data and presenting themes or highlights so that we never have to tell someone's story in a way that dehumanizes or exploits them—and perhaps tell those stories in ways that illustrate resilience while calling attention to real human needs.

Another aspect of trauma porn is failing to frame stories in ways that highlight intersectionality (Crenshaw et al., 1995) or choosing certain stories that may land well with certain audiences. For example, stories of women of color might be exploited to appeal to white donors, as long as the women are not queer or trans (Trott, 2019). We must respect the participants who trusted us with their story by keeping their stories safe and using their stories and experiences in dignifying and humanizing ways that lead to healing and change. If funders or clients insist on sensationalizing a story, it must be done only with a person's explicit consent and with compensation, the likes of which should be determined by the individual.

Even with consent and compensation, we may still transgress our values, ethics, and the principle of Trustworthiness and Transparency. We should steer funders and clients away from engaging in trauma porn and from allowing our participants to be seduced by voyeuristic funders or clients (Trott, 2019). Trauma-informed evaluators and researchers must be prepared to have those hard conversations despite the power trauma porn has to raise awareness and money.

Consider the Audience

Trauma-informed reporting also goes beyond the process and content of the report. It also involves advancing the accessibility of the report to those reading it. Ensuring accessibility is important for inclusion of those with physical, learning, or intellectual disabilities or of lower education levels. It also provides for the maximum comprehension and use by evaluation consumers. If we do not pay attention to issues of equity in report accessibility, then the influence of our work is blunted, which is a disservice to everyone involved. Issues of equity in the presentation of evaluation findings extend to reading level, legibility of colors, symbology, fonts, and the like, as well as the readability of charts, graphs, and tables. Data visualization experts like Stephanie Evergreen and Ann Emery offer online courses to help those charged with portraying data do so in clear and accessible ways.

Additionally, it is good practice to offer different versions of the report calibrated to different populations and uses such as developing a one-page summary, an infographic, an executive summary, and a full report (see Hutchinson, 2017).

Preventing Misuse

Beyond just making sure that our reports are useful and accessible, evaluators need to be savvy about the possibility that our work could be misused by people with ulterior motives. This is especially true when it comes to the evaluative conclusions and recommendations. In Chapter 10, we emphasized the importance of clarifying and aligning the values that would be used in an evaluation to draw conclusions regarding success at the end of the study process. In that case, if this was done well, the conclusions of the report should be well aligned with the interests of the community being studied. If, however, values are tacit, complicit with those in power, or misunderstood, there is a chance that the results could be co-opted by those who do not necessarily want to change the status quo or what is best for the community.

Handle with Care: Emotionally Charged Content

In the summer of 1955, the American public was confronted with the searing image of racially motivated violence. *JET* magazine had published the photographs of Emmett Till, a young Black teenager who was killed while vising family in Mississippi ("When One Mother Defied America," 2016). The boy's mother insisted on an open casket at the funeral and for the presence of the press, stating, "Let the people see what I've seen."[1]

Scholars argue that these images marked a turning point in the Civil Rights Movement. Harold and DeLuca (2005) state, "The incontestable reality of black bodies in pain was used to confer the status of incontestable reality on to the belief in white supremacy" (p. 268). They note that Till's mother, by insisting on the public exhibition of her son's body, "transform[ed] her son from a victim of white racism to an unforgettable symbol that mobilized a generation of activists" (p. 271).

Few evaluators will ever have to convey such devastating images or information in their work. However, this underscores the emotional power of information to motivate action. Sharing data engages emotions, making it a political, powerful, and sensitive act.

Not all information evokes emotions equally. Go to the Rockefeller Institute of Government Mass Shooting Factsheet (*https://rockinst.org/gun-violence/mass-shooting-factsheet*), which is updated regularly. Consider the facts, figures, icons, charts, and colors on the site. How did you feel reading these figures? Although they might be upsetting or cause one to think sad thoughts, these kinds of numbers are nowhere near as disturbing as the anecdote about Emmett Till shared above. They would certainly pale in comparison with the images in terms of their power to evoke and persuade.

How can this be? How can the traumatic story and images of a single person be so much more emotionally powerful than such massive numbers? The suffering contained in those figures, after all, far outweighs the suffering of an individual, and such figures illustrate the suffering of entire communities and populations.

Numbers like those above are sometimes put before the public with the intent to create some kind of call to action or change, but the scale of the atrocity can have the opposite of the desired effect. Psychologists have identified a phenomenon called **psychic numbing**, which decreases people's ability to empathize when they are exposed to larger and larger numbers of people experiencing death, disaster, or suffering (Slovic, Zionts, Woods, Goodman, & Jinks, 2011). Reporting findings in cold numerical terms in this way fails to recognize and empathize with those who have been harmed, set the context for the events, connect the numbers to real human beings, and move people to take actions to alleviate suffering.

[1]We'd differentiate this from trauma porn. Although the traumatic photo and open casket was evidence of violence against Black bodies, it was not done to exploit Till or his family and was not done for profit. Till's mother, who was traumatized herself, transformed her pain into action that changed a movement. It was a personal decision, made by her and her alone. Instead of trauma porn, we see her action as an example of traumatic growth.

Big and Little Data: Infusing Emotions into the Numbers

Despite what many might think, numbers are not neutral, nor are they abstract. Numbers are symbols that represent something or someone real. Researchers must do more than collect, analyze, and report numbers. They, along with their participants and community, must bring those numbers to life, attach them to emotions, and motivate people to take some kind of action. And while traditional, European models of research and reporting so often seen in peer reviewed academic journals require adherence to an uninteresting and stifling outline, we have a responsibility to do better and do more. A bunch of graphs and a bullet list of six recommendations at the end of a report doesn't cut it anymore—not in a world where research and evaluation can play a vital role in our very survival on this planet.

Dr. Echo Rivera is an expert in effective presentations (i.e., sharing data in ways that compel the audience to care and take action). Her work is grounded in psychology, and as a result, she unapologetically deviates from the typical academic model of presenting research, known informally as Death by PowerPoint. In her professional development training courses, Dr. Rivera teaches that even in a data-driven world, people still make decisions based on their emotions. Statistics and facts rarely drive people to take action or cause people to change their minds. Only when emotions are touched and people can relate to data from an emotional place will they genuinely understand what the numbers and trend lines mean and what actions they can take.

Let's use a data narrative from an ACEs study to differentiate between a trauma-informed tone—one that people can connect with emotionally—and one that doesn't.

> Among U.S. adults from all 50 states and the District of Columbia surveyed during 2011–2020, approximately two thirds reported at least one ACE; one in six reported four or more ACEs. ACEs were highest among women, persons aged 25–34 years, non-Hispanic American Indian or Alaska Native adults, non-Hispanic multiracial adults, adults with less than a high school education, and adults who were unemployed or unable to work. Prevalence of individual and total number of ACEs varied across jurisdictions. (Swedo et al., 2023, p. 714)

I (Martha) feel nothing. Apologies to the numerous authors of this study, but seriously—so what? What am I supposed to think, feel, or do with this description of this important public health issue? Are these facts supposed to make me care? Because they don't. These statistics are designed to report, not spur emotions or actions, because, as Echo Rivera (n.d.) says, "it wasn't a study designed to be read by mythical researchers/academics who don't exist, because even researchers/academics find each other boring! But it doesn't even work with this intended audience, because they don't even understand how to communicate effectively to other academics!" And this is exactly how so many of us are trained to report findings.

No wonder research has little influence on policy and practice. What if those findings were reported like this:

> The ACEs study revealed that for every three children, two of them have suffered from and survived at least one traumatic childhood experience. Worse than that, one out of six have survived *four or more* traumatic experiences! Children are suffering. Why is childhood unsafe and traumatic for so many children, no matter where they live or what their culture is? How can communities reverse these trends so that children can develop in healthy ways?

See the difference? Feel the difference? We encourage you to take advantage of the many experts we've mentioned who can teach you how to visualize, report, and present data in ways that ensure your research has value, meaning, and purpose. In the meantime, every one of us should be asking, "If our research cannot evoke an emotional response, like outrage or empathy, why do it? Why would we spend decades (and millions of dollars) researching and evaluating the same issues and programs only to report trends and numbers? Isn't the point to use that data to facilitate positive change and improve lives? Is it any wonder that most initiatives and programs show little to no positive change over time?" Yet researchers and evaluators continue getting government and philanthropic grants that don't result in real, substantial change or life improvement. Perhaps a trauma-informed lens could help facilitate a shift in thinking about how and why we bother to do research.

Our point is that we have an obligation to make the numbers talk if we don't design studies that elicit conversations with participants. How one reacts when exposed to numbers and statistics on human suffering depends on myriad factors, including but not limited to race/ethnicity, socioeconomic status, gender, profession, closeness to the issue, social justice orientation, and political affiliation. Although we cannot control or prevent trauma responses to quantitative data, we can, as empathetic researchers and evaluators who are also human beings, understand the traumatic effects of some statistics and do a better job to humanize them. Given the current sociopolitical trend to discount and distrust facts, we also need to be prepared to defend the validity of our data *and* explain why the findings matter. When groups dispute facts (i.e., it's all fake news, or the government made up the numbers), they discount the very existence of the people (and their families) that the numbers represent.

Quantitative data can be effectively used to highlight discrepancies, inequities, and gaps, which could create opportunities for institutional, structural, and program improvements and social, policy, political, and behavioral changes. It is here that those who work with and use quantitative data have the most opportunity to wear a trauma-informed lens when interrogating and reporting the numbers.

Simply put, it is not enough to put percentages in tables and graphs with descriptors and let others decide what, if anything, to do with them—or leave them on their own to interpret the data through their own lenses. Activity 11.1 gives you an opportunity to practice this skill.

Content Warnings: To Use or Not to Use?

Advocates of trauma-informed practices sometimes encourage people to give **content warnings** (often called *trigger warnings*), which let audiences know something is coming that could unleash stress responses and/or traumatic memories. One might assume that being a trauma-informed evaluator and researcher means universally employing content warnings when sharing data and stories that could be disturbing to people. We have noticed an increase in content warnings everywhere, from the news media to academia, which buys into the current climate of ensuring that no one (particularly white people) feels uncomfortable. However, there is a debate among scholars as to the efficacy of the content warnings, with some high-profile advocates turning about-face on the subject (see Filipovic, 2023). We do not categorically recommend the use of content warnings, as we see some potential issues that give us pause, such as the following:

- They may send a message of expected emotional fragility which is counterproductive to promoting healing and resilience. Avoidance being a core symptom of PTSD, encouraging people to avoid distressing stimuli, thus sidestepping difficult emotions, may get in the way of their making progress.

- They may *increase* anticipatory anxiety of the viewer of the content, as evidenced by a recent meta-analysis (Bridgland, Jones, & Bellett, 2024).

- They may pathologize the experience of difficult emotions, heightening the avoidance response identified above (Newcomb & Venning, 2024). In fact, what many refer to as being triggered or retraumatized in popular discourse seems to be simple discomfort. This would contrast with genuine triggering, which could include dissociation, physiological arousal, crisis behavior, flashbacks, and other extreme psychiatric symptoms (Newcomb & Venning, 2024).

- They may allow for the avoidance of mere discomfort on the part of the privileged (and the mountains moved to keep white people from feeling uncomfortable). In providing opportunities to "look away," we may be offering a way to depoliticize what could otherwise be a powerful force for change or even elevate the status quo. Would a content warning on the Emmett Till images, for instance, have blunted their impact?

Ultimately, while we think there is strong evidence that content warnings may not be universally helpful, we do not have fully developed guidelines. It may take a while for the science to shake out. While we wait for the researchers to do their work, we ask that you use critical thinking when considering their use. We suggest that you ask yourself these questions before implementing them:

1. "Do I know specific information about my audience that would merit a content warning (e.g., presenting on a campus that has recently experienced a shooting may need special care around violent accounts and images)?"
2. "Is this content appropriate for my audience when considering factors such as age, education level, field of practice? If so, why would I need a content warning?"
3. "Do I anticipate that this information could cause real harm? If so, why am I using this content in the first place?"
4. "If this content is disturbing, could I alter it in some way to blunt the impact? Or is the emotion reaction part of the very goal of the content?"
5. "Might a content warning allow some people who really need to confront this reality to avoid it altogether?"
6. "Am I using this content warning because of a legitimate concern for emotional safety, or am I simply doing so to minimize risk to my audience?"

We hope that before slapping a content warning on anything that may seem unpleasant, these questions will help you pause and think critically about it. We may not always do it just right. We'd rather you do it wrong with thoughtfulness and humility than wrong with a simplistic and one-size-fits-all approach. Remember, being trauma-informed is not about avoiding all possible uncomfortable emotions and triggers. As we've said, we can never control or anticipate what a person's triggers may be. The point is treating those in distress with calm and respect. Part of that is conveying a sense of confidence that they can handle difficult emotions, creating safe and brave spaces for them, and being an empathetic person.

Peer Debriefing and Dissemination

After taking trauma-informed steps throughout a study, how then do we exit an evaluation? We believe that every evaluation should be grounded in an authentic relationship between the evaluators, the funders, and the community being served. Just like it's not cool to break up with a partner via text, the technique of breaking up via a 700-page report and invoice delivery should not be evaluators' default exit strategy either. The ideal closure of the "evaluationship" should involve dissemination and peer debriefing in ways that allow processing, interpretation, and action. This allows for maximum use for evaluators to ensure that evaluative conclusions are warranted and give closure to the constituents who are often left wondering whatever happened with that data they provided.

The Corporation for a Skilled Workforce (Williams & Choitz, 2024) recommends that researchers should consider the following practices:

- *Follow up with participants.* If someone was affected by the research experience, then it can be helpful to check in later or offer resources depending on the situation.
- *Follow up with facilitators.* If there was a difficult or emotional situation, then it may also be appropriate to follow up with colleagues as well.
- *Continually confirm the process.* Discuss with other facilitators how the process is going and where there may be a need for tweaks to ensure the safety and comfort of all participating, even if this means not all research activities will be uniform.
- *Disseminate the information collected with care and respect for the participants.* Follow best culturally responsive and participatory practices around dissemination to ensure participants' stories and experiences are thoughtfully reported. Consider if the information being shared were about your mother, father, brother, sister, or children. Would you describe it in the same way?

We advocate, if possible, that evaluators and researchers hold debriefing sessions with the research team and hold multiple community listening sessions for the presentation of results and conversations with constituents *and* that funders build the cost of doing so into the budget during the design phase. This allows the community to give feedback, to process any difficult truths that may have come out, and to decide what actions to take. Treating evaluation and research partnerships like valuable relationships is part of being trauma-informed.

WRAP-UP

In conclusion, contrary to what many of us may believe and practice, analysis and reporting should not be a me-and-my-computer affair. Just like the rest of TIER, we advocate that these evaluation components center the relationship with our beneficiaries and be collaborative. The chance for traumatized people to tell their own stories is a powerful part of healing and developing resilience. And they deserve poststudy follow-up as well. Not only should they be able to participate in the data collection process; telling a collective story can yield added benefits. It also in the end protects us and them and allows for genuine closure and a send-off process. Additionally, we need to do better at how we visualize, report, and present quantitative data so that it addresses the *so what?* and encourages *action.* We have to continue collaborating and engaging with communities to make meaning and use study findings to make people care and want to take action. We hope that by following our recommendations here, your studies can be more useful, more meaningful, and more influential, thus building resilience.

CHAPTER 11 ACTIVITY

The United States government via the Census monitors and reports on child poverty rates. For this activity, we invite you to go directly to the Census website (*census.gov*) and skim through the report titled *Child Poverty Fell to Record Low 5.2% in 2021* (Burns, Fox, & Wilson, 2022). The report, whose primary author is an economist, includes many graphics, tables, and narratives. Find a topic or paragraph and its data visualization, read it, then answer these questions:

ACTIVITY REFLECTION QUESTIONS

1. Did any narrative and chart make you care, or care more, about child poverty and how it could be alleviated? Did any data evoke emotions? If so, what emotions did you feel?
2. Were the root causes of child poverty mentioned or explored?
3. Do you think an economist has a responsibility to expand on the numbers and talk about how reducing child poverty also reduces ACEs and promotes healthy child development?
4. Imagine how the government could publish (and publicize) this very important information in ways that would make the public and/or voters care more about the issue of child poverty and one solution. What collaborations are needed?
5. W. E. B. Du Bois wrote, "When you have mastered numbers, you will in fact no longer be reading numbers, any more than you read words when reading books. You will be reading meanings" (quoted in Thompson, 2022). How does this quote speak to you? How can you get better at reading and reporting meanings?

Activity Discussion

Our concern with the ways in which so much quantitative data is reported is that researchers miss opportunities to call attention to the larger picture or the implications of the findings in ways that matter to policymakers, constituents, taxpayers, or community members. Quantitative analysists and report writers also need to be trauma-informed to do this work. Quantitative studies, especially those relating to social justice, public health, criminal justice, gun and interpersonal violence, educational achievement, and other such topics should be reported and presented in ways that *make people care and want to take action*. In this instance, introductory paragraphs explaining why child poverty is a problem and how it negatively affects health, well-being, safety, longevity, educational achievement, and juvenile delinquency would build a case for why reducing child poverty matters.

Analysts could show the connection between ACEs and child poverty. Explain what people were able to do with the tax credit relief so that the public understands stresses caused by poverty, such as food insecurity and the ability to obtain and keep adequate housing. And because the data were disaggregated by race, why not provide explanations for why Hispanic poverty rates were reduced more than Asian, Black, and white rates? Could the data be visualized differently to call attention to the racial disparities? What equity issues do we not know about? Finally, what barriers remain for families living in poverty that still need to be addressed and cannot be remedied with just the tax credit, and do those barriers differ among the various groups? They disaggregated the data but left so much unaddressed.

Wait, you say. That is not the job of a data analyst—especially an economist. Their job is just to analyze and report the numbers. It's up to program directors and policymakers to decide what to do.

Wrong. Most people are relatively clueless about how to interpret data and statistics. Statistics appear to us as neutral facts (even when we know numbers are easily manipulated). They lack the *so what*? We believe that it is the job of the analysts to report data and findings in ways that make people care. And to care, we need to first understand the problem. The fact that so many American children live in poverty is repugnant given the vast wealth of the nation. Child poverty is a leading cause of ACEs and traumatized brains. How can anyone talk about child poverty without talking about the associated trauma and life-long effects of trauma, as well as the cost of trauma, to society? Perhaps there is an insidious purpose to the silos blocking interagency collaboration.

There are two governmental agencies involved in Activity 11.1: the U.S. Census Bureau and the CDC. However, the CDC's role is invisible because those agencies are not working together to use child poverty data to drive social, structural, systemic, and economic changes. And this is the standard operating procedure in all siloed institutions and systems. Our point is to raise awareness about how data are analyzed and reported; how findings are used, misused, or not used; and how integrating trauma awareness with quantitative data analysis could be a game changer. Additionally, including stories from people whose lives were improved by the tax credit would give power to the numbers—but explaining the benefits of mixed-methods research is beyond the scope of our book.

PART IV
Growing TIER

You've almost made it through the book. Perhaps you consider yourself totally equipped to do TIER, and it would be great if you did! However, the work does not end here. It's not enough for us to be trauma-informed researchers and evaluators when programs, organizations, and entire systems also need to be trauma-informed. The final chapter in this book gives you some insights as to how you—as a person of influence—can expand on the Six Principles in your sphere of influence so that programs, systems, and organizations can also become trauma-informed.

CHAPTER 12

Trauma-Informed Programs, Organizations, and Systems

There is no there or an end to this work.
Being trauma-informed and promoting resilience
is that big a deal. It's gotta get done.

WHAT YOU'LL LEARN

Being a trauma-informed researcher and evaluator is not enough to change programs and systems. In this chapter, we describe what trauma-informed programs, organizations, and systems are (or could be) and once again use a SAMHSA framework for developing a trauma-informed approach to organizational and systems change. Any organization and system that provides services to people can benefit from becoming trauma-informed including but not limited to education, criminal justice, juvenile justice, child welfare, human and family services, physical/mental/behavioral health, government, and the military. All these systems "have the potential to ease or exacerbate an individual's capacity to cope with traumatic experiences" (SAMHSA, 2014, p. 3). We first discuss SAMHSA's domains of a trauma-informed organization. Next, we provide an example of how a single individual—a victim of domestic violence—can potentially come in contact with dozens of agencies within multiple systems, and those contacts can be either triggering and retraumatizing or resilience promoting. We highlight two organizations in the United States that are working toward creating a trauma-informed organization or system and then lead you to some national and regional coalitions working on various aspects of creating trauma-informed systems.

Introduction

Our focus so far has been on an individual researcher's or evaluator's capacity to bring trauma-informed practices into their work, regardless of position or project.

But we know that in many cases, the actual program being evaluated—and/or the organization implementing the program, and/or the funder of the program, and/or the funder of the research/evaluation, and/or the system of which the program is a part of—is not trauma-informed or even aware that they should be and could be. We acknowledge this tension (and many others) and the expanse of the work creating a trauma-informed world. We believe that the work does not begin or end with TIER. However, as evaluators and researchers, we hold power to influence programs, organizations, and systems. In many cases, evaluators and researchers—as either outside consultants or internal evaluators—can raise questions, inform protocol development, rethink desired program outcomes, and recommend system-wide integrations and the applications of findings.

Evaluators and researchers also have a relationship with clients (programs/institutions) and funders, so bringing a conversation about trauma-informed practices to the table is within reach. We know that programs, institutions, and systems cause or have caused harm and trauma at worst and, at best, may not have helped participants and recipients heal and transform their lives in the ways the program had perhaps intended. We also know that programs, institutions, and systems consist of *people* and that people can replicate their own trauma behaviors in their workplace. And we believe most people are capable of change. We encourage evaluators and researchers to take what they learn in this book and the additional resources we provide and use their influence and skills to expand the application of SAMHSA's Six Principles to programs, organizations, and systems.

Expanding the Work in Your Sphere of Influence

As more people understand trauma as a widespread public health problem that is both harmful and costly, it is important to consider how we can transform programs. Organizational factors can play a significant role in the level of compassion fatigue experienced by workers, and risk factors can be helped or exacerbated by the organization itself. Environmental conditions that strain workers' capacity to perform their roles to the best of their ability, such as poor ergonomics and lighting, as well as time crunches that prevent workers from taking needed and necessary time off to create a healthy work–life balance, result in increased rates of compassion fatigue and burnout (Cetrano et al., 2017).

If you have ever interacted with nonprofit organizations or public agencies as a client, you know that sometimes we can walk away feeling dehumanized, unheard, and uncared for, or even completely traumatized and overwhelmed. The more transactional the encounter and the more dehumanizing the process, the more harm is done. It is a vicious cycle. Compassion fatigue, burnout, and STS negatively affect how organizational employees interact with the public, their clients, and colleagues. Rather than "dismantling" these traumatizing systems (and their white supremist/capitalist foundations and structures), we propose transforming systems with equity-focused trauma-informed organizational practices.

SAMHSA's Six Principles imply that organizations and systems must also become more effective, equitable, and trauma-informed. Research by Dr. Ann Masten, a resilience researcher at the University of Minnesota, focuses on resilient systems and how they can affect an individual's ability to be resilient. Masten and Motti-Stefandi (2020) define resilience as "the capacity of a dynamic system to adapt successfully to challenges that threated the function, survival, or development of the system" (p. 95). The COVID-19 pandemic, followed by the second term of U.S. President Donald Trump, have stressed institutional systems (nationally and globally) in unprecedented ways and called on all of us to be resilient in the face of upheaval, chaos, and blatant attacks on democracy. In a 2014 lecture about resistance and transformative politics, Dr. Angela Y. Davis told us that we have to act as if it were possible to radically transform the world, and do it all the time. Let's start with transforming programs.

Trauma-Informed Programs

"Human adaptation and development at the individual or social level arises from interactions of many processes and systems" (Masten & Motti-Stefandi, 2020, p. 99). Humans interact with programs constantly; they are unavoidable. But trauma-informed programs are those that are *intentionally* designed to incorporate the Six Principles and promote resilience. They do not have to be programs explicitly for trauma-affected people, but program designers and managers who have been trained in trauma and the Six Principles can work to integrate the Principles into policy and practice within the boundaries of a program or initiative. Some programs naturally incorporate a few of the Six Principles, even if unintentionally, based on their intended outcomes and the people they serve. The difference between those programs and trauma-informed programs is *intent*. Have program designers and practitioners consciously and carefully integrated the Six Principles and an understanding of trauma into program design and delivery? Or was it happenstance that a few Principles were met without intentionally recognizing the symptoms and effects of trauma, as we saw in our literature review in Chapter 4?

Let's look at the following scenario to see what we mean by intent. Many arts-based programs (summer camps, after-school programs, etc.) offer youth the opportunity to express themselves through their art form (Voice, Choice, and Empowerment). These programs frequently target students of color who live in underresourced neighborhoods or who attend schools with many low-income families (often called Title I schools). However, programs may overlook Historical, Cultural, and Gender Issues by not creating space to address and transform inequities, or program staff may be uncomfortable with certain topics, such as immigration or racial justice. (Or, as is the case in Florida as of 2025, staff are *prohibited* from openly addressing these issues.) The program may provide opportunities for students to co-create or lead projects, develop relationships with peers and adults, and work collaboratively on murals or musical pieces (Mutuality and Collaboration), but there is still little or no awareness of ACEs or how to create a safe space for Mutuality and Collaboration to happen. Some arts-based programs focus on having a professional artist or performer instruct proper technique, and others allow students to choose their own project, to interpret performance style, or to create original music and choreography. Arts camps and after-school programs typically expose and involve students in the arts beyond what is offered in their schools (if the arts are offered at all). This is a good thing, as the arts are healing.

However, if the teachers and teaching artists were trained to be trauma-informed and they intentionally integrated as many of the Six Principles as possible, they could easily implement the program with the intent of being trauma-informed. Such a program would intentionally create space to explore social justice issues; would integrate trust-building activities, such as Circles and games; and would invite participants to determine what they need to feel mentally, emotionally, and physically safe where the classes take place. Students would be offered various options for revising their work, feedback would build on students' strengths, and students would be given options for presenting or performing their work as they are comfortable. But to make this program truly trauma-informed, program designers and instructors must first be able to recognize the effects and symptoms of trauma, incorporate the Six Principles, and even make healing and resilience a desired outcome.

More complex programs, however, such as job readiness programs sponsored by community colleges or state workforce development agencies, would need time to reflect deeply on their practices and policies to determine how to make the job readiness process more trauma-informed. It would be important to understand—and to help job seekers understand—the conditions that support success as well as conditions that may trigger trauma and stress responses. Job readiness programs can be rather mechanized and task oriented: create a resume, learn how to complete a job application, learn how to search for jobs, practice with role-play interviews, and so on. However, looking for a job is extremely stressful, and rejection hurts. Job seekers know that they are being judged and scrutinized by strangers; that they are being measured against standards and expectations, often those of the dominant culture; and that they are competing with others. Job seekers are extremely vulnerable, and the power lies in the hands of employers and recruiters. Thus, successful job seekers must be resilient and able to handle rejection. However, job seekers with unhealed trauma may not know how to practice resiliency. Just think of all the incidents of workplace violence that have occurred after someone has been fired or passed over for promotion. Rejection can be a whopper of a trigger.

To become trauma-informed, the entire workforce readiness system would need to be transformed. All job coaches and volunteers would need training in trauma and trauma-informed practices. The timeline for helping someone find employment—typically 60–90 days in government-funded centers—would have to be extended to allow time to work more compassionately with job seekers and help them cope with the pressures and emotions of a job search in healthy ways. Job coaches and trainers would need to offer authentic, trauma-informed peer support and help job seekers build resiliency skills and handle rejection. They could also help job seekers understand the difference between getting a job and getting the *job right for them.*

Rather than having to mold themselves to an employer looking for someone who is a "good fit," the job seeker would be encouraged and supported in finding a job or career that is a "good fit" for them—perhaps one that does not put them in a situation where they would be easily triggered and stressed. People returning from incarceration and from military service, as well as people with minimal education and skills, would particularly benefit from a workforce readiness system that is trauma-informed. Given the resurgence of work requirements for people who receive federal assistance, now would be a good time for all workforce development and human resources personnel to be trained in trauma-informed practices.

Being a trauma-informed program means that from start to finish, every aspect of the program has been examined—its language, processes, personnel, practices, policies, desired outcomes, service delivery, and so on—to identify and remedy bias, power imbalances, cultural insensitivity, bureaucratic and tedious processes, and other issues. A trauma-informed program considers its messaging; centers people; sees them as worthy and relational; and lives into the values of dignity, mutual concern, and respect for both staff and service recipients (Evans & Vaandering, 2022). Emily Bosk (2023) provided an example of how a program and its evaluation both aligned with SAMSHA's Six Principles, and we encourage you to read and learn from her article.

Trauma-Informed Organizations

In addition to SAMHSA's Six Principles, the frameworks for trauma-informed organizations discussed here can provide program designers and managers with ways to reflect on opportunities to make the organization hosting the program more trauma-informed (see SAMHSA, 2023). Because organizations are composed of people with trauma, they can be toxic work environments that traumatize both staff and recipients. Certainly, burnout and high turnover are signs that an organization can benefit from becoming trauma-informed. There is also a growing effort to make some schools and child-serving organizations more trauma-informed so that they are better equipped to protect children from dangers and promote resilience (Masten & Motti-Stefandi, 2020).

Aligning the Six Principles across an individual program or initiative can be challenging, and doing the same across an entire organization is a highly complex initiative, particularly for large agencies with many departments and locations. SAMHSA offers 10 implementation domains that appear in organizational change literature. We briefly describe them here and encourage you to read *SAMHSA's Concept of Trauma and Guidance for a Trauma-Informed Approach* (2014) and *SAMHSA's Practical Guide for Implementing a Trauma-Informed Approach* (2023) for a deeper explanation and application of the domains.

SAMSHA's Domains for a Trauma-Informed Organization

1. **Governance and Leadership:** Provide support for and be responsible for implementing a trauma-informed approach across the organization.
2. **Policy:** Examine policies for opportunities to make them more trauma-informed.
3. **Physical Environment:** Create a safe and inviting environment for both staff and clients.
4. **Engagement and Involvement of People in Recovery, Trauma Survivors, People Receiving Services, and Family Members Receiving Services:** Ensure Empowerment, Voice, and Choice in all areas of organizational functioning.
5. **Cross-Sector Collaboration:** Expand the work to partnering agencies in the community.
6. **Screening, Assessment, and Treatment Services:** Provide trauma-specific interventions to staff and clients or refer them to an agency that can if these are not in-house.
7. **Training and Workforce Development:** Ensure that all staff across the agency are aware of trauma and its symptoms and provide support for those experiencing secondary or vicarious trauma.
8. **Progress Monitoring and Quality Assurance:** Assess and monitor trauma-informed principles and use trauma-specific screenings, assessments, and treatments if applicable.
9. **Financing:** Assure that training and services can be funded in a sustainable manner.
10. **Evaluation:** Measure initiative implementation using TIER approaches.

This SAMHSA guide also provides questions to consider across each domain that help organizations consider what the Six Principles may look like within each domain.

Trauma-Informed Organizational Assessments

Some organizations may wish to conduct an assessment to determine how much, if at all, it is trauma-informed. Such organizational assessments can create a baseline against which progress and change can be measured. Several assessments are readily available by searching online, and organizations may wish to tailor the assessment so that it is more applicable to its specific context. Of course, the organization should have the ability to analyze and communicate findings of the assessments, either internally or via an outside consultant, followed by the development of an action plan for implementing, strengthening, and sustaining trauma-informed practices and policies. We recommend that organizations that provide direct service include program recipients as well as staff from all levels of the organization in the assessment and action-planning processes.

Here is our story of working with such an assessment. On a pilot project to create a trauma-informed system that involved multiple organizations and public agencies, we used an assessment that had five to seven items per domain that measured respondents' degree of agreement/disagreement with the statements. Given the assessment was an almost 70-item survey, much thought and planning went into preparing staff to take the assessment because it was important to hear from staff across the entire organization. That said, not every staff person could address every item or domain, depending on their role and duties. Some staff used the assessment as an opportunity to attack management and express their unhappiness. We learned that it is important to decide—before conducting an assessment—how such responses will be handled. Confidentiality must be assured for respondents to feel safe, yet issues may come to light that need to be addressed directly. How can leadership work with this tension in a trauma-informed way?

We also faced challenges sharing the results with organizations. The way the analyst aggregated the results eradicated important details in a political move to mitigate some of the more negative findings. There was a clear conflict of interest between the analyst, who worked for the organization's funder, and the organization. (We advised using an outside analyst and were turned down.) Additionally, the data visualizations of the results were confusing and messy. It was difficult for us as well as the teams within the various agencies to make sense of the data, so it was somewhat useless. Had it been analyzed and presented in accessible and transparent ways (as we've previously discussed), the assessment data could have given both the lead organization and the participating agencies more decision-making guidance. We learned that committing to a trauma-informed organizational assessment means that leaders and staff have to be willing to face the results honestly and openly and be serious about leading organizational change. The agency leaders who participated in the assessment wanted to create a trauma-informed workplace and system, but they also struggled with some very real and difficult questions:

- "How can I give my staff time and space to recover from stress and secondary trauma and still get the work done?"
- "How do I onboard and train my 600 employees across 10 departments in trauma-informed practices? Where do funds for training come from? And when do we have the time?"
- "How do we make changes when in so many ways, we are bound by local, state, and federal regulations (which are attached to funding) that would likely hinder some of the changes we want to make?"

These questions are legitimate and illustrate the complexity involved with creating more equitable and trauma-informed organizations and agencies.

Where to Begin

Even though making an organization or agency trauma-informed is difficult and complex, it does not mean we should not move forward and try. Bloom and Farragher (2013) identified key themes for advancing trauma-informed care across organizations:

1. Prioritize organizational culture change.
2. Incorporate patient [or client] voice to guide the process of becoming trauma-informed.
3. Train all staff and review hiring practices to promote a trauma-informed workforce.
4. Encourage and permit self-care to prevent burnout.
5. Screen patients [or clients or staff] for trauma and its symptoms.
6. Deliver trauma-specific services to patients [or clients or staff].

Eastern Mennonite University's STAR program (Center for Justice and Peacebuilding, 2023, p. 120) also offers organizations ways to respond to trauma and promote resilience:

- Create life-sustaining "microcultures." (For example, a professor at a university realized that he could not change the institution, so he made his research center—his sphere of influence—a trauma-informed microculture.)
- Incorporate restorative practices, including Circles, that help transform conflict and redistribute power.
- Acknowledge and understand structural, cultural, historic, and institutional harms that are alive in the organization (i.e., racism, tribalism, imperialism, etc.).
- Destigmatize secondary trauma and providing support, including peer support and professional counseling.
- Enact policies consistent with current knowledge of risk and prevention.

The work is worth doing. Employees in the nonprofit sector suffer from high rates of compassion fatigue, burnout, and turnover due to the stressful and traumatic nature of many nonprofit jobs (Huff, 2025). Becoming more trauma-informed would help organizations recruit and retain good employees, which in turn would make services and programs more effective.

Trauma-Informed Systems

"Resilience can cascade or spread over time by multiple processes, across systems, from one systems level to another, or one generation to another" (Masten & Motti-Stefandi, 2020, p. 99). Trauma-informed practices must extend to entire systems because people in communities often interact with interdependent systems, such as criminal justice and education or health care and child welfare. Imagine moving from agency to agency, system to system, and being treated with respect and dignity. Imagine systems and processes designed *for people*, not for the bureaucracy. Imagine staff and workers being safe and cared for and the resulting effects on services and communities.[1]

Trauma-informed systems are not figments of our imagination. This work has already begun. The cities of Tarpon Springs and Philadelphia and Washington State, to name just a few, have taken steps to center trauma, adversity, and resilience in their policies and programs (SAMHSA, 2014). In Appendix B, you will find a list of many regional, state, and national coalitions and initiatives working in the United States to transform entire systems. The work is hard, slow, and never-ending.

EXAMPLE 12.1 A Trauma-Informed Approach to Meetings

We encourage trauma-informed researchers and evaluators to locate and join existing initiatives and offer their trauma-informed lens to the evaluative processes and research that these coalitions do as they monitor and report change. Here, we present President of Community Evaluation Solutions Ann Price, who shared her trauma-informed approaches in one of her blogs (Price, n.d.):

> Two weeks ago, we completed 3 cross-regional meetings with Resilient Middle Georgia, one of our Resilient Georgia Clients. Our goal was to begin building a coalition identity across the region, to spread the word about PACEs and trauma-informed approaches, and to identify ways the coalition could begin moving forward, together.
>
> Between 30 and 45 community members attended a fast-paced and fun-filled 3-hour session. We learned about trauma-informed communities and imagined what an ideal community could look like. Then we mapped out a journey identifying the systems that touch families, barriers that might impede them, and made personal commitments to the work.
>
> Here is what we did to make this a different experience. Perhaps some of these tips might help.
>
> 1. Set up a warm welcome. Make sure there is someone to greet community members with a smile and maybe a swag bag.
> 2. Have music playing in the background. I learned about Lo-Fi—my new favorite background music.
> 3. Seat people with folks they don't know! Break up groups so that people make new connections and build their network.
> 4. Plan engaging activities that get people moving and laughing. Keep your PowerPoint slide deck to a minimum.
> 5. Be sure and share the benefit of joining the coalition and why they are needed. Make sure they start to see how they can fit into the work and emphasize you aren't asking them to do anything new!
> 6. Share membership packets and a form or QR code they can use to join the coalition. Make it easy for them to say yes, I am in!
> 7. Send a follow up email with highlights, pictures, and quotes from participants. Share with your larger group to show how much fun everyone had. A little FOMO (fear of missing out) never hurts! Be sure you share on social media.

[1]Return on Happiness with JoAnna Brandi is a consulting firm whose purpose (among others) is to "create a feel-good-at-work-place and craft a strong company culture." Imagine if this company integrated SAMHSA's Six Principles and 10 domains into their trainings.

Attendees very much appreciated how Ann incorporated trauma-informed approaches into her coalition evaluation work. If Ann can do it, so can you.

To reiterate, we need to include systems in our quest to make the world more trauma-informed because individuals—who likely have experienced personal or collective trauma—interact with programs, agencies, and organizations at a systems level all the time and those agencies and systems have opportunities to either retraumatize or promote resilience (Masten & Motti-Stefandi, 2020). Let's follow a woman and her two children seeking safety from an abusive husband and father as they navigate complex systems while trying get her needs met and ensure that she and her children are free from violence.

EXAMPLE 12.2 A Domestic Violence Victim's Journey through the System

A traumatized woman with children fleeing a violent relationship will encounter myriad processes and numerous agencies in her quest to be safe. She may first call 911 and thus engage with a dispatcher, law enforcement officers and Victim's Services personnel, prosecutors, and court administrators working in the criminal justice system. She and her children will interact with Child Protective Services, which is overseen by the courts, and they will likely participate in several screenings and assessments in the process of developing a safety plan. She and her children will need safe housing, so she may need the services of a community-based organization that provides emergency housing or may deal with landlords and the Sheriff's department if an eviction is pending. In the likely event the courts determine her to need an Order for Protection (OFP), she may need support from a domestic violence advocate who will help her file the paperwork and navigate the complex journey through the civil and criminal courts. She and her children may need individual and family counseling, and school mental health professionals, teachers, and administrators may be involved in creating a system of support at school. All in all, she may have over 100 encounters with employees at over 14 different agencies.

What would her journey be like if all 14 agencies were living into the Six Principles of Trauma-Informed Care? What would her journey be like if they were not? (which is most often the case). There are several points to consider regarding this example:

- Millions of trauma-affected people interact with programs, organizations, agencies, and systems every day.
- Researchers and evaluators, also likely to be individuals with trauma, typically engage with many of these agencies at programmatic, local, state, and national levels.
- Nonprofit, public, governmental, and/or private individuals (i.e., landlords) are governed and funded differently. There is no single, unifying regulatory or oversight board, yet they are interconnected.
- Each time that a trauma-affected person encounters an employee at any agency is an opportunity to display care, empathy, and support–or an opportunity for retraumatization and revictimization. How clerks, prosecutors, judges, law enforcement officers, social workers, teachers, and advocates interact with trauma-affected people influences a victim's engagement with these systems as well as the outcomes of the case.

How Can Organizations within Systems Change?

Systems change at the scale we are talking about is daunting. It feels impossible. It's not. But it does take a village—and a plan. Although our list in Appendix B is not exhaustive, it points you toward ways to connect. We certainly encourage our readers to seek out coalitions and collaborations near them that may not appear on this list.

Creating trauma-informed systems requires cross-sector collaboration and support from local and state leaders. In many instances, it also requires funding to pay for full-time coalition directors or coordinators. Many coalitions are required to monitor and evaluate progress, which may also require a budget for a trauma-informed consultant. But when two or more organizations break down silos and cross the nonprofit, government, and private sector boundaries, change can happen at an increased scale while being more replicable, resilient, sustainable, effective, and efficient. Let's learn from two very different organizations how they approach trauma-informed systems change. We invite you to reflect on the experiences of both organizations in the Case Study Reflection Questions.

CASE STUDY 12.1 Trauma-Informed Systems Change at the Jewish Federations of North America

CARMEL RABIN

The Jewish Federations of North America's Center on Aging, Trauma, and Holocaust Survivor Care is grounded in the person-centered trauma-informed (PCTI) approach, including in its evaluation efforts. The Center works to intentionally align their programs, subgrantees, training initiatives, research, *and* program evaluations with SAMHSA's Six Principles of Trauma-Informed Care, which are applied through a person-centered lens. The Center defines the PCTI approach as "a holistic model of care that promotes the health and well-being of individuals by accounting for the role of trauma across the life course and by resisting retraumatization, while also focusing on the strength, agency, and dignity of the person receiving care" (Center on Aging, Trauma, and Holocaust Survivor Care, 2024, p. 1). In the Center's *Program Evaluation Workbook*, Rabin (2022) explains that a PCTI evaluation elevates SAMHSA's Six Principles of Trauma-Informed Care *above other evaluation considerations.*

As part of their work, the Center conducted a national survey in 2021 to understand the overall capacity of U.S.-based aging services organizations to provide PCTI care to diverse older adults with a history of trauma. With almost 200 organizations responding to the survey, the Center built an understanding of the awareness of aging, trauma, and the PCTI approach; the capacity of organizations to use the approach; and the benefits of using the approach.

The survey found that 72% of respondents noted their organization was aware of PCTI care before the survey. However, awareness did not translate to capacity, as only 30% of respondent organizations demonstrated a deep capacity to provide PCTI care to diverse care recipients.

Respondents noted a wide range of capacity to serve specific diverse populations. Rates of understanding and capacity were higher among Center-funded organizations, with 93% reporting organizational awareness of the PCTI approach and 70% demonstrating a deep capacity to provide PCTI care, whereas 66% of non-Center-funded organizations reported organizational awareness of the PCTI approach and only 9% of these organizations demonstrated a deep capacity to provide PCTI care. Survey respondents also reported a wide range of benefits as a result of using the PCTI approach in their care, such as improvements to service delivery, client outcomes, and organizational operations.

The Center provides PCTI training for staff, subgrantees, and partner agencies and monitors the growth and influence of organizational understanding and capacity of the PCTI approach over time. Additionally, the Center offers webinars and other free resources where they share what they learn with others who desire to become more PCTI (Center on Holocaust Survivor Care, n.d.). One of the tools the Center provides its subgrantees is a *Program Evaluation Workbook*, listed in our resources in Appendix B.

CASE STUDY 12.2 Trauma-Informed Approaches at Wilder

NORA JOHNSON

Development of the Trauma-Informed Organization Workgroup at Wilder Foundation

The Amherst H. Wilder Foundation (Wilder) works to create lasting, positive change through direct services, research, and community building. Located in Saint Paul, Minnesota, Wilder employs over 400 individuals working in a variety of sectors, including early childhood education, support for older adults and caregivers, culturally specific behavioral care, housing supports, and research. Because Wilder employs and serves a wide range of people with diverse backgrounds and needs, it is critical for its staff to be attuned to the effects of trauma and the histories and experiences of trauma in specific individuals and communities. To this end, Wilder created the Trauma-Informed Organization (TIO) Workgroup in 2014: a grassroots effort composed of a multidisciplinary team from across the foundation.

Initial efforts of the TIO Workgroup were focused on the physical space and building as well as buy-in across the Foundation. Wilder worked with an external vendor to conduct an undercover environmental scan of the main Foundation space, which resulted in a report with recommendations for next steps. The Workgroup then leveraged the scan to advocate for removing sign-in forms and visitor stickers (especially important for individuals experiencing stalking or domestic violence), increasing language capacity among front desk staff, and adding weapons-ban signage on Wilder property. Each of these changes required lengthy conversations and building-wide buy-in to implement, with conversations tending to be very polarized and divided. In addition, many staff involved in decision-making processes were initially unconvinced that trauma-informed efforts could benefit Foundation areas outside of some direct service providers. A few staff were also hesitant to use the word "trauma" in the workgroup name. The TIO leadership spent a lot of time addressing this hesitancy to destigmatize the word and start further conversations throughout the Foundation.

Once Wilder succeeded in taking some initial trauma-informed steps, the workgroup further formalized their work by creating a charter and advocating to be given a budget. Work then focused on building a baseline knowledge of trauma and the effects of trauma and trauma-informed practices throughout Wilder. Other work focused on building buy-in with staff across different parts of the Foundation and encouraging staff in these areas to discuss the trauma-informed efforts in which they were engaging.

After the 2016 fatal police shooting of Philando Castille in a suburb of Saint Paul, Minnesota, the TIO Workgroup incorporated more sessions focused on community self-care, along with their continued efforts to build baseline knowledge of trauma and its effects.

The Foundation TIO Workgroup Today

At the Foundation level, the TIO Workgroup was put on pause from 2020 to 2023 due to the pandemic. As we enter 2024, the Workgroup is in a second round of strategic planning to reorient and align trauma-informed efforts with the Foundation's renewed focus on whole family approaches to meet the interconnected economic, health, and education needs of entire family systems.

Trauma-Informed Efforts within Wilder Research

Until about 2015, trauma-informed work at Wilder Research was project specific, meaning that researchers incorporated trauma-informed practices "as needed" depending on the scope, timing, and budget of a project. As awareness and understanding about trauma and its effects on the human body increased, staff began to think more broadly about how to incorporate trauma-informed practices. In 2015, Wilder Research conducted a literature review on best practices in trauma-informed approaches for organizations, specifically in research settings. Staff used the results of that literature review to present at conferences and to create a tip sheet for trauma-informed data collection.

In addition to the literature review, Wilder Research developed an informal trauma-informed evaluation workgroup, which garnered a significant amount of interest among researchers. However, the workgroup disbanded somewhat quickly, partly because of competing demands on researchers' time and a lack of formal support from organizational leadership at the time. Specifically, no explicit time and budget resources were made available to implement this group, nor was participation for this group considered when deciding on billing expectations for Wilder Research staff.

Development of Trauma-Informed Research as a Strategic Business Area

In 2020, Wilder Research leadership made the decision to implement strategic business areas (SBAs) in an effort to build staff capacity, improve operational efficiency, increase community impact, and sustain or expand business. These SBAs were oriented toward a variety of topic areas and were designed to more formally support researchers in doing work that was not necessarily tied directly to project work. Staff were encouraged to participate in SBAs that aligned with their portfolios and interests. Trauma-Informed Research was one of the original SBAs created in 2020.

Staff expressed a strong need for opportunities to learn more about trauma, as well as opportunities to process difficult experiences resulting from working on projects with sensitive topics. Because all staff are exposed to potentially traumatizing topics, members of the SBA provided training at staff meetings to make sure that everyone—from frontline interviewers to administrative sectors—could participate. A version of this training is also incorporated into the training that Wilder Research provides for incoming staff, with particular emphasis on primary and secondary trauma and opportunities for self-care.

Wilder Research has also built a culture that encourages project leaders to consider the myriad ways trauma can manifest as well as to provide supportive resources to all participants of research after participation, not just the ones that physically appear to be in distress.

Lessons Learned

Trauma-informed efforts throughout Wilder Foundation and Wilder Research have generated valuable lessons.

- Any trauma-informed efforts need formal leadership and organizational support, especially in the form of allotted time and/or budget.
- Any trauma-informed efforts require organization-wide buy-in, and the success of such efforts hinges on multidisciplinary cooperation. These efforts may seem slow and messy, especially at first.
- Trauma can affect staff and clients in myriad ways. Efforts should be taken to minimize primary and secondary trauma for not only direct service providers (including interviewers, counselors, or housing providers, for example) but also individuals exposed to program data and information (including analysts, administrative support, and front desk staff, for example).
- Consider not only trauma that can affect staff and clients within the purview of the organization but also the influence of larger political forces and resulting effects on community feelings of safety.
- It is also important to note that trauma-informed practices are often at odds with capitalist business practices (billing structures, timelines, budgets, etc.). Progress may be incremental within current structures outside of even the organization's control. Celebrate that incremental progress.

CASE STUDIES 12.1 AND 12.2. REFLECTION QUESTIONS

1. Compare the Center and Wilder stories. How are their efforts similar? How are they different? What lessons can be learned from both?
2. In what ways can your organization create more space and time to process secondary trauma (or primary trauma) among your staff?
3. What resources can you dedicate to this work to help bolster and support organizational change?
4. What internal connections can be fostered to move trauma-informed work forward?
5. Who is and is not currently at the table for trauma-informed planning and decision making? How can you engage folks who are not currently at the table?

Time to Go to Work

Becoming a trauma-informed researcher and evaluator requires courage, self-examination, care and empathy for others, and an openness to seeing the world differently. Becoming a trauma-informed program, organization, and system require concentrated and deliberate efforts from trauma-informed leaders willing to set aside time and money for the work. We never said this would be easy.

Wearing the trauma-informed lens changes how you look at and experience the world. Things that you couldn't comprehend now make a little more sense. Patterns of human behavior start to emerge as we trace the roots of historical, intergenerational, and collective traumas that compound the traumas we experience as children and adults. If you've ever wondered why people can't just get along, perhaps we've offered you an explanation: Hurt people hurt people, and hurting people hurts, and this cycle of violence is difficult to interrupt.

That said, it can be done if and only if each of us is committed to doing our own work and healing. As researchers and evaluators, we need to learn to live and work holistically, not just in our heads. As influencers, we need to learn to use *power with* people so that healing and resilience is promoted in our workplaces in the programs and agencies we research and evaluate.

We know that in the past decade, evaluators especially have been charged with being change agents of just about every kind of harm and inequity on the planet. We've often found these lofty goals impractical if not impossible as we question the reality of our own power and sphere of influence. That said, we know that integrating trauma-informed research and evaluation practices will inch us closer to achieving our lofty goals.

We have a moral and ethical responsibility as humans who do research with other humans to ensure that we are all safe, heard, valued, respected, and cared for. With that, we encourage you to form peer support groups that can help you process primary and secondary trauma. We ask evaluation firms of all sizes, and especially those whose specialty is monitoring and evaluating international programs, to build peer support structures into your workplaces and provide trauma and resilience training for all employees. We encourage professors of all courses that teach even the most basic research methods to use this text to supplement the others and to help students integrate TIER early in their undergraduate and graduate educations. Finally, and most important, we encourage you to be good to yourself by developing routine and regular self-care and resilience practices. We believe that recognizing trauma as the ultimate human connector will make us all better people—more resilient, more empathetic, more compassionate, and more willing to use our position and power to influence programs, organizations, and systems.

APPENDIX A

Recommended Literature Referencing the Six Principles

Here are some of the heavy hitters—the articles that deal most directly with trauma and the Six Principles—and we recommend that our readers review them individually. Some deal with issues of trauma head-on, whereas others approach this from a different angle but end up being highly relevant to TIER. During the literature review process, we coded mentions and articles by Principle so that we could count the Principles in the literature. See References for a full citation.

Safety

Safety was the most commonly cited of the Six Principles, with 99 coded segments across 26 articles. Discussions of safety in the context of articles often had to do with protection of participants from retraumatization, especially concerning the means and methods used in collecting data (Andrews et al., 2019; Campbell et al., 2014; Syeda, Fournie, Ibanez, & Crooks, 2021; Wolfe et al., 2020). Authors emphasize the importance of training in trauma-informed practice as being crucial to the protection of participants (Andrews et al., 2019; Bardin et al., 2022; Campbell et al., 2008).

Cultural, Historical, and Gender Issues

Cultural, historical, and gender issues appeared in 56 coded segments across 24 documents. Some authors address these issues from a broad perspective, noting the ways in which issues of power, oppression, and marginalization can interact with our duties as evaluators as well as how evaluators can act more equitably to promote justice (Bosk, 2023; Haugen & Chouinard, 2019; Ward et al., 2018; Wolfe et al., 2020). Discussions of historical and ongoing oppression of indigenous populations are discussed by multiple authors (Andrews et al., 2019; Auger et al., 2019; Cram, 2018; Felt et al., 2022; Martinez, Running Wolf, BigFoot, Randal, & Villegas, 2018; Mawhinney et al., 2023). Waapalaneexkweew (2018) gives an especially thorough review of the legacy of indigenous intergenerational trauma, its effects on evaluation processes with indigenous communities, and evaluators' roles in perpetuating and mitigating these problems. Beyond doing less harm, and repairing harm done, the author emphasizes the role that indigenous knowledge can play in strengthening the evaluation profession as a whole.

Other authors emphasize cultural, historical, and gender issues as they relate to practice with LGBTQ+ populations (Felt et al., 2022; Hartman, Hoessler, Tom, & Camman, 2022; Ismail, Griffiths, & Bond-Gorr, 2022; Phillips et al., 2022; Wright & LaVelle, 2022). Again, these authors emphasize the role that evaluators can play either as those who perpetuate stigmatization, trauma, and injustice or as part of the solution as advocates and allies. Boyce and colleagues (2023) relate the struggles of Black evaluators in light of historical oppression and recent events, such as the murder of George Floyd in 2020.

Collaboration and Mutuality

The concept of collaboration and mutuality in connection with trauma-informed practices was identified in 46 coded segments across 14 documents. Authors most commonly spoke about collaborative efforts (with program staff, service recipients, or alumni) for designing the evaluation processes and instruments, execution of data collection in the hopes of addressing safety concerns, and building trust and reducing power imbalances (Bosk, 2023; Campbell et al., 2008, 2014; Mawhinney et al., 2023; Sikkema et al., 2018; Syeda et al., 2021). Waapalaneexkweew (2018) emphasizes this sort of collaboration and mutuality as critical for righting of historical wrongs against indigenous people in evaluation processes.

Empowerment and Choice

Empowerment and choice are documented in 32 coded segments across 14 documents.

Much of trauma has to do with power dynamics and oppression, so it makes sense that trauma-informed practice would call for emphasizing constituents' own agency and ability to make decisions regarding their involvement in the evaluation process. Authors focused on issues of consent, ensuring that participants are able to easily disengage from the process at any point in the evaluation (Andrews et al., 2019; Wolfe & Price, 2019). Roholt and Baizerman (2012) view the evaluator's role with traumatized populations as one of advocacy and empowerment. Berends and Wansbrough (2023) note that gatekeeping for the sake of protecting vulnerable populations can amount to paternalism and a denial of choice.

Trust and Transparency

Trust and transparency appeared in 19 coded segments across 10 documents. Authors called attention to the importance of developing trust to gain access to information from traumatized individuals (Campbell et al., 2008; Roholt & Baizerman, 2012; Thomas, 2004). Thomas (2004) emphasizes that when working with people who have been systematically marginalized, the evaluator is often viewed as part of that oppressive and traumatizing system. Consequently, evaluators must work hard to give plenty of opportunities "to ask questions, critique their efforts, and provide input in various ways," which "helps to garner the needed trust and respect from stakeholders" (p. 8).

Cohen (2012) uses an anecdote of personal disclosure as a method for building trust and gaining access to traumatized individuals' insights. There is a strong emphasis on collaboration as a vehicle toward gaining trust (Andrews et al., 2019; Thomas, 2004; Ward et al., 2018).

Bosk (2023) emphasizes transparency about the evaluation process as critical for trust.

Peer Support

Peer support is by far the least mentioned SAMHSA Principle, with only nine coded segments across five articles. Berends and Wansbrough (2023) emphasize the importance of participants as experts to the workings of the program. Bosk (2023) underlines the importance of including alumni in advisory boards for the program and evaluation processes while avoiding doing so in a tokenizing way. Brown and Di Lallo (2020) share the idea of talking circles as a specific method for building peer support, aiding in the healing process.

APPENDIX B

Trauma-Informed Coalitions and Organizations

Resource	Lead organization	Geographic area
National Center for Trauma-Informed Care	National Association of State Mental Health Program Directors and its partner, Advocates for Human Potential, Inc.	National
Maryland Essentials for Childhood	State of Maryland	MD
Trauma-Informed Training Roadmap	Resilient Georgia	GA
Trauma-Informed Trainings	Alive & Well Communities	MO
Collective Impact Trauma-Informed Care Team	Wisconsin Office of Children's Mental Health	WI
Adverse Child Experiences Michigan	Michigan Health Improvement Alliance	MI
GNHCC's trauma-informed care	Greater Newark Healthcare Coalition (GNHCC)	NJ—Greater Newark
The Building Community Resilience Collaborative	George Washington Uni. Public Health	OH, KY, TX, OR, DC, MD, WA, VA, MO, and KS
United Way of Greater Philadelphia and Southern New Jersey Trauma-Informed Communities Collective Impact Work	United Way	PA and NJ

Resource	Lead organization	Geographic area
The Resilience Effect	Genentech	Bay Area
Attachment and Trauma Network Inc.	Trauma-informed schools and families	National
THRIVE	System of Care in Maine	ME
TSS	Trauma-informed schools	National
Child Trauma Academy	Child Trauma Academy	Online repository of information
First 5 LA		Los Angeles County
San Francisco Dept of Public Health—Trauma-Informed Systems Initiative		San Francisco
Kaiser Permanente Community Benefits Program Resilience Initiative	Kaiser Permanente	
Virginia Trauma-informed Community Networks	Voice for Virginia's Kids	VA
Trauma-Informed Utah		UT
CTIPP—Campaign for Trauma-informed Policy and Practice		National
The Trauma Stewardship Institute		National

Note. This is not by any means a complete list. We encourage you to seek out coalitions in your region.

APPENDIX C

Resources for Deeper Learning

Foundational Principles of TIER

SAMHSA Trauma-Informed Care, *https://www.health.ny.gov/health_care/medicaid/program/medicaid_health_homes/docs/samhsa_trauma_concept_paper.pdf.*

AEA's Guiding Principles, *www.eval.org/About/Guiding-Principles.*

NIH Introduction to the Principles and Practice of Clinical Research, *https://ocreco.od.nih.gov/courses/ippcr.html.*

Center for Victims of Torture, *CVT.org.*

Equity-Focused and Trauma-Informed Evaluation and Research

RJAE Consulting: Professional development, training, consulting on trauma-informed practices, instruments, programs, organizations, and systems, *www.rjaeconsulting.com.*

Center for Culturally Responsive Evaluation and Assessment, *https://crea.education.illinois.edu.*

Equitable Evaluation, *www.equitableeval.org.*

Racial Equity Tools, *www.racialequitytools.org.*

More on Trauma

Centers for Disease Control and Prevention, ACEs, *www.cdc.gov/violenceprevention/aces/index.html.*

The Body Keeps Score: Brain, Mind, and Body in the Healing of Trauma, by Bessel van der Kolk.

My Grandmother's Hands: Racialized Trauma and the Pathway to Mending Our Hearts and Bodies, by Resmaa Menakem.

STAR: Strategies for Trauma Awareness & Resilience:

Eastern Mennonite University, *https://emu.edu/cjp/star.*

Minnesota Peacebuilding Leadership Institute, *www.mnpeace.org/star-training-5-days.html.*

Self-Care, Empathy, and Resiliency

Headspace App

CALM App

Trauma Stewardship: An Everyday Guide to Caring for Self While Caring for Others, by Laura van Dernoot Lipsky.

Brené Brown on Empathy, *www.youtube.com/watch?reload=9&v=1Evwgu369Jw.*

Greater Good Magazine: Science-Based Insights for a Meaningful Life, greatergood.berkeley.edu/article/item/five_science_backed_strategies_to_build_resilience.

Positive Psychology: How to Develop Empathy: 10 Exercises and Worksheets, *https://positivepsychology.com/empathy-worksheets.*

Secondary Trauma

Both resources below can be used as self-assessments to help you better recognize when you need support.

PRoQOL Quality of Life Survey

The Professional Quality of Life (ProQOL) scale is the most widely employed tool for assessing compassion fatigue, with an extensive history of development and use (Molnar et al., 2017; Stamm, 2010). It is a survey you can take yourself to help you understand what you are experiencing. To take the survey, go to *https://uncg.qualtrics.com/jfe/form/SV aXCF2sA81Zeq6HA.*

Secondary Traumatic Stress Scale

The Secondary Traumatic Stress Scale (STSS) was developed in 2004 by Bride et al. as a way to measure STS. You can find it at *https://theacademy.sdsu.edu/wp-content/uploads/2019/09/STSSwithscoreinterpretation.pdf.*

Restorative Justice and Circles

The Little Book of Circle Processes, by Kay Pranis.

National Association of Community and Restorative Justice, *www.nacrj.org.*

Collection, Analysis, Data Visualization, and Reporting

Engaged Feedback Checklist, by Brené Brown, *https://brenebrown.com/resources/the-engaged-feedback-checklist/.*

Trauma-Informed Evaluation: Tip Sheet for Collecting Information, by Nora Johnson. Wilder Research, *https://www.wilder.org/wilder_research/trauma-informed-evaluation-tip-sheet-for-collecting-information/.*

Equity-Focused Data Visualization with Stephanie Evergreen, *www.stephanieevergreen.com* and *https://stephanieevergreen.com/academy.*

Classes on DataViz and Software—Ann Emery—Depict Data Studio, *https://depictdatastudio.com.*

Classes on Designing Failproof Slides and Presentations—Creative Research Communications with Echo Rivera, *www.echorivera.com.*

Better Reporting: Hutchinson, K. S. (2017). *A short primer on innovative evaluation reporting*, Author.

Trauma-Informed Systems: Downloadable Resources

These downloadable resources are available for those wishing to learn more about trauma-informed systems change.

Bhushan, D., Kotz, K., McCall, J., Gilgoff, R., Dube, S., Powers, C., et al. (2020, December 9). *Roadmap for resilience: The California Surgeon General's report on adverse childhood experiences, toxic stress, and health.* https://osg.ca.gov/wp-content/uploads/sites/266/2020/12/Roadmap-For-Resilience_CA-Surgeon-Generals-Report-on-ACEs-Toxic-Stress-and-Health_12092020.pdf.

Chapin Hall. (n.d.). *Building a multi-system trauma-informed collaborative.* https://www.chapinhall.org/wp-content/uploads/PDF/Multi-System-Trauma-Informed-Care-MSTIC-Guide.pdf.

Connecticut Women's Consortium. (n.d.). *A guide to building trauma-informed practices and organizations*, https://20283716.fs1.hubspotusercontent-na1.net/hubfs/20283716/building-trauma-informed-practices-and-organizations-download.pdf.

Haas, B., & Clements, A. D. (n.d.). *Building a trauma informed system of care toolkit.* TN.gov. www.tn.gov/content/dam/tn/dcs/documents/for-providers/procurement/Building20a20Trauma%20Informed%20System%20of%20Care%20Toolkit.pdf.

Meko, T. (n.d.). *Early adopters of trauma-informed care.* Urban Institute. https://www.urban.org/research/publication/early-adopters-trauma-informed-care.

Ott, J. G., Ithiphol, K., Pinard, R. A., Olwig, T. T., & Center for Collective Wisdom. (2022, October 2). *Trauma and resiliency: A systems change approach.* https://traumainformedla.org/wp-content/uploads/2018/03/lactrisc-final-report-2017-07.pdf.

Rabin, C. (2022). *Program evaluation workbook.* Center on Holocaust Care and Institute on Aging and Trauma, The Jewish Federations of North America. https://holocaustsurvivorcare.jewishfederations.org/resources.

Resonance. (n.d.). *The guide to cross-sector collaboration | Resonance.* Resonance Global. www.resonanceglobal.com/the-guide-to-cross-sector-collaboration.

Schulman, M., Dubay, L., & Burton, R. (2018, October 18). *What does it take to become trauma-informed? Lessons from early adopters* [Blog]. Center for Health Care Strategies. www.chcs.org/what-does-it-take-to-become-trauma-informed-lessons-from-early-adopters.

Substance Abuse and Mental Health Services Administration. (2014). *SAMHSA's concept of trauma and guidance for a trauma-informed approach* [HHS Publication No. (SMA) 14-4884]. https://www.nctsn.org/resources/samhsas-concept-of-trauma-and-guidance-for-a-trauma-informed-approach.

Substance Abuse and Mental Health Services Administration. (2023). *Practical guide for implementing a trauma-informed approach* [HHS Publication No. PEP23-06-05-005]. https://traumainformedutah.org/2024/02/02/practical-guide-for-implementing-a-trauma-informed-approach/.

APPENDIX D

What About Fawning?

A Conversation about the Fourth F—Fawning[1]

Some trauma specialists have added "**fawn**" to the fight, flight, or freeze trauma responses. Brummer and Thorsborne (2021) describe fawning as "appeasing or when the brain has us befriend the threat" (p. 50), whereas Craig (2017) describes a fawner as appearing "overly empathetic, as if they are trying to alleviate their own pain by being overly solicitous of others (p. 40). Fenkel (2023) describes fawning as a trauma response often associated with PTSD that can negatively affect long-term mental health. Clearly, fawning looks very different than a fight, flight, or freeze response, and it is unknown whether it is a response triggered by the amygdala or if it is a learned survival and coping mechanism.

According to Fenkel (2023), these are some key signs of the fawning trauma response:

- You look to others to see how you feel in a relationship or situation.
- You have trouble identifying your feelings, even if you're alone.
- You feel like you have no identity or authentic self.
- You're constantly trying to please other people, whether through flattery, affection, or catering to the demands of others.
- At the first sign of conflict, your first instinct is to "appease" the angry person.
- You ignore your own beliefs, needs, preferences, thoughts, and feelings to please others.
- You have trouble setting healthy boundaries in relationships.

[1]Another possible response is "fainting," or vasovagal syncope, which occurs when the vagus nerve instantly lowers blood pressure and slows the heartbeat (Mayo Clinic, 2026). Vasovagal syncope is caused by many factors and is not exclusive to trauma or threats.

Given this list, there are implications for evaluators and researchers who are fawners themselves or whose study participants are fawners. To gain more insight into how fawning relates to research and evaluation, we spoke with Niki Wood,[2] a professional evaluator, and Erica Staab,[3] an expert in domestic/gendered violence.

MARTHA: Both of you have called my attention to this response called *fawn*. I'm curious. Is fawning specific to victims of domestic violence and other abuse or is it more widespread?

NIKI: I came across it specifically in reference to abuse cases and codependency where fawning is a survival mechanism. Perhaps it is less of a trauma response and more of a symptom of trauma and how one subsequently handles any stressful symptoms.

ERICA: I agree it is unclear. Someone who fawns over an abuser has learned that appeasing them works! Over time, it becomes a habit if not an expectation, but it is a behavior learned because of trauma and as a way to prevent or decrease violence. We also see victims fawning over their children as a way to shield them from the violence and abuse in the home or to make up for it.

MARTHA: I can see fawning as a survival mechanism. But we trauma survivors develop all kinds of coping behaviors, some healthier than others. Fawning seems to be more of a rational choice coming from the cerebral cortex, not the amygdala. Someone has decided rationally that fawning will keep them safe(r). Does it then qualify as a trauma response?

ERICA: When someone repeats a behavior, those neural pathways get established so that it can become an automatic response. She sees him coming and immediately goes into fawn mode. So I think it is etched into the brain just like trauma responses are but in a different way. I mean, does it really matter where it comes from in the brain, or if it starts as a conscious coping mechanism that becomes automatic over time?

MARTHA: Maybe on a physiological level it matters, although I'm sure when a victim is fawning, they are also on high alert for threats and the amygdala is doing its job. Either way, is fawning something researchers and evaluators should pay attention to?

NIKI: Yes, I think we should pay attention. I think you could trigger a fawning response where someone consents when they do not want to or provides responses or impressions that they think are desired. Other challenges with fawning (taking emotional responsibility for everything, for example) could arise as well—if an interviewer behaved poorly, the fawning person might be less likely to report it or come forward, as they may blame themselves. That one is harder to guard against others through the usual safeguards of trauma-informed practices.

---

[2]Niki Wood is a mixed-methods evaluation practitioner specializing in trauma-informed and participatory approaches. She leads the MEL Practice in Chemonics UK, a sustainable development company, and resides in Sweden.

[3]Erica Staab is Executive Director of the HOPE Center in Faribault, Minnesota, and a leading advocate across Minnesota.

AARON: Well, think about it. If someone's default is to please others at any cost and if that person is a study participant who feels unempowered or somehow perceives the researcher to be a threat, then their responses could be entirely based on what they think the researcher wants to hear or what others in the focus group say. They may not even be able to fully identify and describe their feelings and perspectives about a program or treatment.

MARTHA: So fawning could be an exaggerated form of response bias—someone too eager to please the interviewer. What about from the researcher's perspective—are they at risk of fawning over participants?

AARON: I think when we talk about evaluators and researchers who may want to leave participants out of a study because it might be too painful for them, that's a form of fawning. Being overprotective. It could also take the form of being afraid to ask difficult questions. It's hard for me to think that any evaluator or researcher who fawns over participants is doing their work properly—or in a trauma-informed way.

NIKI: I think fawning tends to happen toward those with some form of power over you—that is, an authority figure like your boss or someone in whom you have an emotional investment. As such I think it's much more likely to display it toward the evaluator or researcher if it's a study with multiple interactions with that researcher/evaluator (unless the participant becomes friends with another participant of course). Of course, unhealthy power dynamics can occur, regardless of the hierarchy (i.e., parent toward child or evaluator toward participant), but I wonder if the initial power structure could more likely trigger fawning in a study participant if they had fawning as a previous survival mechanism. I'm really curious about this!

MARTHA: What steps can researchers and evaluators take, if they find a participant has a tendency to fawn, to shift that behavior?

ERICA: It's hard to say because fawning relates to safety, power imbalances, and perceived threats. It all depends on the person and how a researcher uses power. The Principles of Trauma-Informed Care certainly help—making sure they feel safe and supported. But again, it depends on the person. The fawner may not know any other way of being.

REFLECTION QUESTIONS

1. What are your thoughts about fawning? Have you experienced fawning in your personal life? During your research?
2. Why do you think it is important for evaluators and researchers to be aware of fawning behaviors in themselves and in others?
3. If power imbalances trigger fawning responses, what steps can you take to mitigate such imbalances?

TIER Glossary

A

Absolute merit: A judgment about the inherent value or effectiveness of a program or intervention measured against established standards or criteria, without comparison with alternatives. For example, determining that therapy *Z* reduces trauma symptoms by a specific measurable amount.

Acknowledgment: The active practice of recognizing, validating, and responding to what participants share, going beyond simply not judging to demonstrating through words, body language, and facial expressions that their experiences have been heard and valued.

Acute stress disorder: A trauma-related condition that occurs immediately following exposure to a traumatic event, with duration from 3 days to 1 month, serving as a potential precursor to posttraumatic stress disorder (PTSD).

Adjustment disorder: A condition characterized by the development of clinically significant emotional or behavioral symptoms within 6 months of exposure to an identifiable stressor, where the symptoms are either disproportionate to the severity of the stressor or cause significant impairment in functioning.

Adverse childhood experiences (ACEs): Traumatic events occurring before age 18 (e.g., abuse, household challenges, and neglect) that are linked to chronic health problems in adulthood.

American Evaluation Association (AEA): Professional association that provides evaluation competencies and guiding principles for evaluators.

Amygdala: The "lizard brain," or survival center, that controls automatic reactions, including fight, flight, or freeze responses; has no sense of time.

Autonomic nervous system (ANS): The nervous system involved in trauma responses, including sympathetic (activation) and parasympathetic (calming) branches.

Avoidance: Staying away from places, events, or objects that are reminders of a traumatic experience.

B

Brave space: A place where individuals feel encouraged to speak up and share perspectives that might be uncomfortable or challenging, engaging in constructive dialogue while confronting biases and assumptions. Brave spaces empower individuals to take risks, make mistakes, and learn from one another through open and honest conversation.

Burnout: Feelings of exhaustion, frustration, anger, and depression resulting from general work stress.

C

Central tendency: Statistical measures like means and medians that describe the "typical" or average response, which can obscure experiences of marginalized participants.

Clean pain: Term used by Resmaa Menakem for the process of recognizing, accepting, and moving through pain to heal trauma.

Collective trauma: Trauma that affects entire groups or populations, including structural, historical, intergenerational, and participation-induced trauma.

Compassion fatigue (CF): Emotional and physical exhaustion that reduces one's capacity to empathize and feel compassion for those they serve.

Compassion satisfaction: The positive feeling experienced when helping others effectively.

Constructivist evaluation: Emphasizes stakeholder engagement and multiple perspectives in evaluation processes; also known as *fourth-generation evaluation.*

Consumer-oriented evaluation: An evaluation approach developed by Michael Scriven that focuses on providing clear, practical judgments about the merit and worth of programs or products from the perspective of end users or consumers. This methodology emphasizes transparency in evaluation processes and seeks to produce actionable information that helps stakeholders make informed decisions about program value and effectiveness.

Content warnings: Brief notices provided in advance to inform participants about potentially distressing or sensitive material they may encounter, allowing individuals to make informed decisions about their participation and emotional preparation.

Corporate reputation laundering: The practice of using evaluation, research, or other seemingly objective activities to improve a corporation's public image and deflect attention from harmful practices or negative impacts.

Cost analysis: The practical process of calculating the costs of a program, intervention, or investment without necessarily measuring benefits or outcomes.

Criteria: The dimensions used to judge the merit, worth, or value of a program or intervention.

Culturally responsive evaluation and assessment (CREA): An evaluation approach that recognizes and incorporates the cultural contexts, values, and ways of knowing of the communities being evaluated. CREA emphasizes cultural validity, community ownership of the evaluation process, and methods that are respectful of and relevant to participants' cultural backgrounds and experiences.

D

***Dadirri*:** Indigenous Australian philosophy of deep listening and quiet awareness used by researcher Judy Atkinson.

Deep listening: Listening with both head and heart to fully understand participants' experiences and emotions.

Defense cascade: The fear reaction involving arousal, freezing, flight, fight, tonic immobility, and other responses to threat.

Disinhibited social engagement disorder: A childhood disorder characterized by overly familiar and inappropriate social behavior with unfamiliar adults, typically resulting from inadequate care during early development.

Disparities: Systematic differences in outcomes, access, or treatment between different groups, often reflecting underlying inequities based on race/ethnicity, socioeconomic status, or other social factors.

E

Economic evaluations: Evaluation methods that assess programs or interventions primarily through financial metrics such as costs, efficiency, or return on investment. These approaches may overlook broader social, human, or equity impacts when used as the sole criterion for judging program success.

Empathy: The ability to understand and share the feelings and perspectives of others, involving both cognitive recognition of another's emotional state and an emotional response to their experience.

Empowerment evaluation: An evaluation approach that seeks to increase the likelihood of program success by providing program stakeholders with tools for assessing progress and outcomes.

Epigenetics: The study of mechanisms that switch genes on or off without changing DNA; explains how trauma can be passed between generations.

Equity: The condition where everyone, regardless of background, has fair opportunities to achieve optimal outcomes by addressing systemic barriers and providing resources according to need rather than treating everyone identically.

Evaluand: The object being evaluated (e.g., a program, policy, product, or organization).

Evaluation theory tree: Framework by Christie and Alkin organizing evaluation approaches into three branches: methods, use, or values.

Experimental evaluations: Evaluation designs that use controlled conditions, random assignment, and comparison groups to test the causal effects of interventions or programs. These approaches, commonly used in medical research and social science, emphasize rigorous methods to isolate the effects of specific variables while minimizing bias and confounding factors.

Explicit infusion: An approach where values and their application are clearly stated and made transparent throughout the evaluation process from the beginning. This involves openly acknowledging the philosophical, ethical, and value frameworks guiding evaluation decisions and methods.

F

Fawning: A proposed fourth trauma response involving appeasing or befriending the threat; appearing overly empathetic to alleviate one's own pain.

Fight, flight, or freeze: Three primary survival responses automatically triggered by the amygdala when the brain perceives threat or danger.

Four R's: SAMHSA's framework: Realize, Recognize, Respond, Resist Retraumatization

Fourth-generation evaluation: Guba and Lincoln's constructivist evaluation approach emphasizing stakeholder participation and multiple constructions of reality.

H

Hawthorne effect: The phenomenon where individuals change their behavior when they know they are being observed or participating in research.

Healing justice: A framework that integrates personal, community, and systemic healing as essential components of social justice work, recognizing that trauma and oppression are interconnected and require holistic approaches to address. This approach emphasizes collective care, community-led healing practices, and the understanding that individual wellness and social transformation are fundamentally linked.

High-engagement approaches: Evaluation methodologies that actively involve stakeholders, participants, and community members as partners in the evaluation process rather than simply as subjects of study. Examples include utilization-focused evaluation (UFE) and empowerment evaluation, which prioritize meaningful participation, shared decision making, and collaborative knowledge creation throughout all phases of evaluation.

Hippocampus: Brain region controlling memory storage and emotions; helps distinguish between past and present.

Historical, intergenerational, transgenerational trauma: The cumulative emotional and psychological wounding over the lifespan and generations from massive group trauma, including slavery, colonialism, persecution, and genocide, including attempts to eradicate all or part of a culture or people (e.g., Indigenous peoples, European Jews, Palestinians, Cambodians, Armenians).

Homeostasis: The balanced state of a body.

Hyperarousal/hypervigilance: A state where the alert system is overactivated and the body is prepared to defend itself constantly.

Hypothalamic–pituitary–adrenal (HPA) system: System to release stress hormones such as adrenaline and cortisol.

I

Implicit infusion: An approach where values are present and identifiable in the evaluation but are not explicitly stated or discussed. While these values influence the evaluation design and implementation, they remain unspoken assumptions rather than openly declared principles.

Informal evaluation: Subconscious judgment-making and decision processes that occur naturally in human cognition, often without systematic methods or explicit criteria. This approach poses significant risks when applied to important social issues, as it may perpetuate bias and harm vulnerable populations.

Informed consent: A process that ensures participants fully understand the evaluation and what is being asked of them prior to agreeing to participate, allowing them to make voluntary decisions without undue pressure or coercion.

Insensitivity: Disregard for how our actions may or may not affect others.

J

Judgment: The act of forming opinions, making assessments, or drawing conclusions about people, situations, or experiences based on available information and professional expertise. In trauma-informed evaluation, judgment is used wisely and thoughtfully, distinguishing between necessary professional judgments about programs or systems and harmful personal judgments about participants' experiences, choices, or circumstances.

Justice: The principle of fairness and equity that seeks to address systemic inequalities, ensure equal access to opportunities and resources, and remedy historical wrongs.

L

Lens: A conceptual framework that modifies how one views and practices evaluation without replacing the underlying methodology, like glasses that help evaluators see their work differently within whatever approach they're already using.

Logic model: Visual representation showing the logical connections between program inputs, activities, outputs, and outcomes.

M

Member checking: Process of testing hypotheses, data, and interpretations with study participants to ensure accuracy and credibility.

Moral distress: The sense of failing to provide adequate care or achieve valued objectives.

Moral injury: Similar to the concept of participation-induced trauma; trauma as a result of a person inflicting harm on another person and committing a moral transgression.

N

Negative case analysis: Process of revising hypotheses in light of cases that don't fit the pattern, strengthening overall findings.

Neuroplasticity: The brain's ability to heal itself by rewiring neural pathways when provided with safe environments and experiences.

O

Ongoing informed consent: Continuing to ask for permission throughout a study, not just at the beginning.

Outcome hacking: Analyzing data in multiple ways to find any plausible associations, improvements, or outcomes, similar to *p*-hacking in statistics.

P

Parasympathetic nervous system (PNS): The nervous system branch activated when we feel safe, centered, balanced, and resilient.

Participation-induced trauma: Trauma that results from being an active participant in harming others, including committing domestic abuse, police brutality/oppression, child soldiering, gang violence, white supremacy.

Passive response dissociation: A response to danger or threats characterized by complete surrender or passivity; similar to the freeze response.

Peer debriefing: Engaging with neutral colleagues to discuss hypotheses, conclusions, and interpretations during evaluation.

***p*-hacking:** The practice of manipulating data analysis, statistical tests, or research design to achieve statistically significant results (typically $p < .05$), often by selectively reporting favorable outcomes, testing multiple hypotheses without correction, or stopping data collection when desired results are reached. This practice undermines the integrity and reliability of research findings by artificially inflating the appearance of statistical significance.

Positionality: Our understanding of ourselves and what we bring to evaluation work, including how we view, value, and approach situations based on our physical and social background, experiences, upbringing, training, and outlook on life.

Posttraumatic slave syndrome (PTSS): Trauma experienced by enslaved people and its transgenerational effects on African Americans.

Posttraumatic stress disorder (PTSD): A chronic anxiety disorder resulting from trauma that persists over a month and causes extreme distress.

Prefrontal cortex: The rational, thinking brain where executive functions like decision making are housed.

Progressive subjectivity: Process of monitoring evaluator's developing constructions by documenting initial assumptions and comparing with findings.

Protective and compensatory experiences (PACEs): Relational factors that promote child resilience and serve as antidotes to ACEs.

Psychic numbing: People's decreased ability to empathize when they are exposed to larger and larger numbers of people experiencing death, disaster, or suffering.

R

Randomized controlled trials (RCTs): Experimental research design where participants are randomly assigned to treatment or control groups to test the effectiveness of interventions. Although RCTs have strong IRB oversight for safety, they may lack attention to equity, justice, and historical issues affecting traumatized populations.

Reactive attachment disorder: A condition in which young children fail to form healthy emotional bonds with primary caregivers, typically due to severe early neglect, abuse, or frequent changes in caregivers during critical developmental periods (usually before age 5).

Relative merit: A judgment that compares the value or effectiveness of one program, intervention, or approach with another to determine which performs better. For example, assessing whether therapy *X* works better than therapy *Y* in reducing trauma symptoms.

Remembering: Simply recalling a traumatic incident, which may or may not be accompanied by a trauma response.

Resilience: The ability of individuals, communities, or systems to adapt, recover, and maintain functioning in the face of adversity, trauma, or significant stress.

Resilience practices: Specific techniques and activities that help build individual and collective capacity to cope with stress and adversity, such as breathing breaks, mindfulness exercises, or grounding techniques.

Restorative justice: A framework that focuses on repairing harm and rebuilding relationships rather than punishment, emphasizing accountability, healing, and community involvement in addressing wrongdoing. This approach seeks to meet the needs of those harmed while creating opportunities for those who caused harm to make amends and reintegrate into the community.

Restorative Justice Circles: A structured process for organizing effective group communication, relationship building, decision making, and conflict resolution. The process creates a space apart from our normal ways of being together.

Retraumatization: Traumatic stress reactions occurring from multiple exposures to traumatic events, distinguished from triggering or remembering.

Return on investment (ROI): A financial metric measuring the efficiency of an investment by calculating the ratio of net profit to cost, typically expressed as a percentage.

S

Safe space: An environment where individuals feel physically and emotionally secure, free from judgment, harassment, and discrimination, allowing them to express themselves and share experiences comfortably.

Safety: One of SAMHSA's Six Principles: being secure and unthreatened physically, psychologically, spiritually, and emotionally.

Secondary trauma: The emotional distress and psychological impact resulting from indirectly witnessing, hearing about, or working closely with victims of trauma; also known as *vicarious trauma* or *secondary traumatic stress.*

Secondary traumatic stress (STS): Stress occurring when exposure to someone else's traumatic experience becomes traumatizing for the helper.

Sensitivity: The practice of approaching a situation and the individuals involved with an openness to a diversity of reactions while critically examining how our actions and words may be perceived and being flexible and willing to make adjustments as needed.

Self-regulate: The ability to manage one's own emotions, thoughts, and behaviors in response to stress or challenging situations.

Six Principles of Trauma-Informed Care: SAMHSA's framework for trauma-informed care: Safety; Trust and Transparency; Peer Support; Collaboration and Mutuality; Empowerment, Voice, and Choice; and Cultural, Historical, and Gender Issues.

Social desirability bias: Tendency for research participants to answer questions in ways they believe are socially acceptable rather than truthfully.

Somatic: Anything relating to the body as opposed to the mind.

Soul wound: Term describing damage caused by historical, intergenerational, and transgenerational trauma.

Stress-response stimuli: Something external to a person that initiates a stress response.

Structural/functional analysis: Analysis that examines data sources, collection methods, and opportunities for bias (both implicit and explicit) to affect evaluation findings. This approach focuses on understanding how methodological choices and structural factors may influence data quality and interpretation.

Structural trauma: the ongoing violence of poverty and systems that make it difficult to meet basic needs such as health care, jobs that pay wages that can support families, etc.

Substantive analysis: Analysis conducted to understand the "why" behind the data by examining context and additional details that provide deeper meaning. This approach goes beyond surface-level findings to explore the underlying reasons and circumstances that help explain evaluation results.

Sympathetic nervous system (SNS): The nervous system branch activated when sensing threat, mobilizing fight or flight responses.

Systematic approaches: Evaluation methodologies that follow structured, methodical processes with clearly defined steps, explicit theoretical frameworks, and standardized data collection and analysis procedures. Examples include theory-driven evaluation, consumer-oriented evaluation, and experimental evaluation designs.

T

Tacit/obscured infusion: An approach where values are hidden or not openly acknowledged, with evaluators or funders attempting to present the evaluation as "objective" or value-free. This obscures the underlying assumptions and biases that inevitably shape all evaluation work.

Theory: In evaluation contexts, explanations of fundamental issues such as the nature of evaluation, valuing, evidence, and use that provide frameworks for understanding how evaluation should be conducted.

Theory-driven evaluation: Evaluation approach based on explicit program theory or logic model showing how program activities lead to outcomes.

Theory of change: A comprehensive description of how and why a desired change is expected to happen in a particular context, outlining the causal linkages and underlying assumptions between activities and outcomes. It provides the conceptual foundation for program design and evaluation by articulating the reasoning behind how interventions will produce intended results.

Toxic stress: Prolonged activation of stress response that disrupts brain development and increases risk for stress-related disease.

Transformative evaluation: Evaluation approach focused on promoting social justice and addressing issues of power and oppression.

Transformative justice: A framework that seeks to address harm and conflict by transforming the underlying conditions and systems that create violence and inequality rather than relying on punitive or reformist approaches. This approach emphasizes community accountability, systemic change, and building alternative structures that promote healing and prevent future harm.

Trauma: Results from events experienced as physically or emotionally harmful or life-threatening with lasting adverse effects on functioning.

Trauma-affected people: People who are negatively affected in their daily life by trauma, whether or not they have a trauma or stress-related diagnosis.

Trauma-informed approach: An approach that is inclusive of trauma-specific interventions, as well as one that incorporates key trauma principles.

Trauma-Informed Evaluation and Research (TIER): A lens that applies SAMHSA's trauma-informed principles to evaluation and research work.

Trauma-organized individual: An individual whose personality, behaviors, and perception of the world have become fundamentally structured around the need to cope with chronic, repetitive, or overwhelming stress and traumatic experiences.

Trauma porn: Using painful trauma stories for purposes that fail to dignify the individual, often for shocking emotional response or personal gain.

Trauma theory: A scientifically informed understanding of what happens to humans under overwhelming stress; presupposes trauma as injury, not character flaw.

Treatment effect heterogeneity: The degree to which treatments have different effects on different participants; important for identifying who benefits or is harmed.

Trigger: A stimulus that causes memories or reactions to severe or sustained trauma; a stress response to something that has reactivated the trauma memory, setting off a cascade of neurological and chemical events.

Triggering: When a sensory experience or situation reminds someone of trauma and sets off a trauma response.

U

Utilization-focused evaluation (UFE): Patton's approach emphasizing that evaluations should be designed for specific intended uses by specific intended users.

V

Values: Beliefs, principles, or criteria that guide what is considered important, good, or worthwhile; central to making evaluative judgments.

Vicarious trauma: The emotional and psychological effects experienced by individuals who are exposed to the traumatic experiences of others through their work or relationships, resulting in lasting changes to their inner experience and worldview.

W

Window of tolerance (WoT): The zone where the nervous system is relaxed, calm, alert, and engaged; can open or close based on stress levels.

References

Abma, T. A., & Widdershoven, G. A. M. (2005). Sharing stories: Narrative and dialogue in responsive nursing evaluation. *Evaluation and the Health Professions, 28*(1), 90–109.

Ahrens, V., Cruz, E., Pasturczak, M., Bakken, L. L., & Moore, T. R. (2023). Between funding requirements and community priorities: Centro Hispano of Dane County's transformative approach to program evaluation. *Journal of MultiDisciplinary Evaluation, 19*(4), 197–212.

American Evaluation Association. (n.d.-a). *Competencies & standards.* www.eval.org/About/Competencies-Standards.

American Evaluation Association. (n.d.-b). *Guiding Principles for Evaluators.* www.eval.org/About/Guiding-Principles.

American Psychiatric Association. (1980). *Diagnostic and statistical manual of mental disorders* (3rd ed.). Author.

American Psychiatric Association. (2022). *Diagnostic and statistical manual of mental disorders* (5th ed., text rev.). Author.

American Psychological Association. (2018, April 19). Hawthorne effect. In *APA dictionary of psychology.* Author.

Andrews, N. C. Z., Pepler, D. J., & Motz, M. (2019). Research and evaluation with community-based projects: Approaches, considerations, and strategies. *American Journal of Evaluation, 40*(4), 548–561.

APA Dictionary of Psychology. (2026). *Hawthorne effect.* https://dictionary.apa.org/hawthorne-effect.

Astbury, B. (2016). Reframing how evaluators think and act: New insights from Ernest House. *Evaluation, 22*(1), 58–71.

Atkinson, J. (2002). *Trauma trails, recreating song lines: The transgenerational effects of trauma in Indigenous Australia.* Spinifex Press.

Auger, M., Crooks, C. V., Lapp, A., Tsuruda, S., Caron, C., Rogers, B. J., & van der Woerd, K. (2019). The essential role of cultural safety in developing culturally-relevant prevention programming in First Nations communities: Lessons learned from a national evaluation of Mental Health First Aid First Nations. *Evaluation and Program Planning, 72*, 188–196.

Baizerman, M. (2012). Introduction. *Evaluation and Program Planning, 35*(1), 139–147.

Bardin, A., Verma, S., Wagner, J., Ruffier, A., & Morse, D. S. (2022). FOCUS on women: Program evaluation of a pilot probation and primary care transitions clinic collaboration. *Evaluation and Program Planning, 92*, 102088.

Berends, L., & Wansbrough, H. (2023). Enabling young people's involvement in research: Principles for a family youth alcohol and other drug program evaluation. *American Journal of Evaluation, 44*(3), 394–405.

Bergner, L., Eisenberg, M., & Hallstrom, A. (1979). Evaluating emergency medical services: Quasi-experimental outcome studies. *Evaluation & the Health Professions, 1*(5), 3–19.

Bledsoe, K. L. (2021). Evaluation's identity: Who are we, why are we here, and what does our future look like? *Evaluation Matters—He Take Tō Te Aromatawai, 7*, 6–29.

Bledsoe, K. L., & Donaldson, S. I. (2014). Culturally responsive theory-driven evaluation. In S. Hood, R. K. Hopson, & H. T. Frierson (Eds.), *Continuing the journey to reposition culture and cultural context in evaluation theory and practice* (pp. 3–28). Information Age.

Bloom, S. L., & Farragher, B. (2013). *Restoring sanctuary: A new operating system for trauma-informed systems of care.* Oxford University Press.

Bosk, E. A. (2023). Creating a parallel process: A new methodological framework for conducting Trauma-Informed Evaluation and Research (TIER) in mental health settings. *Evaluation and Program Planning, 97*, 102229.

Boyce, A. S., Reid, A., Avent, C., Adetogun, A., Moller, J. R., & Singletary, B. H. (2023). Social justice as ontology: The intersection of Black evaluators' identities, roles, and practice. *American Journal of Evaluation, 44*(3), 528–548.

Boyes-Watson, C., & Pranis, K. (2020). *Circle forward: Building a restorative school community* (Revised ed.). Living Justice Press.

Brave Heart, M. Y. H. (2000). Wakiksuyapi: Carrying the historical trauma of the Lakota. *Tulane Studies in Social Welfare, 21*(22), 245–266.

Briant-Davis, T. (2019). The cultural context of trauma recovery: Considering the posttraumatic stress disorder practice guideline and intersectionality. *Psychotherapy, 56*(2), 400–408.

Bride, B. E., Robinson, M. M., Yegidis, B., & Figley, C. R. (2004). Development and validation of the secondary traumatic stress scale. *Research on Social Work Practice, 14*(1), 27–35.

Bridgland, V. M. E., Jones, P. J., & Bellet, B. W. (2024). A meta-analysis of the efficacy of trigger warnings, content warnings, and content notes. *Clinical Psychological Science, 12*(4), 751–771.

Brounéus, K. (2008). Truth-telling as talking cure?: Insecurity and retraumatization in the Rwandan Gacaca courts. *Security Dialog, 39*(1), 55–76.

Brown, B. (2012a). *Dare to lead: The engaged feedback checklist.* https://brenebrown.com/resources/the-engaged-feedback-checklist/.

Brown, B. (2012b). *Daring greatly: How the courage to be vulnerable transforms the way we live, love, parent, and lead.* Gotham Books.

Brown, M. A. (2015). Talking in circles: A mixed methods study of school-wide restorative practices in two urban middle schools (Doctoral dissertation, Florida Atlantic University). *ProQuest Dissertations & Theses Global* (UMI No. 10154934).

Brown, M. A. (2018). *Creating restorative schools: Setting schools up to succeed.* Living Justice Press.

Brown, M. A., & Di Lallo, S. (2020). Talking circles: A culturally responsive evaluation practice. *American Journal of Evaluation, 41*(3), 367–383.

Brummer, J., & Thorsborn, M. (2021). *Building a trauma-informed restorative school: Skill and approaches for improving culture and behavior.* Jessica Kingsley.

Burke Harris, N. (2021). *The deepest well: Healing the long-term effects of childhood trauma and adversity.* Houghton Mifflin Harcourt.

Burns, K., Fox, L., & Wilson, R. (2022, September 13). *Record drop in child poverty: Child poverty fell to a record low 5.2% in 2021.* U.S. Census Bureau. www.census.gov/library/stories/2022/09/record-drop-in-child-poverty.html.

Cabrera, M. (2002, December). Living and surviving in a multiply wounded country. *Revista Envío*, No. 257. www.revistaenvio.org/articulo/1629.

Caldwell, L. D., & Bledsoe, K. L. (2019). Can social justice live in a house of structural racism?: A question for the field of evaluation. *American Journal of Evaluation, 40*(1), 6–18

Campbell, R., Adams, A. E., & Patterson, D. (2008). Methodological challenges of collecting evaluation data from traumatized clients/consumers: A comparison of three methods. *American Journal of Evaluation, 29*(3), 369–381.

Campbell, R., Adams, A. E., Wasco, S. M., Ahrens, C. E., & Sefl, T. (2010). "What has it been like for you to talk with me today?": The impact of participating in interview research on rape survivors. *Violence Against Women, 16*(1), 60–83.

Campbell, R., Greeson, M. R., & Fehler-Cabral, G. (2014). Developing recruitment methods for vulnerable, traumatized adolescents: A feminist evaluation approach. *American Journal of Evaluation, 35*(1), 73–86.

Cénat, J. M. (2023) Complex racial trauma: Evidence, theory, assessment, and treatment. *Perspectives in Psychological Science, 18*(3), 675–687.

Center for Justice and Peacebuilding. (2023). *STAR: Strategies for trauma awareness and resilience: Level 1 workbook.* Eastern Mennonite University. www.emu.edu/star.

Center on Aging, Trauma, and Holocaust Survivor Care, The Jewish Federations of North America. (2024). *The person-centered, trauma-informed (PCTI) approach.* Author.

Center on Holocaust Survivor Care, The. (n.d.). *Aging with a history of trauma: A guide for providing person-centered, trauma-informed care for older adults.* Jewish Federations of North America. www.jewishfederations.org/blog/all/aging-with-a-history-of-trauma-guides-holocaust-survivor-care-451546.

Centers for Disease Control and Prevention. (1997). *Principles of community engagement.* stacks.cdc.gov/view/cdc/251390.

Centers for Disease Control and Prevention. (n.d.). *Adverse childhood experiences (ACEs).* www.cdc.gov/violenceprevention/aces/index.html.

Cetrano, G., Tedeschi, F., Rabbi, L., Gosetti, G., Lora, A., Lamonaca, D., et al. (2017). How are compassion fatigue, burnout, and compassion satisfaction affected by quality of working life?: Findings from a survey of mental health staff in Italy. *BMC Health Services Research, 17*(1), 755.

Chauvin, L., Mugajuu, J., & Comlavi, J. (1998). Evaluation of the psychosocial trauma recovery programme in Rwanda. *Evaluation and Program Planning, 21*, 385–392.

Chicago Beyond. (2018). *Why am I being researched.* https://chicagobeyond.org/wp-content/uploads/2019/05/ChicagoBeyond_2019Guidebook.pdf.

Chödrön, P. (2009). *Taking the leap: Freeing ourselves from old habits and fears.* Shambhala.

Christie, C., & Alkin, M. (2012). An evaluation theory tree. In M. C. Alkin (Ed.), *Evaluation roots: A wider perspective of theorists' views and influences* (2nd ed., pp. 11–57). Sage.

Chu, B., Marwaha, K., Sanvictores, T., Awosika, A. O., & Ayers, D. (2024). Physiology, stress reaction. In *StatPearls* [Internet]. StatPearls.

Coetzee, S. K., & Laschinger, H. K. S. (2018). Toward a comprehensive, theoretical model of compassion fatigue: An integrative literature review. *Nursing & Health Sciences, 20*(1), 4–15.

Cohen, B. B. (2012). Conducting evaluation in contested terrain: Challenges, methodology and approach in an American context. *Evaluation and Program Planning, 35*(1), 189–198.

Coll, K. M., Sawyer, S., Scholl, S., & Hauser, N. (2019). A logic model development for an adolescent based intervention to improve benefits from therapeutic residential care. *Evaluation and Program Planning, 76*, 101678.

Cook, A., Spinazzola, J., Ford, J., Lanktree, C., Blaustein, M., Cloitre, M., et al. (2003). *Complex trauma in children and adolescents.* National Child Traumatic Stress Network.

Coryn, C. L. S., Wilson, L. N., Westine, C. D., Hobson, K. A., Ozeki, S., Fiekowsky, E. L., et al. (2017). A decade of research on evaluation. *American Journal of Evaluation, 38*(3), 329–347.

Craig, S. E. (2016). *Trauma-sensitive schools: Learning communities transforming children's lives, K–5.* Teachers College Press.

Craig, S. E. (2017). *Trauma-sensitive schools for the adolescent years: Promoting resiliency and healing, grades 6–12.* Teachers College Press.

Cram, F. (2018). Conclusion: Lessons about Indigenous evaluation. *New Directions for Evaluation, 159*, 121–133.

Crenshaw, K., Gotanda, N., Peller, G., & Thomas, K. (Eds.). (1995). *Critical race theory: The key writings that formed the movement.* New Press.

Cruwys, T., Macleod, E., Curll, S., Walker, I., Kurz, T., Western, K., et al. (2025). Is trauma isolating, or does isolation traumatize?: Loneliness and posttraumatic stress mutually reinforce one another in the aftermath of environmental disaster. *Psychological Trauma: Theory, Research, Practice, and Policy.*

Cunningham, V., Mohler, M. J., Wendel, C. S., Hoffman, R. M., Murata, G. H., Shah, J. H., & Duckworth, W. C. (2005). Reliability and validity of the DCP among Hispanic veterans. *Evaluation and the Health Professions, 28*(4), 447–463.

David, P., & Schiff, M. (2015). Learning from bottom-up dissemination: Importing an evidence-based trauma intervention for infants and young children to Israel. *Evaluation and Program Planning, 53*, 18–24.

Davis, A. Y. (2014, February 13). Speech at Southern Illinois University Carbondale, Carbondale, IL.

Dean-Coffey, J. (2018). What's race got to do with it?: Equity and philanthropic evaluation practice. *American Journal of Evaluation, 39*(4), 527–542.

DeGruy, J., & Leary, J. D. (2005). *Post traumatic slave syndrome: America's legacy of enduring injury and healing.* Joy DeGruy Publications.

de Sousa Santos, B. (2014). *Epistemologies of the South.* Routledge.

DeWolf, T. N., & Geddes, J. (2019). *The little book of racial healing: Coming to the table for truth-telling, liberation, and transformation.* Good Books.

Duckworth, M. P., & Follette, V. M. (2012). *Retraumatization: Assessment, treatment and prevention.* Routledge.

Eastern Mennonite University. (2023). *STAR: Strategies for trauma awareness and resilience: Level 1 workbook.* Eastern Mennonite University.

Elliott, D. E., Bjelajac, P., Fallot, R. D., Markoff, L. S., & Reed, B. G. (2005). Trauma-informed or trauma-denied: Principles and implementation of trauma-informed services for women. *Journal of Community Psychology, 33*(4), 461–477.

Equitable Evaluation Initiative. (2024). *EEF expansion: Elements of the EEF.* www.equitableeval.org/post/eef-expansion-eef-elements.

Evans, K. R., & Lester, J. N. (2013). Restorative justice in education: What we know so far. *Middle School Journal, 44*(5), 57–63.

Evans, K., & Vaandering, D. (2022). *The little book of restorative justice in education: Fostering responsibility, healing, and hope in schools* (rev. and updated ed.). Good Books.

Evergreen, S. D. (2019). *Presenting data effectively: Communicating your findings for maximum impact* (2nd ed.). Sage.

Evergreen, S. D. (2023, September 26). Ethical riders in your contract. *Stephanie Evergreen Email Newsletter.*

Felitti, V. J., Anda, R. F., Nordenberg, D., Williamson, D. F., Spitz, A. M., Edwards, V., et al. (1998). Relationship of childhood abuse and household dysfunction to many of the leading causes of death in adults: The Adverse Childhood Experiences (ACE) Study. *American Journal of Preventive Medicine, 14*(4), 245–258.

Felt, D., Perez-Bill, E., Ruprecht, M. M., Petillo, M., Beach, L. B., Glenn, E. E., & Phillips, G. (2022). Becoming an LGBTQ+ storyteller: Collecting and using data on gender, sex, and sexual orientation. *New Directions for Evaluation, 2022*(175), 31–52.

Fenkel, C. (2023, July 30). *Is fawning a trauma response?: What you need to know.* www.charliehealth.com/post/is-fawning-a-trauma-response-what-you-need-to-know.

Fierro, R. S. (2019). Authentic self in evaluation consulting: Reflections after 10 years. *New Directions for Evaluation, 2019*(164), 141–154.

Filipovic, J. (2023, September). I was wrong about trigger warnings. *The Atlantic.* www.theatlantic.com/magazine/archive/2023/09/trigger-warnings-feminism-teen-girls-mental-health/674759/.

Firestone, W. A. (1991). Merit pay and job enlargement as reforms: Incentives, implementation, and teacher response. *Educational Evaluation and Policy Analysis, 13*(3), 269–288.

Ford, J. D. (2005). Treatment implications of altered affect regulation and information processing following child maltreatment. *Psychiatric Annals, 35*(5), 410–419.

Ford, J. D., Grasso, D. J., Hawke, J., & Chapman, J. F. (2013). Poly-victimization among juvenile justice-involved youths. *Child Abuse & Neglect, 37*(10), 788–800.

Gatwiri, K., & Mapedzahama, V. (2022). Pedagogy or "trauma porn"?: Racial literacy as a prerequisite for teaching racially dignifying content in the Australian social work context. *Journal for Multicultural Education, 16*(3), 272–282.

Gerhart, J. I., Canetti, D., & Hobfoll, S. E. (2015). Traumatic stress in overview: Definition, context, scope, and long-term outcomes. In K. E. Cherry (Ed.), *Traumatic stress and long-term recovery: Coping with disasters and other negative life events* (pp. 3–24). Springer.

Gilman, G. (2023, October 18). Frightening events can have lasting effects. *Faribault Daily News*, A5.

Ginwright, S. A. (2016). *Hope and healing in urban education: How urban activists and teachers are reclaiming matters of the heart.* Routledge.

Glines, M., & Cruz, E. (2019, May 19). *Health equity from the inside-out: Centro's employee wellness plan.* Presentation at the 2019 Wisconsin Public Health Association Conference, Madison, WI.

Goldsmith, R. E., Martin, C. G., & Smith, C. P. (2014). Systemic trauma. *Journal of Trauma and Dissociation, 15*(2), 117–132.

Graham, L. (2010, June). The neuroscience of resilience. *Wise Brain Bulletin, 4*, 6. https://s3.us-west-1.amazonaws.com/wisebrain.org/WiseBrainBulletin/WBB4.6.pdf.

Greater Good Magazine. (n.d.). What is empathy? Greater Good Science Center. greatergood.berkeley.edu/topic/empathy/definition.

Greene, J. C. (1997). Evaluation as advocacy. *Evaluation Practice, 18*(1), 25–35.

Guba, E. G., & Lincoln, Y. S. (1989). *Fourth generation evaluation.* Sage.

Guo, J. W., Wallace, A. S., Luther, B. L., & Wong, B. (2022). Psychometric evaluation of the screener for intensifying community referrals for health. *Evaluation and the Health Professions, 45*(3), 270–276.

Harold, C., & DeLuca, K. M. (2005). Behold the corpse: Violent images and the case of Emmett Till. *Rhetoric & Public Affairs, 8*(2), 263–286.

Hartman, A., Hoessler, B., Tom, V., & Camman, C. (2022). Identity as a compass when navigating uncharted equitable spaces: Our queer evaluation practices. *New Directions for Evaluation, 2022*(175), 53–73.

Hatcher, A. M., McBride, R. S., Rebombo, D., Munshi, S., Khumalo, M., & Christofides, N. (2020). Process evaluation of a community mobilization intervention for preventing men's partner violence use in peri-urban South Africa. *Evaluation and Program Planning, 78*, 101727.

Haugen, J. S., & Chouinard, J. A. (2019). Transparent, translucent, opaque: Exploring the dimensions of power in culturally responsive evaluation contexts. *American Journal of Evaluation, 40*(3), 376–394.

Hays-Grudo, J., & Morris, A. S. (2020). *Adverse and protective childhood experiences: A developmental perspective.* American Psychological Association.

Head, M. L., Holman, L., Lanfear, R., Kahn, A. T., & Jennions, M. D. (2015). The extent and consequences of *p*-hacking in science. *PLoS Biology, 13*(3), 1–15.

Herman, J. L. (1992). *Trauma and recovery: The aftermath of violence: From domestic abuse to political terror.* Basic Books.

Hoeper, J. (2013). *Mitigating compassion fatigue among child protection social workers* Master's thesis, University of St. Thomas, Minnesota.

Hood, S., Hopson, R. K., & Frierson, H. T. (Eds.). (2015). *Continuing the journey to reposition culture and cultural context in evaluation theory and practice.* Information Age.

Hopson, R. K., Kirkhart, K. E., & Bledsoe, K. L. (2012). Decolonizing evaluation in a developing world: Implications and cautions for equity-focused evaluations. In M. Segone (Ed.), *Evaluation for equitable development results* (pp. 59–83). UNICEF.

Huff, S. (2023). *Understanding the relationship between evaluator role and compassion fatigue.* Unpublished manuscript, University of North Carolina at Greensboro.

Huff, S. (2025). *Between empathy and exhaustion: Exploring compassion fatigue in program evaluation.* Unpublished doctoral dissertation, University of North Carolina Greensboro.

Huggard, P., & Unit, G. (2013). A systematic review of the measurement of compassion fatigue, vicarious trauma, and secondary traumatic stress in physicians. *Australasian Journal of Disaster and Trauma Studies, 2013*(1), 37–44.

Hundall Stamm, B. (2009). Professional quality of life measure: Compassion, satisfaction, and fatigue (ProQOL) (Version 5) [Software]. https://proqol.org/proqol-measure.

Hutchinson, K. S. (2017). *A short primer on innovative evaluation reporting.* Community Solutions Planning & Evaluation.

Imai, K., & Ratkovic, M. (2013). Estimating treatment effect heterogeneity in randomized program evaluation. *Annals of Applied Statistics, 7*(1), 443–470.

Ismail, Y., Griffiths, D., & Bond-Gorr, J. (2022). Empowering the search for pleasure, health and well-being outside heteronormative definitions: The role of evaluation in shaping structurally sensitive programming for 2SGBTQ+ men who *Party and Play* in Ontario. *New Directions for Evaluation, 2022*(175), 87–107.

Jones, C. P. (2014). Systems of power, axes of inequity. *Medical Care, 52*, S71–S75.

Jones, S. M., Bodie, G. D., & Hughes, S. D. (2016). The impact of mindfulness on empathy, active listening, and perceived provisions of emotional support. *Communication Research, 46*(6), 838–865.

Kahn, J. (2020, January 16). *What "holding space" means + 5 tips to practice* [Web log post]. Gender & Sexuality Therapy Center. www.gstherapycenter.com/blog/2020/1/16/what-holding-space-means-5-tips-to-practice.

Kennedy, M. M. (1983). The role of the in-house evaluator. *Evaluation Review, 7*(4), 519–541.

Kilpatrick, D. G., Resnick, H. S., Milanak, M. E., Miller, M. W., Keyes, K. M., & Friedman, M. J. (2013). National estimates of exposure to traumatic events and PTSD prevalence using DSM-IV and DSM-5 criteria. *Journal of Traumatic Stress, 26*(5), 537–547.

Kim, D. I., Park, S., Park, S., Ye, M., Chen, J. Y., Kang, S. J., et al. (2024). Presynaptic sensor and silencer of peptidergic transmission reveal neuropeptides as primary transmitters in pontine fear circuit. *Cell, 187*(18), 5102–5117.

Kostovicova, D., & Knott, E. (2022). Harm, change and unpredictability: The ethics of interviews in conflict research. *Qualitative Research, 22*(1), 56–73.

Kozlowska, K., Walker, P., McLean, L., & Carrive, P. (2015). Fear and the defense cascade: Clinical implications and management. *Harvard Review of Psychiatry, 23*(4), 263–287.

Kubiak, S. P., Fedock, G., Tillander, E., Kim, W. J., & Bybee, D. (2014). Assessing the feasibility and fidelity of an intervention for women with violent offenses. *Evaluation and Program Planning, 42*, 1–10.

Kübler-Ross, E. (1969). *On death and dying*. Routledge.

LaChenaye, J. M., & McCarthy, S. (2022). The intersection of counseling microskills and qualitative interviewing and reporting in the study of sensitive topics. *American Journal of Evaluation, 43*(2), 255–268.

Ladson-Billings, G. (2000). Racialized discourses and ethnic epistemologies. *Handbook of Qualitative Research, 2*(1), 257–277.

Lederach, J. P., & Lederach, A. J. (2010). *When blood and bones cry out: Journeys through the soundscape of healing and reconciliation*. Oxford University Press.

Ledoux, K. (2015). Understanding compassion fatigue: Understanding compassion. *Journal of Advanced Nursing, 71*(9), 2041–2050.

Levins Morales, A. (1998). *Medicine stories: History, culture, and the politics of integrity*. South End Press.

Lewis, E. F., Hardy, M., & Snaith, B. (2013). Estimating the effect of nonresponse bias in a survey of hospital organizations. *Evaluation and the Health Professions, 36*(3), 330–351.

Madigan, S., Deneault, A.-A., Racine, N., Park, J., Thiemann, R., Zhu, J., et al. (2023). Adverse childhood experiences: A meta-analysis of prevalence and moderators among half a million adults in 206 studies. *World Psychiatry, 22*(3), 463–471.

Malhotra, G., Machado, S., & Aslam, G. (2023, June 27). *The case for building trauma-informed competence for evaluators*. EnCompass LLC.

Martinez, A., Running Wolf, P., BigFoot, D. S., Randal, C., & Villegas, M. (2018). The process of becoming: A roadmap to evaluation in Indian country. *New Directions for Evaluation, 159*, 33–45.

Masten, A. S., & Motti-Stefanidi, F. (2020). Multisystem resilience for children and youth in disaster: Reflections in the context of COVID-19. *Adversity and Resilience Science, 1*(2), 95–106.

Mawhinney, L., Drame, E. R., Bowe, A. G., Duval-Diop, D., Kares, F. R., & Santos, P. (2023). Responding to the times: Adapting an evaluation study during a dual pandemic. *Evaluation and Program Planning, 97*, 1–6.

Mayo Clinic. (2026). *Vasovagal syncope*. www.mayoclinic.org/diseases-conditions/vasovagal-syncope/symptoms-causes/syc-20350527.

McCormack, L., Ballinger, S., Valentine, M., & Swaab, L. (2022). Complex trauma and posttraumatic growth: A bibliometric analysis of research output over time. *Traumatology, 28*(2), 245–255.

Mears, C. L. (Ed.). (2012). *Reclaiming school in the aftermath of trauma: Advice based on experience*. Palgrave Macmillan.

Menakem, R. (2017). *My grandmother's hands: Racialized trauma and the pathway to mending our hearts and bodies*. Central Recovery Press.

Mertens, D. M. (2023, October 13). *Increasing the power of story through transformative culturally responsive mixed methods evaluation*. Paper presented at the annual conference of the American Evaluation Association, New Orleans, LA.

Mertens, D. M., Hall, J., & Wilson, A. T. (2025). *Program evaluation theory and practice: A comprehensive guide* (3rd ed.). Guilford Press.

Miller, K. I., Stiff, J. B., & Ellis, B. J. (1988). Communication and empathy as precursors to burnout among human service workers. *Communication Monographs, 55*(3), 250–265.

Miller, R. L., & Tohme, J. (2022). LGBTQ+ human rights evaluation in the global South: Lessons from evaluating Project ACT. *New Directions for Evaluation, 2022*(175), 139–151.

Molnar, B. E., Sprang, G., Killian, K. D., Gottfried, R., Emery, V., & Bride, B. E. (2017). Advancing science and practice for vicarious traumatization/secondary traumatic stress: A research agenda. *Traumatology, 23*(2), 129–142.

Montrosse-Moorhead, B., Schröter, D., & Becho, L. W. (2024). The garden of evaluation approaches. *American Journal of Evaluation, 45*(2), 164–317.

National Institutes of Health. (2025, June 10). *Guiding principles for ethical research.* www.nih.gov/health-information/nih-clinical-research-trials-you/guiding-principles-ethical-research.

Newcomb, M., & Venning, A. (2024). Defending discomfort: A critical social work case against trigger warnings. *Journal of Social Work Education, 60*(4), 565–575.

Nimmo, A., & Huggard, P. (2013). A systematic review of the measurement of compassion fatigue, vicarious trauma and secondary traumatic stress in physicians. *Australasian Journal of Disaster and Trauma Studies, 2013*, 37–44. trauma.massey.ac.nz/issues/2013-1/AJDTS_2013-1_ Nimmo.pdf.

Okun, T. (2021). *White supremacy culture.* www.whitesupremacyculture.info/progress-quantity.html.

O'Leary, M. R., & Donovan, D. M. (1979). Male alcoholics treatment outcome as a function of length of treatment and level of current adaptive abilities. *Evaluation and the Health Professions, 2*(3), 373–384.

Organisation for Economic Co-operation and Development. (2019). *Evaluation criteria: Adapted definitions and principles for use.* https://one.oecd.org/document/DCD/DAC(2019)58/FINAL/en/pdf.

Parker, T. (2024, June 30). *Uplifting voices: Embedding equity practices as independent consultants* [Web log post]. AEA365. https://aea365.org/blog/independent-consulting-ictig-week-uplifting-voices-embedding-equity-practices-as-independent-consultants-by-tasha-parker.

Partridge, C. (2010). Residential schools: The intergenerational impacts on Aboriginal peoples. *Native Social Work Journal, 7*, 33–62.

Patton, M. Q. (2016). Book review: Cherry Street Alley. *American Journal of Evaluation, 37*(3), 441–447.

Pehlivan, T., & Güner, P. (2018). Compassion fatigue: The known and unknown. *Journal of Psychiatric Nursing/Psikiyatri Hemsireleri Dernegi, 9*(2), 129–134.

Phillips, G., Felt, D., Perez-Bill, E., Ruprecht, M. M., & Elías Glenn, E. (2022). Principles of LGBTQ+ evaluation. *New Directions for Evaluation, 2022*(175), 15–30.

Phillips, P. P., & Phillips, J. J. (2019). *ROI basics.* Association for Talent Development.

Picciotto, R. (2021). Evaluation as a social practice: Disenchantment, rationalities and ethics. *Evaluation and Program Planning, 87*, 101927.

Plant, A., Schladale, J., Neffa-Creech, D., Qaragholi, N., Miller, M., & Montoya, J. (2023). Development, acceptability, and perceived effectiveness of a trauma-informed adolescent self-regulation intervention. *Evaluation and Program Planning, 97*, 1–10.

Plevkova, J., Brozmanova, M., Harsanyiova, J., Sterusky, M., Honetschlager, J., Buday, T., & Buday, T. (2020). Various aspects of sex and gender bias in biomedical research. *Physiological Research, 69*(Suppl. 3), 368–378.

Pranis, K. (2005). *Little book of circle processes: A new/old approach to peacemaking.* Good Books.

Pranis, K., Stuart, B., & Wedge, M. (2013). *Peacemaking circles: From crime to community.* Living Justice Press.

Price, A. (n.d.). *Do things differently!* Community Evaluation Solutions. www.communityevaluationsolutions.com/blog/dothingsdifferently?rq=Resilient%20Georgia.

Purtle, J., & Lewis, M. (2017). Mapping "trauma-informed" legislative proposals in U.S. congress. *Administration and Policy in Mental Health and Mental Health Services Research, 44*(6), 867–876.

Rabin, C. (2022). *Program evaluation workbook.* The Jewish Federations of North America.

Racine, N., Killam, T., & Madigan, S. (2020). Trauma-informed care as a universal precaution: Beyond the adverse childhood experiences questionnaire. *JAMA Pediatrics, 174*(1), 5–6.

RAND. (n.d.). *Homelessness survey* [Software]. www.rand.org/health-care/surveys_tools/homelessness.html.

Rea, L. M., & Parker, R. A. (2005). *Designing and conducting survey research: A comprehensive guide.* Wiley.

Reid, A. M., Boyce, A. S., Adetogun, A., Moller, J. R., & Avent, C. (2020). If not us, then who?: Evaluators of color and social change. *New Directions for Evaluation, 2020*(166), 23–36.

Rivera, E. (n.d.). Dr. Echo Rivera. www.echorivera.com.

Robinson, S. B., & Leonard, K. F. (2018). *Designing quality survey questions.* Sage.

Roholt, R. V. L., & Baizerman, M. (2012). Being practical, being safe: Doing evaluations in contested spaces. *Evaluation and Program Planning, 35*(1), 206–217.

Sadler, J. Z. (1997, December). Recognizing values: A descriptive-causal method for medical/scientific discourses. *Journal of Medicine and Philosophy: A Forum for Bioethics and Philosophy of Medicine, 22*(6), 541–565.

Schwandt, T., & Gates, E. (2021). *Evaluating and valuing in social research.* Guilford Press.

Schwartz, S. H. (2012). An overview of the Schwartz theory of basic values. *Online Readings in Psychology and Culture, 2*(1), 11–20.

Scriven, M. (1991). *Evaluation thesaurus.* Sage.

Scriven, M. (2013). The foundation and future of evaluation. In S. I. Donaldson (Ed.), *The future of evaluation in society: A tribute to Michael Scriven* (pp. 11–44). Information Age.

Scriven, M. (2015). *Key evaluation checklist.* The Evaluation Center, Western Michigan University. https://files.wmich.edu/s3fs-public/attachments/u1105/2023/kec-scriven.pdf.

Scriven, M. (2019). The checklist imperative. *New Directions for Evaluation, 2019*(163), 49–60.

Shern, D. L., Blanch, A. K., & Steverman, S. M. (2016). Toxic stress, behavioral health, and the next major era in public health. *American Journal of Orthopsychiatry, 86*(2), 109–123.

Siegel, D. J. (2009). *Mindsight: The new science of personal transformation.* Bantam Books.

Sikkema, K. J., Choi, K. W., Robertson, C., Knettel, B. A., Ciya, N., Knippler, E. T., et al. (2018). Development of a coping intervention to improve traumatic stress and HIV care engagement among South African women with sexual trauma histories. *Evaluation and Program Planning, 68*, 148–156.

Simon, T. R., Sussman, S., Dent, C. W., Stacy, A. W., Burton, D., & Flay, B. R. (1996). Predictors of misreporting cigarette smoking initiation among adolescents. *Evaluation Review, 20*(5), 552–567.

Skagit Valley College Libraries. (2026) *Restorative and transformative justice guides.* https://library.skagit.edu/justice.

Slovic, P., Zionts, D., Woods, A. K., Goodman, R., & Jinks, D. (2013). Psychic numbing and mass atrocity. In E. Shafir (Ed.), *The behavioral foundations of public policy* (pp. 126–142). Princeton University Press.

Smith, J. A. (2022). Treatment effect heterogeneity. *Evaluation Review, 46*(5), 652–677.

Smith, N. L. (2010). Characterizing the evaluand in evaluating theory. *American Journal of Evaluation, 31*(3), 383–389.

Spiro, S. E., Shalev, A., Solomon, Z., & Kotler, M. (1989). Self-reported change versus changed self-report: Contradictory findings of an evaluation of a treatment program for war veterans suffering from post traumatic stress disorder. *Evaluation Review, 13*(5), 533–549.

Stamm, B. H. (2010). *The concise ProQOL manual* (2nd ed.). ProQOL.org.

Stern, E., Alemann, C., Delgado, G. A. F., & Vásquez, A. E. (2023). Lessons learned from implementing the parenting Program P in Bolivia to prevent family violence. *Evaluation and Program Planning, 97*, 1–8.

Stubbs, V. D. (2023, March 21). *Creating brave spaces vs safe spaces* [Web log post]. KaPri Consulting. https://kapriconsulting.ca/blog/2023/03/21/creating-brave-spaces/.

Stufflebeam, D. L., & Coryn, C. L. S. (2014). *Evaluation theory, models, and applications* (2nd ed.). Jossey-Bass.

Substance Abuse and Mental Health Services Administration. (2014). *SAMHSA's concept of trauma and guidance for a trauma-informed approach.* U.S. Department of Health and Human Services. https://store.samhsa.gov/sites/default/files/d7/priv/sma14-4884.pdf.

Substance Abuse and Mental Health Services Administration. (2023). *Practical guide for implementing a trauma-informed approach.* U.S. Department of Health and Human Services. www.samhsa.gov/resource/ebp/practical-guide-implementing-trauma-informed-approach.

Swedo, E. A., Aslam, M. V., Dahlberg, L. L., Niolon, P. H., Guinn, A. S., Simon, T. R., & Mercy, J. A. (2023, June 30). Prevalence of adverse childhood experiences among U.S. adults: Behavioral risk factor surveillance system, 2011–2020. *Morbidity and Mortality Weekly Report, 72*(26), 707–715.

Syeda, M. M., Fournie, M., Ibanez, M. C., & Crooks, C. V. (2021). Cocreating an evaluation approach for a healthy relationships program with community partners: Lessons learned and recommendations. *American Journal of Evaluation, 42*(4), 466–482.

Taylor, F., & Cahill, L. (2002). Propranolol for reemergent posttraumatic stress disorder following an event of retraumatization: A case study. *Journal of Traumatic Stress, 15*(5), 433–437.

Teasdale, R. M. (2021). Evaluative criteria: An integrated model of domains and sources. *American Journal of Evaluation, 42*(3), 354–376.

Thomas, V. G. (2004). Building a contextually responsive evaluation framework: Lessons from working with urban school interventions. *New Directions for Evaluation, 101*, 3–23.

Thomas, V. G., & Campbell, P. B. (2020). *Evaluation in today's world: Respecting diversity, improving quality, and promoting usability.* Sage.

Thompson, J. (2022, February 6). *Visualizing the color line: DuBois and data storytelling in 1900.* https://medium.com/ibm-data-ai/visualizing-the-color-line-dubois-and-data-storytelling-in-1900-21f565e64a6d.

Thorsborne, M., & Brummer, J. (2020). *Building a trauma-informed restorative school: Skills and approaches for improving culture and behavior.* Jessica Kingsley.

Tibbitts, D. C., Aicher, S. A., Sugg, J., Handloser, K., Eisman, L., Booth, L. D., & Bradley, R. D. (2021). Program evaluation of trauma-informed yoga for vulnerable populations. *Evaluation and Program Planning, 88*, 101946.

Toedter, L. J., Lasker, J. N., & Campbell, D. T. (1990). The comparison group problem in bereavement studies and the retrospective pretest. *Evaluation Review, 14*(1), 75–90.

Trott, V. (2019, October 2–5). *#Metoo And intersectionalism: "Radical community healing" or "voyeuristic trauma porn?"* Paper presented at the 2019 Annual Conference of the Association of Internet Researchers, Brisbane, Australia.

Turner, J. (2020). Creating safety for ourselves. In E. C. Valandra (Ed.), *Colorizing restorative justice: Voicing our realities* (pp. 291–321). Living Justice Press.

Turner, N. R., Hardiman, E. R., Matteson, A. L., & Fletcher, S. (2022). Pathways to program entry: Factors promoting entry and participation in veteran peer-support programs. *Evaluation and Program Planning, 92*, 1–8.

van der Kolk, B. A. (2005). Developmental trauma disorder: Toward a rational diagnosis for children with complex trauma histories. *Psychiatric Annals, 35*(5), 401–408.

van der Kolk, B. A. (2014). *The body keeps the score: Brain, mind, and body in the healing of trauma.* Viking.

Waapalaneexkweew. (2018). Looking backward but moving forward: Honoring the sacred and asserting the sovereign in indigenous evaluation. *American Journal of Evaluation, 39*(4), 543–568.

Walker, R. (2018). Evaluator as observant outsider. *New Directions for Evaluation, 2018*(157), 35–38.

Waller, B. Y., Joseph, V. A., & Keyes, K. M. (2024). Racial inequities in homicide rates and homicide methods among Black and White women aged 25–44 years in the USA, 1999–2020: A cross-sectional time series study. *The Lancet, 403*, 935–945.

Walsh, J. A., & Walsh, R. A. (1982). Behavioral evaluation of a state program of deinstitutionalization of the developmentally disabled. *Evaluation and Program Planning, 5*, 59–67.

Ward, M., Schulz, A. J., Israel, B. A., Rice, K., Martenies, S. E., & Markarian, E. (2018). A conceptual framework for evaluating health equity promotion within community-based participatory research partnerships. *Evaluation and Program Planning, 70*, 25–34.

Weiss, A. (2025). Beyond retraumatization: Trauma-informed political science research. *British Journal of Political Science, 55*(e82), 1–25.

When one mother defied America: The photo that changed the Civil Rights Movement. (2016, July 10). *Time*. https://time.com/4399793/emmett-till-civil-rights-photography/.

Widdershoven, G. (2018). Foreword. In M. Visse & T. Abma (Eds.), *Evaluation for a caring society* (pp. xi–xiii). Information Age.

Williams, M. E., & Choitz, V. (2024, March 19). *An introduction to trauma-informed research* [Web log post]. Corporation for a Skilled Workforce. https://skilledwork.org/an-introduction-to-trauma-informed-research.

Wolfe, S. M., Long, P. D., & Brown, K. K. (2020). Using a principles-focused evaluation approach to evaluate coalitions and collaborative working toward equity and social justice. *New Directions for Evaluation, 2020*(165), 45–65.

Wolfe, S. M., & Price, A. W. (2019). Partnering for social change: Collaborating with clients and communities. *New Directions for Evaluation, 2019*(164), 89–100.

Wolff, T. (2010). *The power of collaborative solutions: Six principles and effective tools for building healthy communities*. Wiley.

Wright, M. M., & LaVelle, J. M. (2022). Evaluator education through an LGBTQ+ lens: Interrogating power and privilege in the classroom. *New Directions for Evaluation, 2022*(175), 153–169.

Yates, B., & Persaud, N. (2024). Michael Scriven and "the missing half of quantitative evaluation." *Journal of MultiDisciplinary Evaluation, 20*(47), 24–27.

Yoder, C. (2005). *The little book of trauma healing: When violence strikes and community security is threatened*. Good Books.

Zehr, H. (2002). *The little book of restorative justice*. Good Books.

Index

Note. f, n, or *t* following a page number indicates a figure, note, or table; page numbers in **bold** indicate glossary terms

Absolute merit, 122, **207**
Abuse, 5, 21. *See also* ACEs (adverse childhood experiences)
ACEs (adverse childhood experiences)
  collective trauma and, 11
  data analysis and, 174–176
  definition, **207**
  overview, 5–7, 22
  reporting and, 170–171
  trauma-informed programs and, 181–182
  See also Individual trauma; Trauma
Acknowledgement, 109, **207**
Activism, 69, 70*f*, 71*t*. *See also* Social justice
Acute stress disorder, 8, 8*t*, **207**
Adjustment disorder, 8, 8*t*, **207**
Adverse childhood experiences (ACEs). *See* ACEs (adverse childhood experiences)
Advocacy, 33, 117–118
AEA (American Evaluation Association), 33–34, **207**
AEA Guiding Principles for Evaluators, 47, 48*t*. *See also* Six Principles of Trauma-Informed Care
Age factors, 6, 45–46
Agency, 86–87
American Evaluation Association (AEA), 33–34, **207**
Amygdala, 16–18, 17*f*, **207**. *See also* Brain
Analysis of data. *See* Data analysis
Audience, 168
Autonomic nervous system (ANS), 19, **208**
Avoidance, 33–34, 49–50, **208**

B

Background knowledge, 50
Behavior, 21–22
Bias
  data analysis and, 163–164
  designing and framing TIER and, 115*t*
  equity-informed approaches and, 83, 83*f*
  implementing an equity-centered, trauma-informed equitable evaluation and, 83–84, 88–89
Black, Indigenous, and People of Color (BIPOC)
  effect of trauma on evaluators and, 25–26
  epigenetics and, 14–15
  experiences of evaluators of color (EOCs), 25–26, 33
  healing trauma wounds and, 98
  See also Ethnicity; Race
Blame, 22, 150
Box breathing, 95–96, **208**. *See also* Breathing
Brain, 16–18, 17*f*, 22, 110. *See also* Neuroplasticity
Brave space, 103–109, 105*t*, 108*f*, **208**
Breathing, 28, 95–96, 109–110
Burnout
  clients and, 34–38, 36*f*, 37*f*
  definition, **208**
  effect of trauma on evaluators and, 28–34
  evaluation and research and, 32–34
  methodology and, 34
  overview, 39–40, 180
  trauma-informed organizations and, 183, 186
  vulnerability to, 30–32

C

Central tendency, 163–165, 208
Cerebellum, 17*f*. *See also* Brain
Change, advocating for, 117–118
Childhood experiences. *See* ACEs (adverse childhood experiences)
Circles, 155–158, 159, 186
Clean pain, 98, 208
Clients, 34–38, 36*f*, 37*f*, 167. *See also* Participants; Stakeholders
Coalitions, trauma-informed, 198–199
Collaboration, 184, 189. *See also* Collaboration and Mutuality principle
Collaboration and Mutuality principle
  data analysis and, 162
  definition, **208**
  evaluation literature and, 62
  implementing an equity-centered, trauma-informed equitable evaluation and, 85, 86, 88
  interrelatedness of the principles, 46–47, 46*f*
  literature referencing, 196
  overview, 45
  See also Six Principles of Trauma-Informed Care
Collective efficacy, 99
Collective trauma
  definition, **208**
  evaluation literature and, 58–59
  healing trauma wounds and, 97–98
  overview, 5, 11–14, 193
  principles-based approach and, 77
  See also Trauma
Colonization, 13. *See also* Decolonization
Comfort, 140–141
Communal trauma, 13, 97–98. *See also* Collective trauma
Communication, 109
Community
  community-driven approaches, 82, 83, 83*f*, 85
  data analysis and, 162, 174–175
  healing trauma wounds and, 97–99
  implementing an equity-centered, trauma-informed equitable evaluation and, 85, 88
  overview, 96
  survey design and, 134
  trauma-informed convening and, 118
Compassion, 33–34, 193
Compassion fatigue (CF)
  clients and, 34–38, 36*f*, 37*f*
  definition, **208**
  effect of trauma on evaluators and, 28–34
  ethical decision making and, 49
  evaluation and research and, 32–34
  methodology and, 34
  overview, 29–30, 39–40, 180
  trauma-informed organizations and, 186
  vulnerability to, 30–32
Compassion satisfaction, 29, **208**
Competence, 48*t*, 115*t*
Complex trauma, 12. *See also* Collective trauma
Confidentiality
  implementing an equity-centered, trauma-informed equitable evaluation and, 85, 87, 88
  reporting and, 167
  survey design and, 130–131
  trauma-informed organizations and, 185
Connection
  conducting surveys and, 140
  deep listening and, 152
  healing trauma wounds and, 99
  interviews and, 150
Consent. *See* Informed consent
Constructivist evaluation, 162–163, **208**
Consumer-oriented evaluation, 73*t*, 75, **208**
Content warnings, 172–173, **209**
Context, 69, 70*f*, 71*t*, 74
Corporate reputation laundering, 116–117, **209**
Cost analysis, 74–75, 74*n*, **209**
Criteria, 123, **209**
Critical theory, 102–103
Cultural, Historical, and Gender Issues principle
  data analysis and, 164
  definition, **209**
  interrelatedness of the principles, 46–47, 46*f*
  literature referencing, 195–196
  overview, 45–46
  See also Six Principles of Trauma-Informed Care
Cultural context
  designing and framing TIER and, 114, 116
  epigenetics and, 15–16
  evaluation literature and, 57–58, 59
  overview, 15–16, 45–46
  survey design and, 137–138
  trauma-informed approach and, 89–90, 186
  See also Cultural, Historical, and Gender Issues principle
Culturally responsive evaluation and assessment (CREA), 25–26, 76, **209**

D

Dadirri, 102, **209**
Data analysis, 87–88, 161–165, 174–176
Data collection
  designing and framing TIER and, 112–113
  equity-informed approaches and, 83
  implementing an equity-centered, trauma-informed equitable evaluation and, 86–87
  mindfulness and, 109
  trauma and, 60
Data disaggregation, 87–88, **209**
Data visualization, 168. *See also* Reporting

Decision making
ethical decision making and, 47–51, 48*t*, 50*t*
evaluation theory tree and, 70*f*, 71*t*
Decolonization, 13, 69, 70, 70*n*, 72
Deep listening
definition, **209**
interviews and, 151–152
mindfulness and, 109
overview, 152
Defense cascade, 18, 22, **209**
Demographic data, 137–138
Design of a study
framing the evaluation and, 121–125
overview, 125–126
power, oppression, and funding and, 112–113
trauma-informed convening and, 114–121, 115*t*
See also Trauma-informed survey design
Diagnosis, 8–9, 8*t*
Diagnostic and Statistical Manual of Mental Disorders (DSM), 8–9
Disaggregated analysis of data, 87–88, **209**
Discrimination, 6, 14–15, 80–81
Disinhibited social engagement disorder, 8, 8*t*, **209**
Disparities, 80–81, **209**
Dissemination, 173–174. *See also* Reporting
Dissociative states, 21–22
Distress, signs of, 50

E

Early experiences. *See* ACEs (adverse childhood experiences)
Economic evaluations, 74–75, **209**
Emotional safety, 87, 88. *See also* Safety
Emotions, 168–173
Empathy
CF, burnout, and STS and, 33
definition, **210**
focus groups and, 153–154
hyperarousal/hypervigilance and, 21
implementing an equity-centered, trauma-informed equitable evaluation and, 86–87
interviews and, 146, 150, 153–154
mindfulness and, 109
overview, 95, 101–102, 193
reporting and, 169
resources for learning more about, 201
Empowerment, 70, 72. *See also* Empowerment, Voice, and Choice (EVC) principle; Empowerment evaluation
Empowerment, Voice, and Choice (EVC) principle
definition, **210**
evaluation literature and, 62
implementing an equity-centered, trauma-informed equitable evaluation and, 85, 86, 88
interrelatedness of the principles, 46–47, 46*f*
literature referencing, 196
overview, 45
survey design and, 138
See also Six Principles of Trauma-Informed Care
Empowerment evaluation, 73*t*, 76, **210**
Engaged Feedback Checklist, 146
Engagement in the evaluation process, 70*f*, 71*t*, 132
Epigenetics, 14–16, **210**. *See also* Genetic factors
Epistemology, 84
Equitable Evaluation Initiative (EEI), 82
Equity
centering through equitable evaluation processes, 81–82
definition, **210**
designing and framing TIER and, 118
evaluation theory tree and, 70, 72
guiding principles and, 48*t*
holding safe and brave spaces and, 104–106, 105*t*
implementing an equity-centered, trauma-informed equitable evaluation and, 83–88
interviews and, 145, 149–150
overview, 69, 80–81, 88
practice and, 76
reporting and, 168
resources for learning more about, 200
See also Equity-informed approaches
Equity-informed approaches
implementing an equity-centered, trauma-informed equitable evaluation and, 83–88
overview, 88–92
trauma-informed approach and, 82–83, 83*f*
See also Equity
Ethical decision making, 47–51, 48*t*, 50*t*
Ethics
implementing an equity-centered, trauma-informed equitable evaluation and, 87, 88
overview, 193
reporting and, 167
trauma-informed convening and, 120–121
Ethnicity
ACEs (adverse childhood experiences) and, 6
epigenetics and, 14–15
experiences of evaluators of color (EOCs) and, 25–26, 33
Six Principles of Trauma-Informed Care and, 45–46
See also Black, Indigenous, and People of Color (POC); People of Color (POC)
Evaluand, 75, **210**
Evaluation and research (E&R)
centering equity in, 81–82, 88–92
effect of trauma on evaluators and, 25–28
ethical decision making and, 47–51, 48*t*, 50*t*
framing the evaluation and, 121–125
Guiding Principles for Evaluators and, 47
implementing an equity-centered, trauma-informed equitable evaluation and, 86–87
methodology and, 34

Evaluation and research (E&R) *(continued)*
overview, 24–26, 41–42, 78–79
resources for learning more about, 200–203
secondary trauma and, 28–29
trauma porn and, 168
See also Design of a study; Evaluators; Literature, evaluation; Researchers; TIER (Trauma-Informed Evaluation and Research)
Evaluation team, 114–121, 115*t*. *See also* Evaluators
Evaluation theory tree, 68–72, 70*f*, 71*t*, **210**
Evaluators
CF, burnout, and STS and, 29–38, 36*f*, 37*f*, 39–40
clients and, 34–38, 36*f*, 37*f*
effect of trauma on, 25–28
experiences of evaluators of color (EOCs), 25–26, 33
Guiding Principles for Evaluators, 47
healing trauma wounds and, 98–99
holding safe and brave spaces and, 103–109, 105*t*, 108*f*
implementing an equity-centered, trauma-informed equitable evaluation and, 86–87
overview, 95, 179–180, 192–193
power, oppression, and funding and, 112–113
recognizing our window of tolerance (WoT) and, 99–101, 100*f*
reporting and, 173–174
resilience practices and, 109–110
role of, 79
secondary trauma and, 28–30
trauma-informed approach and, 101–103, 110–111, 114–121, 115*t*
See also Implementing TIER; Organizations, trauma-informed; Programs, trauma-informed; Researchers
Events, traumatic. *See* Trauma
Executive functions, 16. *See also* Brain
Exercise, 27–28, 109–110
Experimental evaluations, 73*t*, 75–76, **210**
Explicit infusion, 124, **210**. *See also* Values
Extended-family trauma, 13. *See also* Collective trauma

F

Fawning, 204–206, **210**
Fight, flight, or freeze, 17–18, 204, **210**
Flexibility, 21, 99
Focus groups
empathy and, 153–154
interviewing staff and, 145–148
ongoing informed consent and, 131
overview, 145, 159
reflection questions pertaining to, 159–160
trauma-informed practices in facilitating, 155–158
See also Interviews
Four R's of a trauma-informed approach, 41, 42–44, 95, 204–206, **210**. *See also* Fight, flight, or freeze; Trauma-informed approach
Fourth-generation evaluation, 162–163, **210**
Framing the evaluation, 121–126. *See also* Design of a study
Funding
designing and framing TIER and, 112–113, 116–117
interview tool design and, 146–147
trauma-informed organizations and, 184

G

Gender
ACEs (adverse childhood experiences) and, 6
designing and framing TIER and, 114, 116
overview, 45–46
See also Cultural, Historical, and Gender Issues principle
Genetic factors, 14–16, 22. *See also* Epigenetics
Genocide, 13
Goal-Free Evaluation, 123–124, **210**
Grief, 6, 104–106, 105*t*
Guiding principles, 47, 48*t*. *See also* AEA Guiding Principles for Evaluators; Six Principles of Trauma-Informed Care

H

Hawthorne effect, 68, **211**
Healing justice, 78, **211**
Healing trauma wounds, 97–99. *See also* Trauma
Health equity, 104–106, 105*t*
Health problems, 6, 22
High-engagement approaches, 76, **211**
High-risk behaviors, 21
Hippocampus, 16, 17*f*, **211**. *See also* Brain
Historical, intergenerational, transgenerational trauma, 12, 13, 15–16, 102, **211**. *See also* Collective trauma
Historical context
designing and framing TIER and, 114, 116
equity-informed approaches and, 83*f*
healing trauma wounds and, 98
implementing an equity-centered, trauma-informed equitable evaluation and, 84–85
overview, 45–46, 192–193
principles-based approach and, 77
trauma-informed organizations and, 186
See also Cultural, Historical, and Gender Issues principle

Homeostasis, 7, **211**
Hope, 99
Human-centered approach, 33
Hyperarousal/hypervigilance, 20–21, **211**. *See also* Stress response
Hypersensitivity, 49, 50, 50*t*
Hypothalamic–pituitary–adrenal (HPA) system, 19, **211**

I

Identity
  CF, burnout, and STS and, 33
  designing and framing TIER and, 115*t*
  implementing an equity-centered, trauma-informed equitable evaluation and, 88–89
Implementing TIER, 93. *See also* Evaluators; Practice; TIER (Trauma-Informed Evaluation and Research)
Implicit infusion, 124, **211**. *See also* Values
Individual trauma, 5–11, 8*t*, 10*t*, 13. *See also* ACEs (adverse childhood experiences); Posttraumatic stress disorder (PTSD); Trauma
Informal evaluation, 72–74, 73*t*, **211**
Informed consent
  definition, **211**
  guiding principles and, 48*t*
  implementing an equity-centered, trauma-informed equitable evaluation and, 85, 87, 88
  survey design and, 128–132, 136–137
Insensitivity
  definition, **211**
  ethical decision making and, 50, 50*t*
  example of an insensitive interview, 148–149
  overview, 47–48
Institutional harm, 186
Institutional review board (IRB)
  definition, **212**
  empathy and, 101–102
  ongoing informed consent and, 129
  overview, 75–76
Integrity, 48*t*, 116–117
Intergenerational trauma, 12, 13, 15–16, 102, 193
Intersectionalities, 88–89, 167
Interviews
  being trauma informed even when the protocol is not, 149–150
  empathy and, 153–154
  example of an insensitive interview, 148–149
  interviewing staff, 145–148
  overview, 145, 159
  preventing shaming and, 150–152
  reflection questions pertaining to, 159–160

J

Judgment, 122–123, 124, **212**
Justice, 77–78, **212**
Justice-oriented approaches, 77–78, **212**

L

Language
  focus groups and, 155
  interview tool design and, 147–148
  survey design and, 135, 137, 141
Lens
  definition, **212**
  effect of trauma on evaluators and, 26, 39
  equity-informed approaches and, 82
  evaluation literature and, 58, 59, 67–69
  evaluation theory tree and, 72
  interviewing staff and, 145–146
  overview, 42, 47, 67*n*, 96, 192–193
  practice and, 76, 79
  reporting and, 171
Life experiences, 88–89
Listening, 152. *See also* Deep listening
Literature, evaluation
  early patterns in, 57–59
  emerging themes in, 59–63, 62*f*
  overview, 55–56, 63–65
  practice and, 63
  searching and coding, 56, 57*f*
  See also Evaluation and research (E&R); Theory
  systematic transformation and, 63–65
Logic model, 75, **212**

M

Mandatory reporting, 91–92
Marginalized populations
  framing the evaluation and, 122–123
  healing trauma wounds and, 98
  overview, 80–81
  trauma and, 6, 14–15, 22
Medical context, 58
Meditation, 27, 109–110
Member checking, 163, **212**
Memories, trauma, 18
Mental health, 6, 13, 64–65
Metabolized trauma, 11*n*. *See also* Collective trauma
Meta-evaluative criteria, **212**
Methodology
  CF, burnout, and STS and, 34
  evaluation approaches and methodologies, 72–76, 73*t*

Methodology *(continued)*
positionality and, 84
trauma-informed approach and, 77
Mindfulness, 27, 109–110
Misuse of data, 168. *See also* Reporting
Mixed methods, 70*f*
Moral distress, 33, **212**
Moral injury, 12, 114, **212**. *See also* Collective trauma
Movement, 27–28, 109–110
Mutuality, 45. *See also* Collaboration and Mutuality principle

N

Necessity, 50
Negative case analysis, 163, **213**
Neglect, 5. *See also* ACEs (adverse childhood experiences)
Neuroplasticity, 96, **213**. *See also* Brain
Neutrality, 33
NIH Guiding Principles for Ethical Research, 48*t*
Nonsystematic approaches, 72–74, 73*t*
Norms, 86–87, 88
Numbness, 21, 169

O

Ongoing informed consent, 128–132, 136–137, **213**. *See also* Informed consent
Online surveys, 132, 138–139
Ontology, 84
Oppression, 82–83, 112–113
Organizations, trauma-informed
list of, 198–199
overview, 180–181, 183–186
systems change and, 189–192
See also Evaluators; Programs, trauma-informed; Researchers; Trauma-informed approach
Outcome hacking, 165, **213**

P

PACEs (protective and compensatory experiences), 96–97, **213**
Parasympathetic nervous system (PNS), 19, 109, **213**
Participants
equity-informed approaches and, 82, 83*f*
evaluation literature and, 64
healing trauma wounds and, 99
holding safe and brave spaces for, 103–109, 105*t*, 108*f*
implementing an equity-centered, trauma-informed equitable evaluation and, 85, 86–87, 88–89
interviews and, 150–152
practice and, 76
reporting and, 171, 173–174
Six Principles of Trauma-Informed Care, 74
survey design and, 128–132
trauma porn and, 167–168
trauma-informed approach and, 102–103
See also Clients; Stakeholders
Participation-induced trauma, 12, **213**. *See also* Collective trauma
Participatory evaluation, 42, 69, **213**
Participatory trauma, 12. *See also* Collective trauma; Moral injury; Trauma
Passive responsive dissociation, 21–22, **213**
Peer debriefing, 163, 173–174, **213**
Peer Support principle
definition, **213**
evaluation literature and, 62
implementing an equity-centered, trauma-informed equitable evaluation and, 85, 86, 88
interrelatedness of the principles, 46–47, 46*f*
literature referencing, 197
overview, 45–46
See also Six Principles of Trauma-Informed Care
People of Color (POC)
effect of trauma on evaluators and, 25–26
epigenetics and, 14–15
experiences of evaluators of color (EOCs), 25–26, 33
healing trauma wounds and, 98
See also Ethnicity; Race
P-hacking, 165, **213**
Physical safety, 87, 88. *See also* Safety
Planning, 133–134
Positionality
definition, **213**
equity-informed approaches and, 83, 83*f*
implementing an equity-centered, trauma-informed equitable evaluation and, 83–84
Posttraumatic slave syndrome (PTSS), 13–14, **214**
Posttraumatic stress disorder (PTSD)
collective trauma and, 11
definition, **214**
overview, 5, 7–9, 8*t*
trauma-informed convening and, 119
See also Individual trauma; Trauma
Power
designing and framing TIER and, 112–113, 119
evaluation theory tree and, 69, 70*f*, 71*t*
powerlessness, 4
trauma porn and, 114
Practice
evaluation literature and, 63
implementing TIER and, 93

overview, 76, 77–79
resilience and, 50
Predrafting, 133–134
Prefrontal cortex, 16, 17*f*, **214**. *See also* Brain
Principles-based approach, 77. *See also* Six Principles of Trauma-Informed Care
Privacy concerns, 167. *See also* Confidentiality
Program staff, 145–148, 183, 186
Programs, trauma-informed, 180–183, 189–192, 198–199. *See also* Evaluators; Organizations, trauma-informed; Researchers; Trauma-informed approach
Progress monitoring, 184, 189
Progressive subjectivity, 163, **214**
Promoting use, 70*f*, 71*t*
Protective and compensatory experiences (PACEs). *See* PACEs (protective and compensatory experiences)
Psychic numbing, 169, **214**
Psychological context, 57–58

Q

Qualitative research, 164–165
Quantitative research, 141, 161–165, 171. *See also* Surveys
Questions
interview tool design and, 146–147
survey design and, 134–139, 143–144

R

Race
ACEs (adverse childhood experiences) and, 6
epigenetics and, 14–15
experiences of evaluators of color (EOCs) and, 25–26, 33
holding safe and brave spaces and, 104–106, 105*t*
racial trauma, 12, 98
Six Principles of Trauma-Informed Care and, 45–46
trauma porn and, 167
See also Black, Indigenous, and People of Color (POC); People of Color (POC); Racism
Racial trauma and complex racial trauma (CoRT), 12, 98. *See also* Collective trauma
Racism, 6, 14–15, 104–106, 105*t*. *See also* Race
Randomized controlled trials (RCTs), 72, 73*t*, 75–76, **214**
Rapport, 86–87
Reactive attachment disorder, 8, 8*t*, **214**
Realization (R1 in the Four R's), 43
Recognize (R2 in the Four R's), 43
Recognizing symptoms and signs, 19–20
Reflection, 98. *See also* Self-reflection
Relationship and power matrix, 107, 108*f*
Relationships, 21, 107–109, 108*f*
Relative merit, 122, **214**
Religion, 45–46
Remembering, 9, 10*t*, 11, 98, **214**
Reporting, 161–162, 166–176
Research. *See* Evaluation and research (E&R); Literature, evaluation
Researchers
healing trauma wounds and, 98–99
holding safe and brave spaces and, 103–109, 105*t*, 108*f*
overview, 95, 179–180, 192–193
power, oppression, and funding and, 112–113
recognizing our window of tolerance (WoT) and, 99–101, 100*f*
resilience practices and, 109–110
trauma-informed approach and, 101–103, 110–111, 114–121, 115*t*
See also Evaluation and research (E&R); Evaluators; Organizations, trauma-informed; Programs, trauma-informed
Resilience
definition, **214**
healing trauma wounds and, 98
holding safe and brave spaces and, 108–109
mindfulness and, 109
overview, 95–97, 109–110, 111, 181, 193
resources for learning more about, 201
survey design and, 132–133, 136, 141
trauma-informed practices and, 114, 186–187
See also Resilience practices
Resilience (possible fifth R in the Four R's), 44. *See also* Resilience
Resilience practices
definition, **214**
ethical decision making and, 50
overview, 95, 109–110
resilience activity, 111
See also Resilience
Resist retraumatization (R4 in the Four R's), 43, 85, 87. *See also* Retraumatization
Respect for people
equity-informed approaches and, 83, 83*f*
guiding principles and, 48*t*
implementing an equity-centered, trauma-informed equitable evaluation and, 86–87, 88
Respond (R3 in the Four R's), 43
Restorative justice, 77–78, 78*n*, **214**
Restorative Justice Circles, 155–158, **214**. *See also* Circles
Restorative practices, 186
Retraumatization
definition, **215**
evaluation literature and, 64
implementing an equity-centered, trauma-informed equitable evaluation and, 85, 87
overview, 9, 10–11, 10*t*, 43

Return on investment (ROI), 74–75, 74*n*, **215**
Risk–benefit ratio, 48*t*, 50

S

Safe space, 103–109, 105*t*, 108*f*, **215**
Safety
healing trauma wounds and, 99
interviews and, 150
reporting and, 167
trauma-informed convening and, 119–121
See also Safety principle
Safety principle
data analysis and, 162, 164
definition, **215**
implementing an equity-centered, trauma-informed equitable evaluation and, 85, 88
interrelatedness of the principles, 46–47, 46*f*
literature referencing, 195
overview, 44
survey design and, 138
See also Safety; Six Principles of Trauma-Informed Care
SAMHSA (Substance Abuse and Mental Health Services Administration), 183–184, **215**. *See also* Six Principles of Trauma-Informed Care
Secondary trauma, 41–42, 201–203, **215**. *See also* Secondary traumatic stress (STS)
Secondary traumatic stress (STS)
clients and, 34–38, 36*f*, 37*f*
definition, **215**
effect of trauma on evaluators and, 28–34
evaluation and research and, 32–34
methodology and, 34
overview, 30, 39–40, 180
vulnerability to, 30–32
See also Vicarious trauma
Self-blame, 22
Self-care
healing trauma wounds and, 98
overview, 40, 193
resilience practices and, 109–110
resources for learning more about, 201
Self-reflection
healing trauma wounds and, 98–99
interviews and focus groups and, 159–160
resilience practices and, 110
trauma-informed convening and, 114
Self-regulate, 96, **215**
Sensitivity
definition, **215**
ethical decision making and, 50, 50*t*
evaluation literature and, 60
overview, 48
Sexual orientation, 45–46
Sexual violence, 21
Shame, 22, 150–152
Single-criterion econometrics, 73*t*, 74–75
Six Principles of Trauma-Informed Care
data analysis and, 162, 164
definition, **215**
evaluation approaches and methodologies, 72–76, 73*t*
evaluation literature and, 56, 58, 61–62, 62*f*
evaluation theory tree and, 72
implementing an equity-centered, trauma-informed equitable evaluation and, 83–88
interrelatedness of the principles, 46–47, 46*f*
literature referencing, 195–197
overview, 41, 42, 44–47, 46*f*, 51, 79, 80, 95, 181
principles-based approach and, 77
quantitative research and, 141
survey design and, 134, 138
trauma porn and, 168
trauma-informed programs and, 181–183
See also Collaboration and Mutuality principle; Cultural, Historical, and Gender Issues principle; Empowerment, Voice, and Choice (EVC) principle; Peer Support principle; Safety principle; Trauma-informed approach; Trust and Transparency principle
Social desirability bias, 135, **215**
Social justice, 69, 70*f*, 71*t*, 77–78
Socioeconomic status, 45–46
Somatic responses, 19, **215**
Soul wound, 12, **215**
Staff, 145–148
Stages of grief, 104–106, 105*t*
Stakeholders
definition, **215**
designing and framing TIER and, 125
framing the evaluation and, 123–124
funding and, 116–117
trauma porn and, 167
trauma-informed approach and, 102–103
See also Clients; Participants
Storytelling, 151–152
Stress response, 3–5, 7, 7*n*, 19–22, 21*f*. *See also* Stress-response stimuli
Stress-response stimuli, 7, **215**. *See also* Stress response
Structural trauma, 12, 13, 186, **216**. *See also* Collective trauma
Structural/functional analysis, 88, **215**
Substance use, 6, 21, 22, 84
Substantive analysis, 88, **216**
Suicide, 6, 13, 22
Support, 99, 134
Surveys
conducting, 140–141
introduction to, 129–130, 143–144
length of, 132–133
ongoing informed consent and, 128–132
overview, 127–128, 141
phases of survey design and, 133–139
practice activities and, 141–144

quantitative research and, 141
questions on, 134–139, 143–144
trauma-informed survey design, 127–139, 141–144
Sympathetic nervous system (SNS), 19, **216**
Symptoms, 19–22, 21*f*
Systematic approaches, 48*t*, 75–76, **216**
Systematic oppression, 82–83, 112–113
Systemic constraints, 117
Systemic trauma, 12, 13. *See also* Collective trauma
Systems, trauma-informed, 186–188, 189–192. *See also* Trauma-informed approach

T

Tacit/obscured infusion, 124–125, **216**. *See also* Values
Thalamus, 17*f*. *See also* Brain
Theory
definition, **216**
evaluation theory tree and, 68–72, 70*f*, 71*t*
framing the evaluation and, 122, 123
overview, 66, 67–68, 79
See also Literature, evaluation; TIER (Trauma-Informed Evaluation and Research)
Theory of change, 75, **216**
Theory-driven evaluation, 73*t*, 75, **216**
TIER (Trauma-Informed Evaluation and Research)
CF, burnout, and STS and, 29–34
definition, **216**
empathy and, 101–102
epigenetics and, 14
evaluation approaches and methodologies, 68–76, 70*f*, 71*t*, 73*t*
Four R's of a trauma-informed approach and, 42–44
framing the evaluation and, 121–125
healing trauma wounds and, 99
holding safe and brave spaces and, 107
overview, 9, 24–26, 41–42, 51, 53, 68, 78–79, 80
principles-based approach and, 77
quantitative research and, 141
resources for learning more about, 200–203
Six Principles of Trauma-Informed Care and, 44–47, 46*f*
trauma-informed convening and, 114–121, 115*t*
See also Evaluation and research (E&R); Theory; Trauma-informed approach
Toxic stress, 7, **216**
Transformative evaluation, 76, 77–78, 108–109, **216**
Transformative justice, 73*t*, 77–78, 78*n*, **216**
Transformative social justice oriented approach, 73*t*, 77–78. *See also* Social justice; Transformative justice
Transgenerational trauma, 12, 13, 15–16, 102, 193
Transparency, 44–45, 86–87. *See also* Trust and Transparency principle
Trauma
brain's response to, 16–18, 17*f*
cultural context of, 15–16
definition, **217**
designing and framing TIER and, 115*t*
effects of, 25–26, 41–42
epigenetics and, 14–15
evaluators and, 26–28
framing the evaluation and, 122–123
healing trauma wounds, 97–99
overview, 3–5, 22, 55–56, 80–81, 193
principles-based approach and, 77
resources for learning more about, 201
trauma memories, 18
traumatic events, 3–5
traumatic stress, 7, 7*n*
See also ACEs (adverse childhood experiences); Collective trauma; Individual trauma; Posttraumatic stress disorder (PTSD); Trauma-informed approach
Trauma informed, 41–42, **217**. *See also* Trauma-informed approach
Trauma porn, 114, 167–168, **217**
Trauma symptoms. *See* Symptoms
Trauma theory, 5, **217**
Trauma-affected people, 7, 20, **217**
Trauma-informed approach
contracting and convening and, 114–121, 115*t*
cultural context of, 89–90
definition, **217**
equity-informed approaches and, 82–83, 83*f*
evaluation approaches and methodologies, 72–76, 73*t*
evaluation literature and, 55–56, 59–65
evolution of, 56–59, 57*t*
framing the evaluation and, 121–125
implementing an equity-centered, trauma-informed equitable evaluation and, 83–88
interviews and, 145–148, 149–150
overview, 41–42, 77, 88–92, 179–180, 186–187
power, oppression, and funding and, 112–113
practice and, 63
reporting and, 166–174
researchers and evaluators, 101–103, 110–111
resources for learning more about, 200–203
self-reflection of evaluators and, 26–28
See also Organizations, trauma-informed; Programs, trauma-informed; Six Principles of Trauma-Informed Care; Systems, trauma-informed; TIER (Trauma-Informed Evaluation and Research); Trauma; Trauma informed; Trauma-informed survey design
Trauma-Informed Evaluation and Research methods (TIER). *See* TIER (Trauma-Informed Evaluation and Research)

Trauma-informed interviews. *See* Interviews
Trauma-informed survey design
ongoing informed consent and, 128–132
overview, 127–128, 141
phases of, 133–139
practice activities and, 141–144
survey length and built-in resilience breaks and, 132–133
See also Design of a study; Surveys; Trauma-informed approach
Trauma-organized individual, 20, **217**
Traumatic stress. *See* Stress response
Treatment, 18, 27, 184
Treatment effect heterogeneity, 164, **217**
Trigger, 19–20, 172–173, **217**
Triggering, 9, 10*t*, 11, 172–173, **217**
Trust
equity-informed approaches and, 83, 83*f*
implementing an equity-centered, trauma-informed equitable evaluation and, 86–87, 88
interviews and, 150
practice and, 76
Trust and Transparency principle
data analysis and, 162
definition, **217**
implementing an equity-centered, trauma-informed equitable evaluation and, 85, 86–87, 88
interrelatedness of the principles, 46–47, 46*f*
literature referencing, 197
overview, 44–45
trauma porn and, 168
See also Six Principles of Trauma-Informed Care

U

Utilization-focused evaluation (UFE), 73*t*, 76, 123–124, **217**

V

Validity, 48*t*, 171
Values
definition, **217**
evaluation theory tree and, 70*f*
framing the evaluation and, 123–126
implementing an equity-centered, trauma-informed equitable evaluation and, 86–87, 88–89
positionality and, 84
reporting and, 168
Valuing
definition, **217**
evaluation theory tree and, 70*f*, 71*t*
framing the evaluation and, 122–123
Vicarious trauma, 30, 34, **218**. *See also* Secondary traumatic stress (STS)
Violence, 5–6, 13–14, 21
Visualization, data, 168. *See also* Reporting
Voice, 74, 85. *See also* Empowerment, Voice, and Choice (EVC) principle
Vulnerability, 102–103, 109

W

Window of tolerance (WoT), 19, 99–101, 100*f*, **218**

About the Authors

Martha A. Brown, PhD, is an independent evaluation consultant in Minnesota. Her interests and expertise include trauma-informed practices, restorative justice, and culturally responsive evaluation approaches. She has applied these various methods and philosophies to her work as well as to her own healing from adverse childhood experiences and other traumas. As president and founder of RJAE Consulting, Dr. Brown helps individuals and organizations become restorative and trauma-informed through online courses, workshops, and coaching sessions.

Aaron W. Kates, PhD, LCSW, is an Indiana-based evaluation consultant with Effect X, where he works with a range of for-profit and nonprofit organizations designing and implementing program evaluations. As a social worker, mental health counselor, evaluation scholar and practitioner, and survivor of childhood trauma, Dr. Kates brings a wealth of experience and knowledge to trauma-informed evaluation and research. He worked as a trauma therapist with unaccompanied minors before pursuing his doctoral education.

Contributors

Vivien Ahrens is a PhD candidate in Civil Society and Community Studies at the University of Wisconsin–Madison. Drawing on participatory, culturally responsive, action-oriented, and multisensory methods, she works toward making research and program evaluation more accessible, restorative, and fun.

Katrina Bledsoe, is principal of Global Equity, Diversity, and Inclusion at Abt Global, where she is responsible for developing strategies that center on culturally responsive and equity-centered research and evaluation approaches, theory-driven evaluation, and organizational learning. Her evaluation work has focused on community-based social services, health and education evaluation and programming, mixed methodology and methods, theory-driven evaluation, culturally responsive and equity-focused approaches, and topics in applied social psychology.

Evelyn Cruz is Director of Esperanza at Centro. Esperanza is a mental health equity set of strategies based on radical healing models and reawakening ancestral wisdom as pathways to community healing and wellness. For over 20 years, she has worked on state- and community-level development, implementation, and evaluation of public health programming.

Celena Donahue is Pueblo Indian, and her family is Hupa, Yurok, and Karuk. She was raised on the Hoopa Valley Indian Reservation in rural northeastern Humboldt County. She graduated from California State University, Sacramento, in 2008 and currently is a Cancer and Health Disparities Eliminator, Public Health Equity Advocate, and Talking Circle Facilitator.

Stephanie Evergreen is a data visualization and design expert. She is the author of three books and a popular blog on data visualization. She also trains aspiring entrepreneurs.

Carrie Fisher is a research and evaluation scientist at the Institute for Community Health. She is trained as a medical anthropologist and has a particular interest in trauma, behavioral health, and the health care system.

Elyse Fuerst currently helps human service organizations understand their impact with data. She is certified in Restorative Justice and actively participated in the Racial Justice Network while at the University at Buffalo. She brings a trauma-informed and restorative lens to the field of evaluation, specifically with children and families and advocating for racial justice and mental health.

Rachael Jackson is monitoring, evaluation, research, and learning specialist at NORC at the University of Chicago. Most of her 15-plus years of evaluation/research work has focused on vulnerable and hard-to-reach populations. Ms. Jackson specializes in engaging communities through trauma-informed, community-based participatory approaches.

Nora Johnson is a research scientist at Wilder Research, with over 15 years of research experience. She manages evaluation projects on a range of topics, including substance abuse prevention and recovery, mental health, violence prevention, and health equity. She specializes in trauma-informed evaluation methods with a variety of communities, including individuals with disabilities and veterans.

Erika Keaveney is a senior research scientist at NORC at the University of Chicago, where she leads research on child labor, forced labor, forced recruitment into illegal armed groups, commercial sexual exploitation, and other forms of human trafficking. She is a member of NORC's Institutional Review Board and spearheaded the development of NORC's trauma-informed research toolkit, an initiative directed at promoting best practices in conducting ethical research with survivors of posttraumatic stress disorder and other mental health disorders.

Kareem Kysia is Director of Vulnerable and Hard-to-Reach Population Studies at NORC at the University of Chicago. Mr. Kysia provides technical oversight on multiple extensive research projects funded by the U.S. Department of Labor, the U.S. Department of State, and the International Labour Organization, among others. He has completed successful projects on commercial sexual exploitation of children, forced labor, child labor, and child soldiers over the last 20 years.

Sofía Alejandra Ladner is a research and evaluation project manager at the Institute for Community Health (ICH). She also supports the Leah Zallman Center for Immigrant Health Research, a research center at ICH focused on immigrant health and well-being, as the Community and Staff Engagement Manager.

Rucha Londhe is an equity champion focused on developing and advancing human-centered, intersectional approaches to evaluation, research, and project delivery practices. She is an experienced qualitative researcher and excels in establishing collaborative relationships with and within public, private, or nonprofit service delivery agencies.

Carmel Rabin is Director of Research and Evaluation at the Center on Aging, Trauma, and Holocaust Survivor Care. She specializes in empowering and participatory evaluation of socioeconomic development programming. She holds an MA in development studies from Erasmus University and an MA in international relations from Syracuse University.

Melanie Ward is a public health scientist with a focus on embedding equity in all stages of the evaluation process. Her training spans community-engaged research, social justice, and equity-centered strategic planning. She is currently a health equity strategist with the Michigan Public Health Institute.

Marian Ware is a skilled evaluator with a decade of experience in inclusive development, supporting human rights, and enhancing citizen-driven politics. She specializes in dynamic facilitation and participatory approaches that inform decision making and amplify impact.